The Twilight of the British Empire

Intelligence, Surveillance and Secret Warfare
Series editors: Richard J. Aldrich, Rory Cormac, Michael S. Goodman
and Hugh Wilford

Published and forthcoming titles
The Arab World and Western Intelligence: Analysing the Middle East,
    1956–1981
Dina Rezk

Chile, the CIA and the Cold War: A Transatlantic Perspective
James Lockhart

The CIA and the Pursuit of Security: History, Documents and Contexts
Huw Dylan, David Gioe and Michael S. Goodman

www.edinburghuniversitypress.com/series/isasw

The Twilight of the British Empire

British Intelligence and Counter-Subversion in the Middle East, 1948–63

Chikara Hashimoto

Edited by Rory Cormac

EDINBURGH
University Press

Edinburgh University Press is one of the leading
university presses in the UK. We publish academic
books and journals in our selected subject areas across
the humanities and social sciences, combining cutting-
edge scholarship with high editorial and production
values to produce academic works of lasting
importance. For more information visit our
website: edinburghuniversitypress.com

Edinburgh University Press Ltd
The Tun – Holyrood Road
12(2f) Jackson's Entry
Edinburgh EH8 8PJ

Typeset in 11/14 Sabon by
Servis Filmsetting Ltd, Stockport, Cheshire

A CIP record for this book is available from the
British Library

ISBN 978 1 4744 1045 8 (hardback)
ISBN 978 1 4744 1046 5 (webready PDF)
ISBN 978 1 4744 1047 2 (epub)

Contents

Two-Part Tribute Foreword

Dr Chikara Hashimoto
24 October 1975–22 September 2016

Part One

Dr Chikara Hashimoto died suddenly on 22 September 2016 at the age of forty. *The Twilight of the British Empire: British Intelligence and Counter-Subversion in the Middle East, 1948–63* was completed in 2016 and is here taken forward to publication in Edinburgh University Press's Intelligence, Surveillance and Secret Warfare series. Some drafting amendments were made by the series editors, Richard J. Aldrich, Michael S. Goodman, Hugh Wilford and, in particular, Rory Cormac. These efforts, and those of Jen Daly at Edinburgh University Press, have expedited publication of Dr Hashimoto's first and, tragically, last book.

Chikara arrived at Aberystwyth University with his wife, Sawa, in 2004. He studied intelligence as an undergraduate and as a Master's student, before embarking on his PhD in 2009, the year that Sawa gave birth to their daughter, Miyaka. The family lived in Aberystwyth until they moved to the University of Sharjah when Chikara become an Assistant Professor in the Department of International Relations. At Aberystwyth he established himself as a central figure in the Centre for Intelligence and International Security Studies in the Department of International Politics. At Sharjah his academic career flourished as a teacher and scholar, and his contribution to the field of intelligence studies gathered further momentum.

The Twilight of the British Empire: British Intelligence and Counter-Subversion in the Middle East, 1948–63 is an important book for three main reasons. Firstly, it is a notable contribution to understanding Britain's role in the Middle East. It provides the first systematic study of the neglected aspect of intelligence and counter-subversion policy during a critical phase of the Cold War and the demise of British imperialism. It provides significant insights into Britain's relationship with states that were mostly tangential to Britain's colonial heritage but whose potential Cold War role London sought to cultivate.

Secondly, it casts light on the intelligence perspectives and practices of countries whose domestic and regional agendas were often at variance with British Cold War priorities. The book illuminates the development of bilateral and multilateral security and intelligence relationships and provides new perspectives on intelligence liaison within the region. The analysis of the relationships between Western democracies and non-democratic states resonates with contemporary challenges in international relations. Much of the research is drawn from Chikara's doctorate, which won the prestigious Leigh Douglas Memorial Prize in 2014, awarded by the British Society for Middle East Studies to the best PhD thesis on a Middle Eastern topic.

Thirdly, it demonstrates Chikara's formidable qualities as a researcher, including his commitment to multi-archival and international research, and to meeting the challenges of studying secret intelligence. The book is both testimony to his academic vision and evidence of his ambitions to further the scope and methodological horizons of intelligence studies.

At Aberystwyth, and in his work as Assistant Editor of the journal *Intelligence and National Security*, Chikara became a very highly respected and well-liked figure, admired for his integrity, kindness and exemplary diligence. As a colleague he was universally popular and unfailingly dependable. His commitment to the life of the PhD community in the Department of International Politics was recognised by his receipt of the Jana Fritzsche Award in 2012 for his outstanding contribution to the community.

Notwithstanding the tragedy of his early death and the sense of loss felt by his family, friends and colleagues, Chikara achieved so much in so short a time in his professional and in his personal life. *The Twilight of the British Empire: British Intelligence and Counter-Subversion in the Middle East, 1948–63* is an important contribution to international history and intelligence studies and testament to Chikara Hashimoto's ability, efforts and achievements.

Len Scott
Emeritus Professor of International History and
Intelligence Studies
Aberystwyth University
31 January 2017

Part Two

Chikara Hashimoto's untimely death is a terrible loss to his devoted wife, Sawa, his beautiful young daughter, Miyaka, his loving mother, Shoko, brother, Makoto, and wider family, friends, students, colleagues and the world of intelligence studies. Chikara was a historian of much promise and this book should have been only the beginning of a fine career; instead, it must serve as a memorial to him. He greatly admired scholarship, loved his research and was fascinated by the history and current operations of intelligence agencies. His dream was to become a scholar and teacher. He achieved it – but for too short a time.

This book began as a third-year undergraduate dissertation and became a Master's dissertation and then a PhD thesis. I supervised all three, and it was an honour to mentor such a kind, good-humoured, thoughtful, diligent and intelligent man. I will cherish Chikara's memory for as long as I live.

Chikara's determination is reflected in his career path. He began undergraduate study relatively late in life, at Aberystwyth University in 2004, at the age of twenty-eight. He prepared for his undergraduate studies by learning English for two years, first in Salisbury and then in Reading. It was in Salisbury in 2002 that he met his wife, Sawa, who gave unstinting support to his efforts to become, first, a student and then a scholar in the field of international history. His PhD thesis, entitled 'British

Intelligence, Counter-Subversion and "Informal Empire" in the Middle East', was awarded the Leigh Douglas Memorial Prize in 2014 for the best PhD thesis on a Middle Eastern topic by the British Society for Middle Eastern Studies. The Society's judges rightly considered it to be 'an original and thoughtful exploration of a little-studied subject' and praised the good judgement it displayed and the 'exemplary determination' with which it had been researched.

Chikara's thesis would eventually become this book, which sheds much new light on Britain's attempts in the early Cold War to use security cooperation with the police forces and security services of key Middle Eastern states to combat Soviet Communism and maintain British influence. It is an important addition to the historical literature on British intelligence and the international relations of Middle Eastern states in the early Cold War.

Had Chikara lived longer, he would have become a significant historian of intelligence. When he died, he was already a successful teacher, admired by his students and valued by his colleagues. In 2012 he won an award for teaching excellence at Aberystwyth University, where he taught for several years as a graduate teaching assistant (2009–14), before moving to the University of Sharjah in the United Arab Emirates, where he worked for the last two years of his life as an Assistant Professor of International Relations.

The key to Chikara's success as both teacher and colleague was his outstandingly pleasant and considerate nature. I never heard him say a bad word about anyone. In their tributes to him after his death, his students said how fondly they remembered his 'bright smile', and they recalled a question he often asked them in his classes: 'Are you with me?' His colleagues remembered him as a man with a striking concern for their welfare. This remarkable consideration for others was the source of Chikara's great charm. Every supervision with him was a pleasure; his presence brightened up every room he was in.

Chikara was ambitious, both intellectually and professionally. His ambition helped him to write an original and significant book. Sawa's help was also valuable to him; she photographed the documents on which this book is based. He could not have found a better partner. He leaves behind him friends from all over the world who valued his great qualities and will miss him for the rest of their lives. May he rest in peace.

Dr Paul Maddrell
Lecturer in Modern History and International Relations
Loughborough University
31 January 2017

Acknowledgements

An enquiry into state secrets inevitably faces methodological hurdles. It is a risk of a journey to unknown destinations. My journey could not have been completed without a lot of help. My journey would have not been embarked upon without the financial support of the Department of International Politics, Aberystwyth University, which funded my PhD research substantially through an E. H. Carr Studentship. I was also supported by generous grants: the Caroline Adams Travel Bursaries of the Department (twice in row); the Aberystwyth Alumni Student Hardship Fund; the Royal Historical Society; and the Founders Fund Award for 2012 of the British International Studies Association.

I would secondly like to thank my PhD supervisors, Len Scott, Paul Maddrell and James Vaughan, for their invaluable expertise and their support throughout my studies in Aberystwyth. Their experiences and expertise helped me a lot in finding the right way in a dark tunnel where I was often unsure of which direction I should take. Particular thanks also go to Len, not as my supervisor, but as my employer for his generosity in sustaining my family in the final year of my PhD.

I would also like to acknowledge my friends, colleagues and others whose identities remain anonymous for their assistance and support for my research. Amongst these, Peter Jackson, Gerry Hughes, Martin Thomas, Michael Goodman, James Simpson, Mustafa Ozcan, Hamid Soorghali and Youmna Asseily have helped me in one way or another in invariably shaping my research project. Any mistakes that may appear in the book are of course entirely my own.

I am much obliged to the publishers and editors who have kindly allowed republication. This book is derived in part from articles published in *Intelligence and National Security* on 30 October 2012, available at <http://dx.doi.org/10.1080/02684527.2012.722763>; *The International History Review* on 7 January 2014, available at <http://dx.doi.org/10.1080/07075332.2013.828644>; and *Middle Eastern Studies* on 27 May 2016, available at <http://dx.doi.org/10.1080/00263206.2016.1175344>.

Last, but not least, I would like to thank my family for their support. Thanks must go to my mother, Shoko, for her financial and moral support for my academic career in the UK. Above all, my deepest gratitude goes to my wife, Sawa, who trusted me and accompanied me even before this journey started, for her continuous and dedicated support for my entire academic career, without which I could not have completed my journey.

Chikara Hashimoto
Sharjah, the UAE
August 2016

Abbreviations

AC (M)	Ministerial Committee on Communism
AC (O)	Official Committee on Communism (Overseas)
ALO	Area Liaison Officer
AOC	Air Officer Commanding
BAOR	British Army of the Rhine
BDCC/ME	British Defence Co-ordination Committee in the Middle East
C	Code for the Chief of MI6
CENTO	Central Treaty Organisation
CIA	Central Intelligence Agency (USA)
CICI	Combined Intelligence Centre Iraq/Iran
CID	Criminal Investigation Department
CPGB	Communist Party of Great Britain
CRPO	Combined Research and Planning Office
CSE	Committee of Security Experts
CSO	Counter-Subversion Office
DIB	Delhi Intelligence Bureau
DSO	Defence Security Officer
DTC	Defence Transition Committee
D/WP	Directorate of War Planning
FOIA	Freedom of Information Act
G-2	Deuxième Bureau, security organisation of the Iranian armed forces
GC&CS	Government Code & Cipher School
GCHQ	Government Communications Headquarters
GHQ/ME	General Headquarters of the Middle East
ICP	Iraqi Communist Party
IRD	Information Research Department

ISLD	Inter-Services Liaison Department
ISOS	Intelligence Section, Oliver Strachey
JIB	Joint Intelligence Bureau
JIC	Joint Intelligence Committee
JIC (ME)	Joint Intelligence Committee in the Middle East
JID	Joint Intelligence Division
KDP	Kurdistan Democratic Party
KDPI	Kurdistan Democratic Party of Iran
LCP	Lebanese Communist Party
MES	Moslem Ethical Society
MI5	Security Service
MI6	Secret Intelligence Service
NATO	North Atlantic Treaty Organisation
NSA	National Security Agency (USA)
NSC	National Security Council
PUSD	Permanent Under-Secretary's Department
RAF	Royal Air Force
SAVAK	Iranian National Intelligence and Security Organisation
SCP	Syrian Communist Party
SEATO	Southeast Asia Treaty Organization
SIA	Security Intelligence Adviser
SIFE	Security Intelligence Far East
SIGINT	signals intelligence
SIME	Security Intelligence Middle East
SLO	Security Liaison Officer
SOE	Special Operations Executive
SPA	Special Political Action
UAR	United Arab Republic
USIS	United States Information Service

Introduction

The history of the British presence in the Middle East between 1948 and 1963 is one of failure. During this period, from a time of much British influence to the twilight of its Empire, various socio-political factors challenged – and ultimately brought down – most of the partner regimes over which the British had enjoyed their influence. By the late 1950s, despite its once imperial position, Britain had lost all reliable allies, such as Egypt and Iraq, as well as other friendly regimes, such as Jordan and Iran, themselves also increasingly challenged by domestic and international political upheavals. The culmination of the British preoccupation with maintaining influence in the region can be seen in the Suez Crisis of 1956, where Prime Minister Anthony Eden's personal endeavour against the Egyptian leader, Colonel Gamal Abdul Nasser, included collusion with France and Israel.[1]

Intelligence and security was a vital realm in which Britain sought to engage with the Middle East, maintain its regional influence and support friendly regimes. Britain's intelligence and security services and its secret propaganda apparatus – the Information Research Department (IRD) of the Foreign Office – conducted counter-subversion across the Middle East, including in Egypt, Iraq, Jordan, Lebanon, Turkey and Iran. Such activity in foreign countries inevitably raised sensitive issues surrounding cooperation with local authorities, and the murky world of intelligence liaison between British intelligence and security services and their Middle Eastern counterparts. Based on newly declassified and hitherto unexploited records, as well as Middle Eastern sources, this book reveals the history of Britain's subterranean engagement in the post-war Middle East.

At the end of the Second World War, the Middle East consisted of both colonial territories (Cyprus, Aden Colony, the Palestine Mandate and the Arabian/Persian Gulf) and independent states. Britain's interactions with the latter, and its desire to influence their policies, have sometimes been referred to by imperial historians as Britain's 'informal empire'.[2] Despite the loss of the British mandate in Palestine in 1948, Britain enjoyed unparalleled political influence throughout the Arab world, where many, according to Sir Anthony Parsons, a former British diplomat who served there, heralded Britain as 'the lion'.[3] Enjoying such reputation and influence, Britain strove to maintain close connections with Middle Eastern governments – and their intelligence services.

Britain's role in the region has long caught the attention of diplomatic, imperial and military historians emphasising the importance of the Middle East to Whitehall.[4] Indeed, defending the region against Soviet attack formed one of the pillars of post-war strategy,[5] whilst the retention of the British Empire was 'part of the habit and furniture' of Whitehall minds.[6] And yet these histories rarely consider the role of intelligence and counter-subversion when discerning the long-term trends of Britain's engagement with the post-war Middle East.[7] Even academics specialising in secret affairs have neglected Britain's intelligence power. The authorised history of the British Security Service, MI5, only covers the colonies in the region,[8] when, in reality, its activities expanded beyond the imperial boundary to cover liaison with Middle Eastern governments and collaboration with MI6 (Secret Intelligence Service).[9] Some discussion of signals intelligence in the Middle East exists,[10] whilst special political actions, or attempts to covertly shape internal developments, in the region have begun to attract some serious scholarly attention; the most famous example being the 1953 coup in Iran, which Britain's foreign intelligence service – MI6 – orchestrated with its American counterpart.[11] Other cases of event shaping, such as in Syria and Yemen, have recently come to light[12] but remain underexplored. Meanwhile, the literature is particularly thin on the important, and sensitive, subject of intelligence liaison between Britain and Middle Eastern regimes.[13]

This book reveals that, in the twilight of the Empire in the Middle East, British policymakers saw intelligence as a tool to preserve strategic and economic interests in the region. In particular, intelligence could supposedly counter the spread of Communism; a goal shared by many of the regional governments. Sensing their common interest, the British pushed for secret liaison with Middle Eastern security agencies. However, the friendly Arab States as well as Iran struggled to reciprocate. The regimes faced more imminent socio-political challenges and battled even to retain legitimacy. As British influence faded during the period between 1948 and 1963, intelligence liaison with Middle Eastern counterparts was a short-term success but a long-term failure.

In revealing the hidden history of intelligence liaison with Middle Eastern regimes, this book demonstrates three core ideas. Firstly, the relationships bridged democratic and non-democratic governments, thereby reflecting differences in political and cultural values which extended to counter-subversion. Secondly, and following on from this, the nature and activities of the Middle Eastern intelligence and security partners were important in the relationship. It is necessary to move intelligence studies beyond the overwhelming focus solely on Western intelligence organisations.[14] Thirdly, intelligence liaison encompassed more than merely sharing resources or information. It also could – and did – influence foreign governments. Accordingly, Britain sought to influence the policies of Middle Eastern governments through clandestine means.

These are important matters, shedding light on both past and present. In recent years, the 'War on Terror' has raised the public profile of controversial British intelligence liaison with Middle Eastern governments.[15] This is not a new phenomenon, however. Sir Stephen Lander, former Director-General of MI5, for instance, reminds us that the British intelligence services maintained a relationship with their Middle Eastern counterparts long before 2001.[16] Yaacov Caroz, a former Deputy-Chief of the Israeli Intelligence Service, Mossad, also testified over three decades ago that the British intelligence services had been instrumental in developing the Arab security services.[17] In the post-war period, this took place against the backdrop of anti-Communism.

The significance of Britain's counter-subversive measures in the Middle East cannot be underestimated. Referring to MI5's domestic role, Bernard Porter once remarked that without counter-subversion, 'we would be a very different country from what we are today'.[18] This idea is also applicable to the Middle East. Local counter-subversion efforts, conducted by strong domestic security forces in secret partnership with British intelligence, ensured that Communist Parties were largely prohibited. As a result of counter-subversion efforts, Communist influence in the region was less prominent than elsewhere throughout the Cold War.[19]

Counter-subversion liaison extended to multilateral cooperation. The Central Treaty Organisation (CENTO), formerly known as the Baghdad Pact (1955–8), was a military alliance which has received far less attention than its European equivalent, the North Atlantic Treaty Organisation (NATO).[20] Even Air Marshal Sir Neville Stack, who served as British Representative of the Permanent Military Deputy (1970–2) to CENTO, described it as 'the unknown alliance'.[21] Few realise that CENTO states' security forces in fact worked together to contain internal subversive activities within the Pact area. Below the highest body, the Council of Ministers, CENTO was primarily comprised of four 'major' Committees: the Military Committee, the Economic Committee, the Counter-Subversion Committee and the Liaison Committee.[22] The latter two are particularly interesting. They were distinctively political, incredibly secretive and, more importantly, targeted the internal affairs of the Pact signatories.

Unaware of the significance of these two committees, military historian Panagiotis Dimitrakis argues that, unlike NATO, CENTO was a 'failed alliance', asserting, above all, that 'there was no real threat to be deterred in the first place'.[23] Owing to the nature of the Middle East, however, where political intrigues, assassinations and coups d'état were commonplace, most regional governments were more concerned about internal subversion than Soviet invasion. In addition, the Middle Eastern leaders' perceptions of regional affairs were driven by what Daniel Pipes has called the 'conspiracy mentality'.[24] Nevertheless, although some works on the importance of the Cold War to post-war

British imperial strategy have suggested that these Cold War and End of Empire historiographies overlap,[25] the significance of the potential danger that these movements might be exploited by Communists, or that they might adopt Communist tactics – a perception resulting from the complex picture of the Cold War and the decolonisation process in the region – has yet to be adequately addressed by historians.[26] Moreover, little is known about how the local police and security services dealt with Communists and subversive activities.[27]

Finally, British intelligence has also been in the spotlight over the last few years in the context of its alleged complicity in human rights abuse during the so-called War on Terror.[28] At the same time, a darker side of decolonisation has emerged with evidence of torture and excessive violence during Britain's counter-insurgency campaigns, for example in Kenya.[29] Historians now know about how MI5 sought to export a 'Commonwealth intelligence culture' throughout the British Empire, often through training courses,[30] and how particular techniques and methods were transported with the movement of MI5 officers from one colony to another.[31]

This dark side of the Cold War is not confined to the territories of the British Empire. Britain also facilitated the development of security advising and police training in anti-Communist measures in the post-war Middle East. A distinct characteristic of Middle Eastern states was that they were politically non-democratic in the Western sense, with domestic politics dominated by a strong security force, often labelled a secret political police.[32] This raises important questions surrounding the extent to which Britain was involved in training Middle Eastern security services, alongside their level of complicity in oppressive anti-Communist measures conducted by Middle Eastern governments, which often engaged in human rights abuses. These issues remain relevant and controversial today.

Counter-Subversion

Subversion is sometimes treated as an area of irregular warfare and the term is often interchangeably used with *insurgency*.[33]

However, according to Frank Kitson, a first-hand practitioner as well as classic theorist, insurgency refers to 'the use of armed force by a section of the people against the government', whereas subversion means 'all measures short of the use of armed force' to overthrow the government.[34] Subversive activities therefore include political and economic pressure, strikes, protest marches, propaganda and 'the use of small-scale violence for the purpose of coercing recalcitrant members of the population into giving support'.[35] Importantly, the British government also made this distinction during the period.

Counter-subversion is political in nature, which makes it inherently subjective. As a result, Britain and Middle Eastern governments understood and applied counter-subversive measures differently. For the British, they were primarily directed against Communist activities in the region, whereas for Middle Eastern governments, counter-subversion targeted any anti-governmental political activities. The difference becomes more apparent when countering subversion through propaganda. For the British, the purpose of propaganda was essentially to broadcast and publicise information to expose the methods and tactics of Communist subversive propaganda. It was meant, by exposing the reality of life in the Communist bloc, to dispel any illusion about the Soviet Union as a 'workers' paradise' throughout the world.[36] For Britain, counter-subversion was purely a reactive and defensive concept.

However, Iraq, Turkey, Iran and Pakistan adopted a more aggressive definition: they believed that proactive counter-subversion was necessary to eradicate the threats coming from outside the Pact area – from not only the Soviet Union, but also Egypt and Saudi Arabia – as well as the activities of minority groups, such as the Kurds. Counter-subversion was above all understood by the regional members as more physical activity, such as imprisoning targets.[37] Thus, the inherent nature of the term itself, *counter-subversion*, connotes both offensive and defensive meanings. In addition, owing to the subjectivity of the meaning, the demarcation line between subversive elements and anti-British sentiment also caused confusion even among MI5 officers in the region, who were responsible for counter-subversion but found it difficult to distinguish between anti-British nationalist movements and legitimate anti-British governments.[38]

The core forms of counter-subversive activities to be addressed in this book are: policing, intelligence sharing, protective security, security training, special political action (so-called covert action) and propaganda, all of which were pursued and clandestinely implemented through MI5, MI6 and the IRD. These services had different roles in counter-subversion. MI5 was responsible for defensive counter-subversive activities, such as collecting security intelligence, protective security and security training. Similarly, the IRD exclusively conducted propaganda campaigns. MI5 and the IRD did not engage in special political action, such as para-military operations and overthrowing a foreign government by clandestine means, for which MI6 was responsible. These services were engaged in different degrees of intelligence sharing with local authorities. As the book illustrates, these defensive and offensive counter-subversive activities sometimes overlapped or were incompatible with one another.

Organisation of Book and Chapters

This book considers Britain's relationship with independent countries in the early Cold War. It excludes Britain's colonies and protectorates, such as Cyprus, the Aden Colony and the Arabian/Persian Gulf. Britain's engagement in these colonies is mainly a story of counter-insurgency rather than counter-subversion.[39] Archival research indicates that MI5 was also involved in the protective security of oil companies in the Arabian/Persian Gulf, but its involvement was passive and minimal – mainly advising on their vetting procedures (i.e. excluding Communist elements from the oil companies).[40] Meanwhile, MI5's security liaison intended to maintain law and order, such as in cases of disturbances and riots, rather than to achieve political goals – fighting Communist activities there.[41]

Likewise, this book does not cover Israel. Although some informal personal connections existed between British intelligence and its Israeli counterparts after 1948, there was not much official cooperation in counter-subversion during the period.[42] According to Tom Bower, the biographer of Sir Dick White, both former Director-General of MI5 and Chief of MI6, 'anti-Semitism' amongst senior MI6 officers and 'pro-Arab sentiments' within the Foreign Office prevented MI6's cooperation with the Israeli Intelligence Service, Mossad.[43]

The book consists of six chapters, divided into thematic topics. Chapter 1 shows the development of Britain's anti-Communist policy overseas from the Attlee Government of 1945–51 to the Macmillan Government of 1957–63, and how the role of intelligence was understood by policymakers when dealing with the difficulties Britain faced in maintaining its positions and influence overseas, and especially in the Middle East. Based on records declassified under the Freedom of Information Act of 2001 (FOIA), the chapter demonstrates that counter-subversion – anti-Communist measures, in other words – preoccupied British thinking throughout the period, and shows that policymakers such as Prime Minister Harold Macmillan saw intelligence as the solution.

Chapter 2 investigates the introduction of British security/police liaison officers and their role in instituting anti-Communist measures on the part of Middle Eastern governments up to the mid-1950s. With the Chiefs of Staff contemplating a potential war against the Soviet Union, this was the period in which police training became particularly necessary.

Chapter 3 examines the role of a hitherto unexplored organisation, Security Intelligence Middle East (SIME), the regional headquarters of MI5, in counter-subversion in the region. It shows how SIME operated in the region to liaise with local authorities, and examines its relationship with MI6.

Chapters 4 and 5 reveal the nature of intelligence and propaganda cooperation with the Baghdad Pact countries. Chapter 4 examines the preconditions for intelligence sharing. It shows that one of the British concerns about operational security contributed to establishing the Iranian National Intelligence and Security Organisation, known as SAVAK. Chapter 5 demonstrates conflicting interests between Britain and Middle Eastern governments in counter-subversion through propaganda. It shows that the

British were primarily concerned with Communist activities, but this did not necessarily accord with the concerns of the regional members. A schism in propaganda approaches can be seen as a microcosm of the problems affecting regional cooperation as a whole.

Based on the findings from the preceding chapters, Chapter 6 examines the general extent to which Britain was involved in the conduct of anti-Communist measures by Middle Eastern governments, and Britain's attitudes towards their security measures which often violated of human rights. It also discusses the efficacy and limitations of the intelligence liaison.

1 Fighting the 'Communist Menace' Overseas[1]

The term 'counter-subversion' is used in this paper to mean clandestine activities, whether by propaganda or by operations, directed against Communism or, in the Colonies, against subversive forms of nationalism.

Prime Minister's Memorandum, 10 December 1955[2]

The principal object of our Middle East policy has recently been stated by Ministers to be the security of the oil on which the United Kingdom so greatly depends. The main instrument by which we hope to achieve our policy is the Baghdad Pact. Its value to the United Kingdom is primarily as a means of improving the Western position in the cold war and retaining the goodwill of two of the oil producing countries, namely, Iran and Iraq.

The Chiefs of Staff Committee, 13 July 1956[3]

Introduction

The British government was greatly concerned by subversive activities. In 1958, for example, the Joint Intelligence Committee (JIC) viewed 'subversive threats' to 'British interests throughout the world' as the highest priority intelligence targets, alongside a strategic nuclear attack by the Soviet Union against Great Britain.[4] This chapter looks at the development of Britain's post-war overseas anti-Communist policy and the organisational structures that shaped it. Since anti-Communist, or counter-subversion, policy in the Middle East developed in parallel with other foreign and colonial territories, this chapter starts with the origins of Britain's post-war anti-Communist policy overseas in the late 1940s. It shows that Whitehall departmental infighting over waging Cold War included stark disagreement about the role, conduct and severity of anti-Communist measures. The chapter then outlines the mechanisms of counter-subversion in the Middle East and discusses Britain's relationship with the United States in anti-Communist measures in the region.

The Origins of Post-War Counter-Subversive Activities Overseas

The origins of Britain's counter-subversive activities overseas can be traced back to the late 1940s. The first post-war British government envisaged a potential war against the Soviet Union and adopted a very strong anti-Communist policy to fight the 'Communist menace' overseas.[5] Britain's first post-war Foreign Secretary, Ernest Bevin, decided to establish three bodies within the Foreign Office directing anti-Communist activities in order to fight the Cold War against the Soviet Union: one committee and two departments. The first, in 1946, was the Russia Committee, a body in charge of political warfare activities and consisting of senior FO officials.[6] The second, established in 1948, was the IRD, an anti-Communist propaganda apparatus, which one historian dubbed 'Britain's secret Cold War weapon'. The IRD was responsible for researching and conducting anti-Communist propaganda activities overseas.[7] The third was the Permanent Under-Secretary's Department (PUSD), created in 1949, to liaise with MI6 and MI5 and coordinate their activities in accordance with Foreign Office policy.[8]

An even more secret body has only recently come to light. Records declassified in October 2010 reveal that an interdepartmental official committee, the Official Committee on Communism (Overseas), or AC (O), was established in December 1949.[9] The AC (O) Committee replaced the existing interdepartmental committee, named 'Committee on Communism' at the Cabinet Office,[10] and was formed in response to mounting pressure from the Chiefs of Staff, specifically Air Chief Marshal Sir John Slessor, who suggested that the Attlee Government take stronger action against the spread of International Communism movements overseas.[11] According to Bevin, it conducted both 'offensive and defensive' actions against the 'Soviet and Communist menace in all spheres, political, military, economic and social, at home and abroad'.[12]

The AC (O) was chaired by a senior official from the PUSD of the Foreign Office: Sir Gladwyn Jebb (1949–50); Sir Pierson Dixon (1950–3); Sir John Ward (1954–5); and Sir Patrick Dean (1955–6).[13] The permanent members included the Chairman of the JIC, the Chief of MI6, and representatives of the Ministry of Defence and of the Chiefs of Staff, and were later joined by a representative of MI5.[14] Members of relevant departments, including the Colonial Office and the Commonwealth Office, were invited to committee meetings on an ad hoc basis. The purpose of the committee was the coordination and initiation of 'any measures' which 'appeared desirable in the conduct of the Cold War'. 'Any measures' included propaganda by the IRD; clandestine para-military operations by MI6; and security training of both foreign and colonial police forces supervised by MI5.[15] The activities of the committee were supervised by a newly established Ministerial Committee on Communism, or the AC (M), chaired by Prime Minister Clement Attlee himself.[16]

Britain's planners learned techniques from their own wartime experience, but also borrowed from Britain's post-war enemies, the Soviet Union and International (Soviet-sponsored) Communism. Air Chief Marshal Sir John Slessor, an influential figure in setting up the AC (O) Committee, who was also one of the architects of Britain's plans for the liberation of the Eastern bloc through special operations in the late 1940s, for instance, commented on countering Communist threats overseas that, although 'we should never descend to their levels', it would be 'profitable to borrow certain methods from our enemies' and 'we should not hesitate to adopt measures against them which would not be warranted in dealing with a Civilized Power'.[17]

The AC (O) produced myriad proposals, including, in December 1950, for MI6 to conduct 'certain activities' behind the Iron Curtain in 'full co-operation with the Americans'.[18] Around this period, the Chiefs of Staff were lobbying to use MI6 as a tool for 'Cold War fighting' through special political action, including paramilitary operations against Albania, codenamed Operation VALUABLE.[19] A parallel development, and also very similar thinking to that of the Doolittle Report (a report on covert activities of the United States), was also taking place on the other side of the Atlantic, where the Central Intelligence Agency (CIA) was empowered in 1948 under National Security Council (NSC) Directive 10/2 to engage in special operations, including 'subversion against hostile states', in other words, what is well known as 'covert action'.[20] This was also largely a response of American policymakers to the threats from the Soviet Union and International Communism.

Quarrelling over the Conduct of the 'Cold War'

There was no major development in anti-Communist policy and its underpinning machinery from the Attlee Government to the Churchill Government. After Stalin's death in March 1953, the Soviet Union adopted the traditional Leninist critique of the West; the rise of nationalism in the colonial territories and the emergence of the non-alignment movement loomed large, and 'colonialism' became the pretext under which the Soviet Union was attacking European empires. Accordingly, in the mid-1950s, there was an important shift in British government anti-Communist policy overseas.

Despite the committee approach, and the broader appearance of consensus and collegiality,[21] departmental infighting over Britain's conduct of the Cold War was a common occurrence. In fact, Britain's post-war foreign, defence and security policies often arose from civilian–military disputes, especially in the early period of the Cold War.[22] Richard Aldrich argues that while the Chiefs of Staff had dominated Britain's foreign policy and MI6's special political action after the war, the Foreign Office took control of the conduct of the Cold War from 1950 onwards.[23] However, this departmental infighting continued in the first half of the 1950s up until February 1956, when the AC (O) was officially disbanded.

In October 1955, echoing the point made by Air Chief Marshal Sir John Slessor five years earlier, the Chiefs of Staff pointed out the need for 'a world-wide strategic policy', including foreign and colonial territories and also at home, to initiate 'whole-hearted' counter-offensive operations against 'communist subversion'. Noting a change of the Soviet tactics from direct military confrontation with the West to 'the intensification of subversion' all over the world, the Chiefs of Staff considered that their anti-Communist measures so far had largely been 'by way of ad hoc measures aimed half-heartedly at the stopping of gaps', and warned that this was 'the reverse of a winning policy'.[24] As one of the 'fundamental requirements for our success in the cold war', the Chiefs of Staff noted, 'we should vigorously combat and counterattack subversion by clandestine and all other related means'.[25] However, while this recommendation by the Chiefs of Staff triggered a change in anti-Communist policy, it took the policy in a different direction from what they actually desired.

This recommendation preceded by a week a separate suggestion by Foreign Secretary Harold Macmillan for forming new anti-Communist committees.[26] Macmillan sought to revise Britain's anti-Communist policy overseas and to review the activities of MI6, MI5 and the IRD in the context of decolonisation and on the basis of Britain's financial limitations. Around this time, anti-Communist measures were chiefly targeted at Eastern European countries. Similar to Operation VALUABLE in Albania, MI6 had conducted paramilitary operations through various émigrés, and the IRD had attempted to destabilise the legitimacy of these newly established Communist regimes. Such anti-Communist 'rolling-back' measures were also conducted with the Americans.[27] Instead of directing anti-Communist measures behind the Iron Curtain, which were yielding unfruitful results and only wasting Britain's resources, Macmillan suggested Eden pay more careful attention to colonial problems as well as maintaining British interests abroad, especially in the Middle East, where the Soviet Union was exploiting anti-British nationalist movements.[28]

Sir Norman Brook, the influential Cabinet Secretary, supported Macmillan's proposals as being 'more cautious' than those of the Chiefs of Staff, which he labelled 'rather feverish and muddled'.[29]

In line with Macmillan's framework, Brook made more specific and clearer recommendations on subsequent anti-Communist policy, officially termed 'counter-subversion' from this point (thus the terms 'counter-subversion' and 'anti-Communist measures' were used interchangeably in official papers hereafter). Firstly, anti-Communist activities conducted by MI6 and IRD against the countries behind the Iron Curtain were to be suspended for the time being.[30] Secondly, Whitehall was to mobilise 'all our available resources' to distinguish between Communist and nationalist movements and ensure 'Communism is held in check and nationalist movements are guided along sound lines'. In order to counter 'Communist encroachment' in the colonies, Brook noted that 'sound' colonial administration, 'good' police forces and an 'efficient' intelligence system were necessary.[31]

Brook also expressed his views on the way in which the AC (O) Committee, and more specifically the Chiefs of Staff, handled counter-subversion abroad, and noted that ministerial responsibility was 'being weakened by allowing the clandestine activities in this field to be "stimulated" by an interdepartmental committee of officials including a representative of the Chiefs of Staff'.[32] Around the same time, the Chiefs of Staff also attempted to initiate a survey under the pretext of the 'Cold War' on 'Communist infiltration in schools, both in the United Kingdom, and all foreign and colonial territories' as a 'general exercise by the JIC'.[33] Once this was known to Brook, who thought it an inappropriate action by the Chiefs of Staff, he intervened in the matter and stopped it.[34] He then insisted to Eden that the use of the term 'Cold War' in any official minutes and memoranda should be banned as the term was, in Brook's words, 'responsible for a lot of muddled thinking – or, worse still, lack of thinking', which 'led the Chiefs of Staff to suppose that they are in some way responsible for matters which are essentially the business of the Foreign Secretary'.[35]

Senior officials in the Foreign Office shared Brook's frustration with the Chiefs of Staff. As a result of 'a clear cleavage' in the AC (O) Committee between the Chiefs of Staff, who wanted to 'get cracking', and those representing the Foreign Office, who preferred 'a more cautious approach', Sir John Ward, Chairman of the AC (O) Committee (1954–5), consequently found himself in the 'invidious position of acting as a brake rather than an accelerator on the Committee machine'.[36] In addition, Sir Patrick Dean, the successor to Sir John Ward as Chairman of the AC (O) Committee (1955–6), who also chaired the JIC, recorded in his minute in December 1955 to Sir Ivone Kirkpatrick, the Permanent Under-Secretary of State, that:

> there would be no objection to telling General Templer and the Chiefs of Staff generally about what was going on [about counter-subversive policy in the FO], but the trouble was that they conceived it their duty to 'stimulate' action and were always interfering in the details of the special operations which were not their concern. We are always having difficulty on this with the Chiefs of Staff representative.[37]

Moreover, 'in my experience', Sir Ivone Kirkpatrick noted to the Foreign Secretary, Selwyn Lloyd, when the Chiefs of Staff were arguing that stronger counter-subversive activities were necessary, they mostly relied on 'hearsay' from their low-level representatives and did not 'always know what they [were] talking about'.[38]

The reforms revised the inappropriate machinery of the AC (O) and, by extension, revised the meaning of counter-subversion itself by emphasising that it must be directed by broader foreign or colonial policy: it was stated that the Foreign Secretary must be responsible for all counter-subversion in foreign countries, and the Colonial Secretary must be similarly responsible for counter-subversion in the colonies.[39] Following Cabinet approval on 24 February 1956, the AC (O) Committee was disbanded and replaced by new counter-subversive committees.[40] Unlike the old AC (O) Committee, these new committees excluded the Chiefs of Staff.

The Official Committee on Counter-Subversion in the Colonial Territories was formed as an interdepartmental committee at the Cabinet Office to cover the colonial territories, supervising all counter-subversive activities in the colonies, and some Commonwealth countries, under the direction of the Colonial Policy Committee.[41] The other committee, the Overseas Planning Committee (1956–7), often referred to as the 'special' committee, was established in the Foreign Office and was directly concerned with foreign countries, including Middle Eastern states. From 1957, after absorbing the Russia Committee, it was renamed the Political Intelligence Committee.[42]

The newly appointed Foreign Secretary, Selwyn Lloyd, who had been the Minister of Defence until December 1955, was, however, concerned about the exclusion of the Chiefs of Staff, who were 'very strongly opposed' to Eden's memorandum which proposed the formation of these committees, and decided to include Major-General William G. Stirling on the Overseas Planning Committee as a representative of the Ministry of Defence and the Chiefs of Staff.[43] Despite an earlier decision that the new committee be chaired by a senior official from the PUSD, Selwyn Lloyd instead selected his Parliamentary Under-Secretary of State, Douglas Dodds-Parker, as chairman.[44] Lloyd thought that 'it would be useful for a Minister to be closely concerned because he could then talk to the Chiefs of Staff and the Minister of Defence as well as discussing with the Secretary of State himself'.[45] The chairing of the Foreign Office's special committee by Dodds-Parker was formally accepted by the same Cabinet meeting that approved Eden's memorandum on 24 February 1956.[46] Ministerial responsibilities and positions in directing counter-subversion overseas would become consolidated and enhanced.

These developments are important: they shaped broader British thinking and action in numerous ways. Firstly, they established a clear government policy to maintain British interests overseas, shifting the focus of anti-Communist measures away from the Soviet Union and its satellite countries to other territories, most notably Middle Eastern states, where Britain had national interests – oil in particular.[47] Eden stated that in shifting the focus from the Eastern bloc, 'we should be ready to make more use of counter-subversion in the smaller countries in the Middle East and in South-East Asia which are seriously threatened with Communist infiltration'.[48] Secondly, the Eden Government recognised that while nationalist movements in the colonies were not necessarily Communist, they had the potential to be exploited by the Soviet Union or local Communist Parties. The recognition of this long-standing problem at the highest level not only led to developments in the Foreign Office, but was also a prelude to the subsequent 1957 development that saw the JIC placed in the Cabinet Office with a representative from the Colonial Office as an official member.[49]

Around the same time, there had been a parallel shift of emphasis in Foreign Office intelligence from 'a possible global war' against the Soviet Union and its satellite countries to 'present and increasing' subversive activities overseas, such as in the Middle East. Observing this shift, Sir Patrick Dean, the JIC Chairman, noted that 'nearly all the intelligence now considered by the Joint Intelligence Committee in its weekly review is of a political/ economic nature' rather than to do with military threats.[50] Dean also commented that:

the JIC are considering whether some part of the considerable effort put by our collecting agencies (particularly JIB [Joint Intelligence Bureau], our friends [MI6] and GCHQ) into obtaining intelligence about the military organisation, capabilities, state of preparedness, etc., of the Sino-Soviet bloc could not be switched more profitably and successfully to these 'grey' territories [such as the Middle East and the colonies] where the politico/economic/cultural threat is more imminent. If some of the effort directed to obtain order of battle and similar types of intelligence could be dropped, the resources thus freed could be used to obtain intelligence about Communist plans for subverting and penetrating the 'grey' areas.[51]

While a possible change in the allocation of intelligence collection efforts was being discussed at the JIC level, Dean noted that:

there is a strong case for seeing what steps can be taken by the Foreign Office to improve immediately the organisation for collating and assessing Sino-Soviet intentions and plans, both general and particular, for attacking and increasing their influence in these 'grey' territories.[52]

Thirdly, the developments defined counter-subversion as one of the 'clandestine activities' to be conducted by MI6, MI5 and the IRD, and reiterated that all counter-subversive activities were to be directed by government policy: the Foreign and Colonial Secretaries were 'responsible for all counter-subversion' in their respective spheres. Eden's memorandum also noted that 'subject to the Prime Minister, the Foreign Secretary should retain sole control over C's organisation [MI6]. C's activities in support of foreign policy should remain subject to the Ministerial control of the Foreign Secretary.'[53] This was mainly intended to prevent any further interference by the Chiefs of Staff in counter-subversive activities conducted by intelligence and security services.

Once the government's counter-subversive policy was made clear, Sir Ivone Kirkpatrick despatched a top-secret and personal letter by diplomatic bag to all ambassadorial and ministerial positions in foreign countries, instructing them to pay more careful attention to 'signs of Communist or other subversive activities'. He wrote:

> We have decided, in view of the new type of threat, that counter-subversion, i.e. clandestine activities whether by propaganda or by special operations, will have an increasing part to play in support of foreign policy . . . We have accordingly tried to draw up a broad list of priorities for such action . . . Action is most urgently required in the Middle East and South-East Asia . . . Her Majesty's Representatives are in the best position to suggest ways of countering dangerous activities and of reinforcing the influence of those well-disposed towards us and their ability to resist hostile subversive activities; and you should not hesitate to put forward such suggestions, whether they are for overt anti-Communist measures or for ways in which the policies of Her Majesty's Government might be furthered by clandestine means.[54]

The Overseas Planning Committee also clearly set out the use of 'covert operations' by MI6 as counter-subversive measures. In his minute to the Foreign Secretary Selwyn Lloyd, Sir Patrick Dean reported that:

> We are preparing a circular letter to Her Majesty's representatives abroad informing them that the increased use of clandestine means to further foreign policy has been approved and requesting them to bear this constantly in mind and to submit recommendations for such

activities in consultation with the local representatives of our friends [MI6]. We recommend that this should be followed up by more detailed instructions as appropriate to individual posts, asking for more reports on Communist penetration and prospects and recommendations for counter-action.[55]

The approval by the Eden Government of the increased use of covert operations suggests that such activity was considered a useful and cost-effective tool to implement foreign policy.

Policymakers understood covert operations as being less costly than sending troops overseas. This point was made by Harold Macmillan – who used the example of sending British troops to Kenya, British Guiana and Cyprus, which incurred huge expenditures of money and manpower – to suggest to Anthony Eden a wiser use of intelligence.[56] Furthermore, Macmillan may even have suggested this increased use of covert operations, informing Eden in 1955 that:

> there is sometimes reluctance to contemplate the use of covert means until it is rather too late for the proper planning to take place. I think therefore we should examine our present procedures and organisation to ensure that the possibility of using covert means to achieve our ends and in support of our overt policy is constantly borne in mind and the necessary planning carried out wherever possible well in advance.[57]

As discussed below, Macmillan saw the use of intelligence services as an instrument of policy as a valid proposition. In short, these various bureaucratic debates and reforms had real impact: they drove an intensification of British covert counter-subversion in the Middle East.

Counter-Subversion in the Middle East

Since the post-war Middle East was regarded as, in the words of Ernest Bevin, 'of cardinal importance to the United Kingdom, second only to the United Kingdom itself', British policymakers had a particular attachment to defending British interests against subversive activities in the region.[58] Until the mid-1950s, mostly under the Attlee Government, British interests were more associated with its defence policy and military planning; Wm. Roger Louis describes it as 'a region honeycombed with British military installations'.[59]

The Middle East consisted of both colonial and foreign territories with which Britain had military commitments under defence treaties, such as Egypt, Jordan and Iraq. The post-war Middle East was also a region in turmoil, in which Britain was under attack in various ways – the military presence in Egypt was seriously threatened by growing anti-British sentiment; and then by the 1954 Anglo-Egyptian Agreement, under the terms of which British military forces were to be evacuated from Egypt. The centre of gravity of British foreign and defence policies in the region had already shifted from Egypt to the Iraqi–Jordanian axis.[60] From the mid-1950s, British foreign and defence policies in the region depended on the Baghdad Pact, which had been formed in April 1955,[61] and, through counter-subversion cooperation, became 'the main instrument' to achieve 'the security of the oil' and the retention of 'the good will' of the oil-producing countries, such as Iraq and Iran.[62]

Although Britain had different defence, foreign and colonial policies towards the various Middle Eastern countries, the urgency for anti-Communist measures in the region came from the need to prepare for a possible war against the Soviet Union in the early post-war period. The defence of the Middle East was then considered by the British military as a pillar of Britain's post-war defence strategy.[63] The necessity of anti-Communist measures in the region was, in essence, primarily guided by the Defence Transition Committee (DTC) and the 1948 Government War Book.[64] The 1948 War Book set procedures for all departments, including the intelligence and security services, to deal with the possible event of war against the Soviet Union.[65] In this context, the role of MI5 was to inform security authorities of 'lists of persons' who should be detained under draconian defence regulations.[66] To ready itself, MI5 prepared its own in-house war book, which was constantly reviewed and circulated internally.[67]

The 1948 Government War Book was also the key driving policy for MI5's activities in the Middle East. The regional headquarters of MI5, SIME, the prime security authority in the region, prepared security measures in case of an emergency or war.[68] Since the Chiefs of Staff envisaged the possibility of a Soviet invasion of the region, SIME was particularly important because the integrity of the Middle East was essential for British defence planning.[69] In the same way, their activities were further directed by foreign and colonial policies in the region.[70]

A distinctive characteristic of the Middle East was that Communism had been made illegal in most Middle Eastern countries by the late 1940s.[71] Despite Communist activities being prohibited by local authorities, Communism remained a cause for concern, especially for the Chiefs of Staff, who had to plan a potential war against the Soviet Union. Although Communist Parties had not gained popular support in the region, the Communist movements were by no means non-existent and merely existed underground. According to the first comprehensive post-war survey conducted by the JIC, these underground Communist movements sought to exploit nationalist elements for 'opposition to the interests of "Anglo-American Imperialism"'.[72] Local Communist Parties and their sympathisers were inevitably regarded by the Chiefs of Staff as 'potential fifth columnists', whose activities might threaten an allied war effort in the event of war with the Soviet Union.[73]

Secondarily, since its establishment in 1949, the AC (O) Committee became the most important body not only for coordinating Britain's anti-Communist activities in the Middle East but also for stimulating anti-Communist measures to be conducted by local authorities. Countries such as Iran, Syria and Lebanon were identified as flashpoints vulnerable to Communist exploitation of local conditions, such as low standards of living and unequal distribution of wealth.[74] For instance, Sir Michael Wright, Assistant Under-Secretary at the Foreign Office and the chief expert on Middle Eastern affairs, was frequently invited to the committee's meetings to express his opinion. Wright pronounced in June 1950 that the danger of the spread of Communist influence in the Middle East was 'very real'.[75] In addition, the AC (O) considered the local security services ill-prepared for war, especially as far as their anti-Communist security measures were concerned. The AC (O) encouraged close security liaisons with Middle Eastern countries, as a means of implementing anti-Communist measures in the region.

Like the post-war Labour Government, the subsequent Conservative (Churchill, Eden, Macmillan) administrations continued to place particular importance on the region. The Overseas Planning Committee of the Foreign Office coordinated counter-subversive measures in foreign countries and its first meeting noted that 'the Middle East and South-East Asia, *in that order*, are the areas most immediately threatened and where counter-action both overt and covert is most urgently needed'.[76] From the mid-1950s, as the possibility of a conventional third world war faded away, anti-Communist measures in the region shifted from war planning to the pursuance of regional alliances through the Baghdad Pact.

Under the umbrella of anti-Communist policy, MI5, MI6 and the IRD conducted a range of activities including police training, propaganda and disruptive actions. At the regional level, there was also a Joint Intelligence Committee in the Middle East, JIC (ME), where SIME and MI6 were both represented. Although the JIC (ME) was chaired by an FO representative, it was more associated with the Chiefs of Staff than the one in Whitehall, on which the intelligence services continued to be represented.[77] The relationship between MI5 and MI6 in the region merits brief attention here. MI5's role of defending the realm against espionage, subversion and sabotage extended to the colonial territories.[78] In conditions laid out under the Attlee Directive (also known as the 'Attlee Doctrine') of 1948, MI6 operated in foreign countries.[79] Nevertheless, the post-war Middle East, consisting of both colonial territories and foreign countries, proved an exception. MI5 and MI6 operated on an ad hoc basis, partly governed by the broadly defined SIME Charter,[80] and also directed by the objectives set by the AC (O) Committee and the Baghdad Pact.

It is worth mentioning MI6's anti-Communist activities in the region in particular. From 1949, MI6's link with the Foreign Office was maintained through the PUSD.[81] In the early post-war period, however, MI6 had an even closer relationship with the Chiefs of Staff as the 'primary customers',[82] who used MI6 for 'Cold War fighting'.[83] MI6's special political action was also favoured by Prime Ministers, such as Winston Churchill, Anthony Eden and Harold Macmillan, as an instrument of foreign policy. Winston Churchill's penchant for secret intelligence and his use of it is well known.[84] Notable examples include Churchill's support for Operation BOOT/TPAJAX, to overthrow the Iranian Premier in 1953.[85] Anthony Eden also sought to use MI6 as his personal tool against Gamal Abdul Nasser.[86]

Harold Macmillan was in fact one of the key decision makers who set the direction of counter-subversive activities, especially in the Middle East. Concerning Macmillan's approach to defending 'British interests in the Middle East', Nigel Ashton remarked that he 'was not only the foremost of the Cabinet hawks over Suez' but also he was, 'if anything, even more radical' than his Cabinet colleagues.[87] In October 1955, Macmillan told Eden that the 'supply of oil' from the Middle East was vital for reviving Britain's exhausted economy, and therefore, maintaining Britain's position in the region was necessary 'at almost any cost'.[88] He seemingly favoured MI6's special operations in the Middle East region to achieve this.[89] In his memoirs, Christopher 'Monty' Woodhouse, the chief planner on the MI6 side of the 1953 Iranian coup, records that it was Macmillan, not Anthony Eden, who was keen to know more about the operational details of that coup. According to Woodhouse, Macmillan was 'clearly looking to the future possibilities' of using such an operation elsewhere.[90] In their conversation about problems with the colonial insurgency in Cyprus at a party in the Ministry of Defence in December 1954, Macmillan said to Woodhouse, 'We ought to be trying some of your [MI6] stuff there.'[91]

In addition to the use of special operations, Macmillan also had a clearer plan for the conduct of the Cold War. He saw intelligence as a cost-effective tool in implementing British policy overseas especially when facing Soviet exploitation of anti-colonial nationalist movements on the one hand, and the lack of economic and defence resources on the other. Macmillan noted that:

To accomplish this our first line of defence in these territories [refer-ring to the Middle East and South Asia] must be to build up wherever possible adequate reliable intelligence/security forces from the local population and resources so that ... these forces are *in situ* and capable of preventing a relapse into Communism or anarchy ... I am convinced that the sooner we get to work in some of these foreign ter-ritories and British Colonies the easier our task will be and the cheaper to us in terms of manpower and money.[92]

Macmillan was referring to the problems not only in the colo-nies but also in the Middle Eastern countries on which Britain's national interests depended. He simultaneously decided to 'make available technical advice on Communist subversion' to members of the Baghdad Pact (Iran, Iraq, Turkey and Pakistan), and pro-posed the formation of multilateral intelligence/security coop-eration for intelligence sharing and fighting against Communist problems in the Pact area.[93]

This proposal was significant in at least two ways. Firstly, by consolidating local security services through sharing intelligence on the methods of Communist subversion, local authorities were more likely to resist it. Thus, pro-British regimes, such as in Iraq, would remain in power. Indeed, declassified records from the Overseas Planning Committee confirm that bolstering Britain's closest ally, Iraq, against subversion was at the centre of counter-subversive measures in the region. In addition, the Baghdad Pact was considered a defence against the growing influence of the Egyptian leader, Gamal Abdul Nasser, who became a symbol of anti-British agitation in the region from 1955. The first report by the Overseas Planning Committee in March 1956 noted that:

The retention of Iraq as a firm base is of the greatest importance to Her Majesty's Government, and we should ensure that member-ship of the Baghdad Pact is seen to be more profitable than Egyptian 'neutralism'. Although no drastic covert action is urgently needed, we recommend that: ... our friends [MI6] and the Security Service should be asked to pay particular attention to forces acting in Iraq against Nuri Pasha and our interests, and to put forward suggestions for counter-measures.[94]

Secondly, liaising with other intelligence/security services allowed Britain to obtain intelligence that might not otherwise be available. Sir Patrick Dean noted that it was 'one of the functions of the Security Service; to obtain secret intelligence by its own means'.[95] Thus, the arrangement for sharing intelligence with local authorities would in turn enable Britain to 'check the growth of Communism' in the region.[96]

The nature of the post-war Middle East, which became more hostile to British presence and its influence, as well as the multiple layers of intelligence customers at different levels directing anti-Communist measures in the Middle East, made anti-Communist measures more difficult to be concerted in practice. Above all, while anti-Communist measures in the region were planned by policymakers in Whitehall, the policymakers were less concerned with the implementation, let alone the implications, of these measures in the region. In addition, the compartmentalisation of the services also contributed to the lack of coordination in practice on the ground.[97]

Britain's Relationship with the Americans in the Middle East

Britain's relationship with the United States in the Middle East was not a zero-sum game.[98] Britain enjoyed a relatively independent position in the Middle East, where the United States was seen as a new and inexperienced actor soon after the Second World War.[99] However, Britain's established 'paramount power' was rapidly fading away by the mid-1950s, and by Britain's invitation the transfer of power to the United States was completed by the early 1960s.[100] In the wider context of British decolonisation, the British Empire was also 'transformed as part of the Anglo-American coalition' in the Cold War.[101] Harold Macmillan was important in cementing the so-called special relationship after the Suez debacle and welcomed American interference in the region.[102] When American officials were deliberating possible collaboration with the British on clandestine special operations in the Syrian Crisis in September 1957, the Secretary of State of the United

States, John Foster Dulles, noted that there was 'genuine, intimate and effective cooperation, stemming directly from Macmillan'.[103]

At departmental and intelligence levels, Britain had a different degree of cooperation with the Americans.[104] Amongst all, perhaps, the closest cooperation was maintained at the military level, thanks to the Second World War, which also included intelligence sharing.[105] This was particularly true in the case of the post-war Middle East, where joint military planning saw the highest level of cooperation.[106] Security intelligence reports on Middle Eastern affairs compiled by SIME were periodically shared with the Americans after the end of the Second World War.[107] MI6 also enjoyed fairly close cooperation with the Americans. A notable example of this is the aforementioned 1953 coup in Iran.[108] The reasons for cooperation with the Americans on the British side were both financial and practical. When diplomatic relations were ended in October 1952, the British Embassy staff, including the MI6 station, were expelled from Tehran, where MI6's agents were contacted and maintained by the CIA, such as Roger Goiran, CIA station chief in Tehran, and Kermit Roosevelt, who carried out the operation with American finance.[109]

The Overseas Planning Committee also referred to future cooperation with the Americans. Sir Ivone Kirkpatrick addressed all posts abroad, encouraging more active counter-subversion in foreign countries, and noted that 'even in cases where counteraction is not possible by ourselves owing to lack of resources', 'it may still be possible to do something in consultation with our allies, e.g. the Americans'.[110] Sir Patrick Dean noted to Foreign Secretary Selwyn Lloyd in March 1956 that 'we must cooperate even more closely in all "cold war" activities' with the Americans, and reminded him that the Americans would 'certainly welcome a more robust attitude on our part', and the British 'should not scruple to ask them for financial help'.[111] In the case of countersubversive measures in Jordan, for instance, which had maintained a close connection with the British since the end of the First World War, a number of problems were identified – such as an influx of refugees that caused the collapse of the Palestine Mandate and the establishment of Israel, growing Communist influence, and all forms of hostile propaganda from the Soviet

Union and Egypt. In March 1956, Douglas Dodds-Parker, the Charmain of the Overseas Planning Committee, suggested to Selwyn Lloyd that counter-measures in Jordan be carried out by the Americans, which Lloyd approved.

By the beginning of 1958, the United States had assumed 'financial responsibility' from Britain for the Jordanian Army, with which the American Military Attaché acted as a liaison officer and made 'successful' efforts to influence the Jordanians.[112] The financial assistance to Jordan was indeed a part of the so-called Eisenhower Doctrine, which provided American assistance to Middle Eastern states that were prepared to resist Communist threats.[113] Reporting on the American activities in Jordan to the Foreign Office, Sir Charles Johnston, the British Ambassador in Jordan (1956–60), noted that this caused him 'no misgivings' since 'our relations with the Middle Eastern side of CIA are very close at present', and that 'we are agreed that it is a Western interest to keep the Jordan Arab Army both strong and efficient'.[114] Jack O'Connell, the former CIA station chief in Jordan (1963–71), who liaised directly with King Hussein of Jordan, recalls that the CIA's long relationship with Jordan started from his arrival in Jordan in the summer of 1958.[115]

Despite American involvement in certain countries, such as Egypt and Jordan, their overall policy towards the region was mostly dominated by the so-called Project ALPHA from 1954 until early 1956, concentrating on the means of achieving peace between the Arab states and Israel, and their oil interest in Saudi Arabia.[116] The ambiguous attitude of the Americans towards the region was clearly seen in the context of the American attitudes towards the Baghdad Pact – while the United States was a full member of some important committees of the Pact, such as the Economic and Military Committees (it joined in 1957), it was not a member of the Pact itself until 1959.[117] More importantly and specifically, in dealing with subversive activities in the Pact area, the United States remained officially neutral as an 'observer' and its ambiguous attitudes continued throughout the period. Elie Podeh has suggested that 'all these mixed signals created the impression that Washington did not consider the Baghdad Pact as a major instrument of policy'.[118] A report by the British Chief of the Imperial General Staff confirmed in August 1958 that, 'up to the present time', from their point of view, 'the United States have had no wish to support or protect British interests'.[119]

The American accession to the Pact in 1959 largely resulted from British efforts to maintain the Pact as a regional defence/security organisation. When the Baghdad Pact lost its headquarters, after Iraqi withdrawal, Britain faced difficulties in persuading the remaining regional members to maintain the rationale for and morale of the Pact. Britain was especially concerned about Iran, which belonged to the Baghdad Pact but not to any another Western security organisations, unlike Turkey (a member of NATO) and Pakistan (a member of the Southeast Asia Treaty Organization, SEATO). The CIA noted that 'the British are anxious to boost the Shah's morale', and also recorded that Selwyn Lloyd insisted in September 1958 on the United States becoming a full member and expressed his concern that 'Iran might go neutralist if the Shah does not receive the material and moral support he deems necessary.'[120]

Until the Iraqi Revolution on 14 July 1958, Britain's policy towards the region had maintained a strong anti-Nasserite stance, paying particular attention to 'the region-wide task of diminishing Egyptian and Saudi influence' and 'breaking the Egypt/Saudi axis'.[121] Soon after Britain 'lost' Iraq, its closest ally in the region, Harold Macmillan reconsidered Britain's position, dropping its outright anti-Nasserite policy, and reformulated a new policy towards the region.[122] In order to maintain good relations with the Baghdad Pact members, who were unlikely to welcome such a policy, the British government decided that the Americans 'should be induced to join the new organisation'.[123] Consequently, the United States joined CENTO, which was the Baghdad Pact renamed, and they participated in counter-subversive activities from 1959 onwards.

Conclusion

Anti-Communist measures overseas dominated debates inside the British government about the conduct of the Cold War throughout the period between the late 1940s and the mid-1950s. As the Cold War intensified, diplomats faced greater pressure to instigate ever more active measures, and counter-subversion gradually intensified. Whitehall planners created elaborate machinery which drove the new agenda. Late 1955 was a key date for the Middle East in particular. Before then, the Chiefs of Staff prioritised the region, given its likely importance in any third world war. From the mid-1950s, counter-subversion became seen more as a tool of foreign policy – under the Baghdad Pact, regional cooperation in counter-subversion was regarded as necessary to check and prevent the spread of Communism in the region. Policymakers in London increasingly saw intelligence and security services as having a core role to play in anti-Communist measures as a central part of the burgeoning Cold War policy. As will be shown in the following chapters, MI5, MI6 and the IRD had particularly important functions to play in such activity, but there were also implications for the internal security of the regional governments.

2 Security Training and Liaison in Anti-Communist Measures

People in the Arab world were intrigued by the Communists . . . The old political parties all over the Arab world were bankrupt of ideas and influences because the world was changing and they were not prepared for change. So there was a vacuum of power and the idea of Communism was potentially attractive . . . When the Communist Manifesto was smuggled into Egypt it caused a sensation. Intellectuals read it and thought that they had come upon a key which could open all the political and social doors.

Mohamed Heikal[1]

It is in countries where social unrest and resentment may be exploited that Communism gains a hold. The Middle East, as long as it remains under the imperialist yoke, took the line of least resistance to Communism. In Egypt, at this time, we were witnessing the birth of a new fanaticism – Communism – and the revival of the old fanaticism of the Muslim Brotherhood. At first taking parallel courses, the two creeds finally converged and united.

Anwar El Sadat[2]

Introduction

Mohamed Heikal, an Egyptian journalist writing on the potential appeal of Communism, illustrates a common sentiment amongst Egyptians immediately after the Second World War. More importantly, these ideas could be found throughout the Middle East, where many dominant political parties enjoyed close ties with Britain and were increasingly being challenged by a public growing frustrated with their local politics. While the idea of Communism never became popular in the region, as a result of measures adopted by the strongly anti-Communist governments, frustrated nationalists adopted a revolutionary tendency often associated with International Communism and engaged in subversive activities to change the status quo. Sometimes anti-colonialists did work with the Communists to achieve shared goals. Anwar El Sadat, as quoted above, has pointed out that the Muslim Brotherhood, an anti-British militant group, conducted subversive activities against the pro-British Egyptian government in tandem with Communists.

This chapter reveals firstly, how the British government came to conclude that training Middle Eastern security services in anti-Communist measures was necessary, and secondly, the way in which these measures were implemented in Lebanon, Iran, Iraq and Jordan. It also shows that British anti-Communist policy and concerns about the Communist movements in the region dovetailed with the demands of Middle Eastern governments for British advice on anti-Communist measures.

Setting a Policy of Security Advising and Police Training

The origins of Britain's security advice to, and training of, colonial security forces can be traced back to before the Second World War when Whitehall despatched a number of security officers to the colonies and Commonwealth as a precautionary measure for maintaining internal security.[3] However, it is wrong to assume that the training courses conducted by MI5 in the post-war period merely involved the maintenance of law and order. These courses were more specifically geared towards enhancing the intelligence and security capabilities of local authorities. When General (later Field-Marshal) Sir Gerald Templer, the Chief of the Imperial General Staff, conducted a survey of the status of internal security machinery throughout the British Empire in the early 1950s, intelligence was considered 'our Achilles heel'.[4] Referring to the ongoing counter-insurgency in Malaya, he insisted that 'the emergency will be won by our intelligence system – our Special

Branch'.[5] British advice and training courses were designed specifically for anti-Communist measures, and MI5 was the chief organiser from the outset.

Sir Percy Sillitoe, the first post-war Director-General of MI5, made twelve substantial trips to British territories overseas, advising and liaising with local authorities on enhancing internal security.[6] MI5 officers were also sent to colonial territories under the title of Security Liaison Officer (SLO) to work with local security forces to prevent Communist influence and ensure that newly independent states would not fall to Moscow's influence.[7] Such service formed a sizeable part of the lives of MI5 personnel who were expected to spend 'a quarter to a third of their careers on overseas posting in the Empire and Commonwealth' to advise local authorities on security matters.[8]

Drawing on Templer's recommendations for enhancing colonial security, the Colonial Office formed its own Intelligence and Security Department in 1955. Meanwhile, three MI5 officers were seconded to the Colonial Office under the title of Security Intelligence Adviser (SIA) and, between 1954 and 1957, paid fifty-seven visits to twenty-seven colonial territories, helping to found some twenty-one Colonial Special Branches.[9] A. M. MacDonald, a chief SIA (1954–7), noted that:

> the aim is to build towards an indigenous professional intelligence service, able to stand on its own feet when self-government is attained in meeting the intelligence needs of the territory . . . Such an organisation is not only a valuable legacy to a territory achieving independence, but the best guarantee of maintaining H.M.G.'s intelligence interests in the longer term.[10]

MI5 regularly organised a series of training courses designed for senior police officers, such as the heads of Special Branch or equivalent ranks, of all colonial and protectorate territories. The total number of colonial and Commonwealth police and administrative officers trained in Britain by MI5 averaged 250 per year from 1954 to 1958; at the height of decolonisation the following year, it peaked at 367.[11] Colonial security officers attending the training courses were also greeted by Colonial

Secretary Alan Lennox-Boyd.[12] The purpose of providing such training was, in Templer's words, for the 'stepping-up of intelligence activity' against the spread of Communist movements overseas.[13]

MI5's police training appears mainly to have consisted of two different curricula: one was a series of lectures conducted by senior MI5 officers, and the other was a number of Special Branch training sessions run by Scotland Yard. MI5 designed the lectures to foster common understanding of the nature and scale of International Communist movements throughout the world and included a range of topics, such as 'Why Communists are subversive'.[14] Sir Dick White, later the Director-General of MI5 and Chief of MI6, delivered a lecture on the links between the Soviet Intelligence Service and International Communism, entitled 'The Methods of Soviet Subversion throughout the World', and one on 'The Objects and Capabilities of the Communist Party of Great Britain' (CPGB).[15] According to Peter Wright, a former MI5 officer, Dick White 'believed in the fashionable idea of "containing" the Soviet Union, and that MI5 had a vital role to play in neutralizing Soviet assets', meaning that successful counter-subversive measures could prevent the spread of Communist movements.[16] The training sessions run by Scotland Yard dealt with tradecraft and techniques of counter-intelligence and counter-subversion, including how to detect secret writing hidden in a letter and how to discreetly open and re-seal mail.[17]

There was an additional development in the colonies. In the mid-1950s, again on Templer's recommendation, several Regional Training Colleges, also known as Special Branch Training Units, were established for the purpose of anti-Communist training.[18] By November 1957, these colleges hosted the majority of anti-Communist training courses.[19] Such training was not, however, confined to Britain and the Empire but also took place in the Middle East more broadly.

British Security/Police Liaison in Anti-Communist Measures in the Middle East

The British realised that Communists had successfully infiltrated Eastern European police forces. As a result, training foreign police officers in preventing such infiltration was key to stopping the spread of Communist movements overseas. This logic had already driven the British to enhance colonial security, but extended to the Middle East more broadly.[20] The task of prioritising, directing and supervising Britain's anti-Communist measures fell to the aforementioned highly secret Cabinet committee, the AC (O). Target partner countries spanned Western Europe, Southeastern Europe, Southeast Asia and Latin America.[21] Above all, however, Whitehall officials considered the Middle East the most important region to be protected and that it required anti-Communist measures to be implemented most urgently.

In the 1920s and 1930s, local Communist Parties in the Middle East were founded under the direction of the Comintern, and adhered to a Soviet Marxist-Leninist ideological doctrine.[22] While using subversive propaganda to undermine the reputation of local authorities, these Communist groups attempted to infiltrate armies and security services. But the local governments were well aware of such activity and authorised rigorous counter-measures against them, enforced by domestic laws. According to the Iraqi Penal Code, for example, expression of approval or dissemination of Communist doctrines would be punished by penal servitude, and if the offence occurred in the 'presence of more than one member of the armed forces or the police', it would be 'punishable with death'.[23] Similar measures were enforced in other Middle Eastern countries, including Egypt and Turkey.[24] By the late 1940s, Communist activities were outlawed throughout the region, except Israel.

Despite these legislative settings, the attitudes of Middle Eastern governments towards Communists varied from country to country. Iraq, Britain's closest ally, which had maintained a strong policy since the 1920s, was the leading anti-Communist government in the region until 1958. Despite being resilient since its establishment in the early 1930s, the Iraqi Communist Party

(ICP) was consistently suppressed by the Iraqi authorities.[25] These security measures were conducted by the Criminal Investigation Department (CID) of the Iraqi Police, led by Colonel Bahjat Beg Attiyah since the 1930s.[26]

Meanwhile, in Lebanon, which was considered to have the most liberal government in the region, the authorities were more reluctant to take firm action. Emir Farid Chehab, the Chef de Sûreté (Head of the Lebanese Sûreté Générale) (1948–58), once told a Western journalist that 'They [Lebanese politicians] will tell you they are fighting Communism, but it is only because they think it will please [the West] to hear that.'[27] When Chehab visited Captain Guy Liddell, the Deputy Director-General of MI5, at Leconfield House in London in 1951, he lamented the fact that he had received virtually no support from his Ministers to conduct anti-Communist measures in the country. In addition, Chehab had only a handful of officers whom he could trust in his organisation, and also believed that the Lebanese Police had been penetrated by Communists or their sympathisers. Whenever Chehab warned the police about a forthcoming Communist demonstration in the country, 'the information reached the Communist Party within an hour'.[28]

Since the Middle East was considered of paramount importance to Britain's post-war strategy, the AC (O) paid close attention to Communist activities in the region. The problem with the Communist movements in the Middle East, from the British point of view, was that, since they had been forced underground, it was difficult to obtain a clear picture of their extent and influence. Regardless of their size and popularity, the danger of Communist activities was noted by General Sir John Bagot Glubb, Commander of the Arab Legion, known as Glubb Pasha: 'communism does not wait until it secures a majority', and 'a small group of fanatics carry out the coup d'état'.[29] This fear of the Communist menace was exacerbated by the fact that the region was full of intrigue, conspiracies, and assassinations by internal opponents and external enemies.[30] Glubb Pasha also warned the Foreign Office in 1950 with an Arab proverb that 'the enemy of my enemy is my friend' – both Britain and pro-British regimes were easily targeted by propaganda from Communists and the Soviet Union, and Communists could be seen as allies by non-Communist anti-British groups.[31] In November 1948, the Foreign Office had already contemplated sending Graham Mitchell of MI5, an expert in International Communist movements, to countries such as Iran, Iraq, Transjordan, Lebanon and Egypt, to 'tender advice to those countries on communist methods and tactics'.[32] This earlier proposal was eventually turned down as no requests had been made by the local authorities.

Once the Korean War broke out in June 1950, the AC (O) grew particularly concerned about the situation in the region as, despite Communist Parties being prohibited, local authorities were not deemed particularly aware of the 'insidious nature of methods used by Communists' outside the region.[33] The Foreign Office considered that even the most diligent security forces, such as those of the Egyptians and Iraqis, were 'not particularly well-conceived or effective' as they tended to 'make arrests too soon, thus losing valuable intelligence'.[34] The AC (O) agreed that local authorities lacked experience in anti-Communist security measures in the event of a third world war.[35]

The first group to attend MI5's security training courses was not colonial police officers but, in fact, an Iranian delegation. Convinced of the inefficiency of Iran's own methods to fight Communism in the country, General Hadj Ali Razmara, the Chief of the Iranian General Staff, approached the British Embassy in Tehran via a British Military Attaché in 1950. He asked the British to assist in conducting anti-Communist measures in his own security organisation, the Deuxième Bureau (also known as the G-2), and also requested his military officers be trained in London. Once his request reached policymakers in London via the Foreign Office, the AC (O) welcomed Iran's interest in enhancing anti-Communist measures and asked MI5 to meet the requests.[36] Accordingly, Captain Guy Liddell arranged specially designed anti-Communist courses for the Iranians, in consultation with Jack Easton, the Vice-Chief of MI6.[37] The delegation of four senior Iranian officers (two from the police and two from the G-2), all of whom had also been vetted by MI5 prior to their visit, arrived in London in late October 1950.[38]

During the anti-Communist training course, senior MI5 officers delivered a series of three lectures to the Iranians.[39] In order to meet their guests' specific requests, a four-week-long practical training session, run by Scotland Yard, was held at the Metropolitan Police Training School, Hendon. The Iranians stayed in Britain nearly a year as further ad hoc training followed at a War Office Field Security course and one of the higher police training courses at Hendon.[40] However, there was a practical difficulty in training the Iranians: communication. When Guy Liddell gave the lecture to the Iranian officers in November 1950, he had to speak 'very slowly' and repeat it 'at least three times' as 'none of them understood much English'.[41]

Despite this difficulty, similar training courses were arranged at the request of other Middle Eastern governments. Senior Middle Eastern security chiefs, such as Emir Farid Chehab, Chief of the Lebanese Sûreté Générale, and Colonel Bahjat Beg Attiyah, Director of the Iraqi CID, also attended such courses.[42] Jordanian senior officers were also regular attendees at the request of Glubb Pasha.[43] These training courses were also made available to Iraqis sent by Duncan MacIntosh, the British Police Adviser to the Minister of the Interior, in the mid-1950s.[44] Britain decided which countries to train as a result of both requests from local authorities and strategic consideration within the AC (O).

After providing anti-Communist training to a number of Middle Eastern police officers, another approach was adopted by 1951. Working to a different standard and practice, anti-Communist training in Britain had 'little chance of improving national security services' in the Middle East. Guy Liddell then instead suggested the AC (O)'s anti-Communist measures be implemented 'through local liaison by Security Service trained personnel or by Police advisers'.[45] The introduction of the British adviser had at least two objectives: the first objective was to try to control the spread of Communism; the second was to obtain information on Communist movements in the region. Chairman of the JIC, Sir Patrick Reilly, also a permanent member of the AC (O), recorded:

> Apart from the obvious value of this to our general anti-communist effort, any such strengthening of links with foreign police authorities

can be of great advantage both to [MI6] and the Security Service, by paving the way to the exchange of information and operational liaison.[46]

Thus, a two-track approach was adopted: while providing anti-Communist training courses to Middle Eastern security services, liaison officers visited the region to advise the local authorities on measures directly. By 1951, while still providing anti-Communist courses in London, posting security advisers to local governments had become the preferred method for advising local authorities on more effective administrative and legislative measures against the local communist problem. It sought to check the spread of Communism in the region through liaison with the local police of 'strategically important countries'.[47]

In addition to the introduction of British security advisers in the region, the AC (O) decided in June 1951 to use Britain's closest ally in the region, Iraq, to encourage other Middle Eastern authorities to take 'legislative and administrative action to combat Communist activities' through the sharing of Iraqi experience and information. The British Ambassador in Baghdad was instructed to suggest that the Iraqi government cooperate with other local authorities to 'take steps to segregate and re-educate political persons held on charges of Communist activities'.[48]

In 1956, the importance of security training was restated under Eden as one of the pillars of counter-subversive measures. The Overseas Planning Committee, the successor to the AC (O), quickly stated: 'We consider that the value of training in security and anti-communist techniques cannot be overemphasised.' The Eden memorandum provided the financial resources (£25,000 a year) needed for security training especially for foreign security forces; a stark contrast to earlier efforts hampered by a lack of funding. In addition to arranging such training courses for foreign security/police officers either in Britain or in host countries, this made it easier to conduct anti-Communist measures through a residential security/liaison officer, attached to a foreign government, free of charge to the host government. It had previously been very difficult for the Foreign Office to persuade the Treasury to authorise payments to despatch British advisers to foreign countries to conduct security training on an ad hoc basis.[49] By the mid-1950s, and demonstrating the importance of the threat, this had changed dramatically.

The Lebanese Sûreté Générale and Ousting the French Influence

Lebanon is normally regarded as part of the French sphere of influence owing to its colonial legacy.[50] Nonetheless, the British had compelling reasons to undertake robust anti-Communist measures in the country. Lebanon housed the highest number of Communist Party members (12,000) and sympathisers (50,000) in the Middle East.[51] The Lebanese Communist Party (LCP) was also believed to have been cooperating very closely with the Syrian Communist Party (SCP) under a Joint Higher Committee. The strength of the SCP was estimated at around 2,000–2,500 members.[52] According to British intelligence, the LCP also 'kept in close touch with the Soviet Legation', through which it was believed that the Soviets maintained close ties with regional Communist Parties.[53] When the chief expert on Middle Eastern affairs, Sir Michael Wright, then Assistant Under-Secretary of the Foreign Office, was invited in June 1950 to an AC (O) meeting to express his opinion on Communist influence in the Middle East, he insisted on the need to 'stimulate' the Lebanese government to take necessary action as they were showing 'very little vigour in tackling this problem'.[54]

It is noteworthy that, by the time the anti-Communist measures in Lebanon were discussed at the AC (O) in London, the Lebanese had already approached Britain for advice. In March 1949, the Lebanese Minister of Foreign Affairs, Hamid Franjieh, approached Sir William Houstoun-Boswall, the British Minister in Beirut, to ask for a British expert on anti-Communist measures. Houstoun-Boswall then reported the Lebanese request to London with great secrecy, as 'nobody including the chief of secret police knows anything of this move which it is desired to keep secret and quite unofficial'.[55] The reason for the secrecy was mainly due to the presence of a French security adviser to the

Lebanese government in Beirut. Since 1920, Lebanon had hosted French advisers who intervened in every single matter of internal security, including operational aspects, recruitment of personnel and promotions.[56] Since countering French influence in Lebanon had been a British concern since before the end of the war, the Lebanese approach presented Whitehall with a unique opportunity to establish influence in the French sphere by placing a senior police officer in the heart of the Lebanese government with access to the Prime Minister and the chance to impart personal advice on anti-Communist measures.[57]

L. G. Thirkell, a senior official of the Eastern Department of the Foreign Office in charge of Syrian and Lebanese affairs, noted that appointing such an expert without informing the French 'would arouse the worst suspicions', but it was decided not to tell them as notification would 'invite serious criticism and such an appointment would presumably have to be kept secret or have some form of cover'.[58] A meeting was soon held in the Foreign Office, where officials decided that 'the best man' for the assignment, an MI5 expert in International Communism, Graham Mitchell, was to be sent to keep the Lebanese government on track.[59] Mitchell's mission was to secure a position in Lebanon; his failure to do so might cause the Lebanese government 'to approach another Power instead, such as the Americans or even the French'.[60]

In post-war Lebanon, the internal security system was inherited from the French Mandate, in which the Sûreté Générale, the Lebanese Security Service, was responsible for internal security, including counter-espionage and counter-subversion.[61] The Sûreté Générale comprised sectarian factions reflecting the structure of the Lebanese government.[62] The complexity of the Lebanese security apparatus as a result of sectarianism also hampered effective security work. One such 'petty annoyance' which Emir Farid Chehab, then newly appointed as Head of the Sûreté Générale, complained about to Major David Beaumont-Nesbitt, Assistant Military Attaché at the British Embassy in Beirut, was that his official telephone line in the Sûreté was 'tapped by agents of the President's brother'.[63] Major Beaumont-Nesbitt, serving as the representative of MI5 in Lebanon and Syria, seconded from the Army on a temporary basis, reported to MI5 headquarters that 'the mechanics of this preposterous operation, if true, are, as one may imagine, highly complex and there are the usual wheels within wheels, the agents concerned being simultaneously employed by various organisations'.[64]

Mitchell's visit in May 1949 was an appreciable success. During the visit, he convinced the Lebanese Prime Minister, Riad el-Solh, that the Communist movement was a 'formidable enemy', able to act as 'a fifth column in the event of war with Russia'. He also managed to obtain an oral promise to appoint a British adviser to Farid Chehab. Mitchell wrote in his report that:

> Repeated reports from various sources have emphasised that from the Russian Legation in Beirut there springs a multitude of espionage and other subversive activities ... British control, direct or indirect, of a local Security Service [Sûreté Générale] working on efficient lines would therefore hold out a promise of producing material of considerable intelligence value.[65]

In addition, Mitchell noted that it was essential to meet with Farid Chehab, with the permission of Riad el-Solh, to discuss the subject, as Farid Chehab was 'thoroughly friendly to British interests and ready to co-operate'. He was above all 'a close contact of our [MI5] representative in Beirut'.[66]

Farid Chehab, still remembered as 'Bay al Amn al Aam [Father of the Sûreté Générale]' in Lebanon, retained the post of Chef de Sûreté for over a decade until September 1958.[67] He served his country diligently, but most of all, Farid Chehab was an anti-Communist, believing with Britain that Communism was a real threat which was detrimental to the values and traditions of the Middle East. He directed and prioritised anti-Communist measures over other issues, which he considered of lesser importance.[68] He once explained to a Middle East correspondent of *TIME*, Keith Wheelock, the reasons for his, and other Middle Eastern governments', association with the West:

> If it comes to war, the Middle East will fall to the Communists inevitably. Just as inevitably you'll have to take it back. The West could not

abide Russia controlling the Middle East. It'll be a lot easier to take it back if the people are on your side. If they're not on your side it will be almost impossible to take it back.[69]

Moreover, Farid Chehab was clearly pro-British, as opposed to being pro-American – he regarded the Americans as being 'temperamentally incapable of understanding the complexities of the Levant'.[70] Farid Chehab had an intimate relationship with the British: after his imprisonment by the Vichy French, he had, though indirectly, cooperated with Colonel Sir Patrick Coghill, the head of the British Security Mission in Lebanon during postwar independence from French rule; in August 1947, he attended a three-month training course, including counter-espionage, at Scotland Yard's Superior Police Training College in Britain. Once he was back from Britain, he was appointed Head of the Sûreté Générale.[71]

Mitchell left written recommendations with Riad el-Solh regarding steps to take in combating Communism. He suggested Riad el-Solh enhance the capabilities of the Sûreté Générale – giving Farid Chehab a 'free hand' for internal security; allowing him to have a technical liaison with the Minister of Posts and Telegrams with the 'object of putting at the disposal of the Sûreté means for the interception of communications of suspects'; and to set up effective control of frontiers and of 'Russian and satellite aliens' by ensuring that 'no alien enters or resides in the Lebanon' without the knowledge of the government. These were deliberately written in French to conceal 'evidence of British origin'.[72] Wiretapping, as recommended by Mitchell, became an integral part of maintaining internal security for the Sûreté Générale under the direction of Farid Chehab.[73]

In his report, Mitchell recommended that the Foreign Office respond quickly should the Lebanese formally request an adviser, and to make the necessary appointment while 'the iron is hot'. If not, an alternative possibility was to insert a 'technical officer at a lower level' into the Sûreté to 'be elevated gradually by Farid [Chehab] as opportunity offers'.[74] Soon after Mitchell's visit, administrative developments indeed emerged: Farid Chehab acquired a new building for the Sûreté Générale and strictly compartmentalised sections were established for organisational efficacy.[75]

After initial hesitation by the Lebanese President, Bechara El Khoury, who favoured a French connection, a formal request for an adviser from the Lebanese government eventually reached the Foreign Office via the British Embassy in Beirut.[76] J. M. Kyles – the former Commissioner of Police in Sudan, and a fluent Arabic speaker with some twenty years of experience in Palestine – was appointed Security Adviser in May 1950.[77] J. M. Kyles was tasked by the AC (O) to 'stimulate' the Lebanese government 'to repress' the Communist menace.[78] In September 1950, about four months after the appointment of Kyles, Riad el-Solh issued a new secret decree for the formation of a special Anti-Communist Bureau, to be headed by Farid Chehab as the Chef de Sûreté.[79] Shortly after its establishment, Farid Chehab was once again in Britain, this time for training in anti-Communist measures.[80]

Nevertheless, anti-Communist measures in Lebanon through both J. M. Kyles and Farid Chehab ended with mixed results. Following the formation of the Anti-Communist Bureau, Sir William Houstoun-Boswall despatched a letter to Ernest Bevin:

> Mr Kyles, the Police Adviser whose task, as you can well imagine, is not an easy one here, has been trying to influence the authorities to work along more systematic lines. The trouble is, as you will not be surprised to hear, that Mr Kyles' advice is very rarely sought and when given is not acted upon ... But now they have at least begun – if only dimly – to appreciate the very real danger presented by Communism. And I do not propose to allow them again to relapse into their pipe dream that Communism must be dead just because it is outlawed.[81]

This indicates that the influence of a British SLO in the implementation of legislative measures was limited as the final decision was always in the hands of the Lebanese government. In fact, the anti-Communist Lebanese government was short-lived. When Riad el-Solh was assassinated in July 1951, the implementation of these anti-Communist measures became more strained. It also caused the termination of Kyles's advisory post.[82]

As noted earlier, when Farid Chehab met with Guy Liddell during his training in Britain in June 1951, he told Liddell that Kyles's advice had rarely been sought owing to constant changes in government policy, which also cut the manpower of Chehab's organisation from '200 to 100', of which Chehab felt he could rely on 'barely 5 per cent' as the organisation, he believed, had been penetrated by Communist sympathisers and hampered by sectarianism.[83] In addition, Farid Chehab noted that he received little support from his ministers, and even when he reported that someone in the government was 'working for the Russians', no action was taken.[84] Despite the opportunity to challenge French influence, and the risk of going behind French backs, British attempts to shape Lebanese policy ultimately came to little.

Iranian G-2 and General Razmara

Iran had caused Cold War concerns since the end of the Second World War, and, by 1950, the JIC estimated that the strength of the Tudeh Party was around 10,000–12,000 members.[85] Again though, the initial approach for liaison came not from the British but instead from Tehran. General Hadj Ali Razmara, the Chief of the Iranian General Staff, secretly contacted the Military Attaché at the British Embassy in January 1950.[86] This was not the first attempt. As noted earlier, a proposal to send Graham Mitchell of MI5 to Tehran in November 1948 to 'obtain information about Communism' and share the British experience of combating Communism in Malaya was rejected due to the lax security of the Iranian government and fears that news of the contact might leak to the Russians.[87] In addition, in March 1949, when the Iranian Police informally contacted Scotland Yard requesting counter-espionage training, MI5 saw an opportunity 'to exploit' but the Iranian government never made a formal request.[88] The 1950 approach therefore formed Britain's opportunity to train the Iranians in anti-Communist measures, as well as to obtain information about Communist activities in Iran.

Razmara's decision to approach the British came after debriefing a Soviet walk-in, named 'Vassilev', who defected to the Iranian authorities with some documents on the subversive activities of the Tudeh Party.[89] Convinced that Iran's own methods of fighting Communism had been insufficient, General Razmara hoped to improve his own security organisation, the G-2, with help from Britain. Razmara regarded the G-2 as 'the only effective organisation in the country' in combating the continued underground activity of the Tudeh Party, and believed that the police had been penetrated by the Communists.[90] Despite the presence of a large American military mission in Iran, Razmara later noted to Haldane-Porter of MI5 that he did not consult with the Americans on this matter since the Americans had 'no understanding of the Asiatic mentality', and it would therefore be 'a waste of time to have a resident American Adviser' in Tehran.[91]

Since no one was available from MI5 Headquarters at the time, it was considered that Brigadier William Magan, Head of SIME, the regional headquarters of MI5, would be an ideal candidate to visit Tehran for a discussion with General Razmara, as Magan spoke Persian and knew the country well from his experience there during the Second World War.[92] Magan's task was to find out whether the long-term appointment of a British residential adviser was necessary.[93] The proposal was, nevertheless, turned down by Foreign Secretary Ernest Bevin, who was content to advise the Iranians on anti-Communist measures in principle, but unhappy with the 'likelihood that the Russians would know who Mr Magan is'.[94] It was then decided that Haldane-Porter, a senior officer of MI5's OS (Over-Seas) Division, whose real identity was 'certainly not known to the Russians', would travel to Tehran via Cairo in late March 1950 in the guise of 'a member of the Foreign Service'.[95] The US Embassy in Tehran was informed of Haldane-Porter's visit in advance.[96]

In the course of his four-day-long discussions with General Razmara, which were conducted in French owing to Razmara's lack of fluency in English, Haldane-Porter was fully briefed on Razmara's G-2 organisation with a chart of its organisational structure; it had been given particular responsibility for watching and countering the activities of the Tudeh Party under a special law passed after the attempted assassination of the Shah of Iran in February 1949.[97] From Haldane-Porter's view, the G-2 was an 'ambitiously large' organisation – while being responsible for intelligence collection and analysis for the Iranian military services, it also functioned as an internal security service, responsible for espionage, counter-espionage, anti-subversive activities and censorship. Haldane-Porter also learned of the activities of the Tudeh Party and the difficulties Razmara faced in countering their activities: 'Russian agents of all kinds were continually being sent across the Persian [Iranian]/Soviet frontier with money, with arms, and with propaganda material.'[98] During the discussions, he was handed classified up-to-date reports on the activities of the Tudeh Party, and on a member of the Soviet Embassy in Tehran, Daniel Semyonovich Komissarov, a Russian Iranologist who was believed to be connected with the Tudeh Party.[99]

General Razmara then requested his military officers be trained in anti-Communist measures in Britain, and a British security adviser be stationed in Tehran. This was the context mentioned earlier in which Iranian officers were sent to and trained in London. The discussion also touched upon what the British government could receive in return. In the current arrangement, the British Military Attaché had been granted limited access to 'some Russian defectors' in Iranian hands. General Razmara agreed to extend this to allow the British completely free access to 'any Russians who either defected from the Soviet Union into Iran or were captured by the Iranians'. Haldane-Porter was also promised that General Razmara would prepare for him 'a long detailed report', setting out 'the sum of [Razmara's] knowledge of the Tudeh Party'. Haldane-Porter commented on the rationale behind this arrangement in his report:

> In all our discussions on the subject of Russians, Razmara adopted a surprisingly sensible and realist attitude. He said that the Soviet Union was a very big, powerful country which could easily occupy Persia [Iran] by force; he was therefore not really interested in what went on inside the Soviet Union, except in the immediate area of the Soviet/Persian frontier. We, however, were extremely interested in the Soviet Union and he was glad to help us in obtaining information about it.[100]

General Razmara's mentality, which Haldane-Porter described as having 'an exaggerated but understandable phobia of the Russians', perhaps also added to his rationale.[101]

Besides the appointment of a British security adviser, Haldane-Porter later proposed to MI5 headquarters that a Russian-speaking Assistant Military Attaché should be appointed to the British Embassy in Tehran for the purpose of this new arrangement, instead of using a representative from either MI5 or MI6. This was owing to the fact that, to Haldane-Porter's surprise, General Razmara was unaware of the presence of an MI6 officer operating in Tehran at the time.[102] Thus, without raising General Razmara's suspicions, Haldane-Porter noted that the appointment of a 'genuine' Russian-speaking Assistant Military Attaché was ideal, someone who would be able to use 'his knowledge of Russian to interrogate Russians in Persian [Iranian] hands' in addition to carrying out his normal duties as an Assistant Military Attaché.[103] The appointment is unclear from documentary evidence, but was probably Alexis Kougoulsky Forter, a former RAF officer, who had emigrated from Russia. Alexis Forter had been in the Middle East in the late 1940s as a junior SIME officer, and he was also present in Tehran in the tumultuous year of 1953 as not an MI5 but an MI6 officer. He later became the Head of Station in Baghdad in the late 1950s.[104]

Appointing a British security/police adviser to Tehran, however, did prove difficult owing to an agreement with General Razmara, who insisted on absolute secrecy about the arrangement, with the exception of the Shah. In addition, Razmara made it clear that there would never be formal contact between the British and Iranian governments. The *maison de rendezvous* for the intelligence liaison was to be somewhere in Tehran, where an Iranian military official, chosen by Razmara, and the British security adviser 'could meet frequently for the discharge of their business'.[105] Razmara also noted that the adviser should be protected by diplomatic immunity as a member of the British Embassy staff in case of arrest by the Iranian Police.[106] Given the growing anti-British sentiment throughout Iran as a result of the internal political situation at the time, Razmara's obsessive secrecy was understandable. Razmara was above all a military officer, but also a calculated politician. Intelligence historian Stephen Dorril notes that Razmara was 'well aware that any suspicion of British meddling and influence could spell political suicide'.[107]

The AC (O) strongly endorsed the arrangement as a 'valuable means of combating subversive Russian activities' in Iran, and recommended to Ernest Bevin the appointment of Sir George Jenkin as a British adviser to the Iranians on anti-Communist measures.[108] Bevin was content with the proposal in principle but turned it down, as 'there might be a risk that the Russians would be given a good excuse for complaining strongly to the Persians [Iranians] about our activities'.[109] Nevertheless, consideration was given to the fact that General Razmara was the most likely to become the next Prime Minister of Iran.[110] On 26 June 1950, five days after Clement Attlee approved the proposal, General Razmara indeed became Prime Minister.[111] The main difficulty of this arrangement was MI5's chosen candidate – Sir William 'George' Jenkin, former Deputy Director of the Intelligence Bureau in India (1930–50).[112] There were 'large Indian and Pakistani Embassies in Tehran' whose staff were well aware of Sir George Jenkin's career in India, and so creating a diplomatic cover for him – without exposing his contact with the Iranians – was 'impossible'.[113]

The substitute for Jenkin was John Albert Briance, the former head of the CID of the Palestine Police until 1948.[114] Guy Liddell noted in his diaries that Briance was operating in the guise of Political Adviser in Iran and provided '90 per cent' of the information on the internal political situation, mostly concerning the activities of the Tudeh Party, in Iran.[115] Christopher 'Monty' Woodhouse also remembers that, when he visited Tehran during the turmoil of 1952, there was 'a useful liaison, approved by the Shah, with the chief of the Security Police, who was well informed about the Tudeh Party'; Woodhouse was likely also referring to John Briance.[116]

During his tenure as premier, Razmara was an ardent anti-Communist, acting as the Minister of the Interior and controlling the Iranian Police at the same time. Razmara undertook a series of both legislative and administrative initiatives to counter subversion, including improving prison discipline to control the activities of Tudeh prisoners; giving the government discretion to proclaim martial law; and taking action against subversive publications. Sir Francis Shepherd, British Ambassador to Tehran, reported to Bevin that 'these measures have been reasonably effective'.[117]

In addition, as noted earlier, under the agreement reached with Haldane-Porter, Razmara sent four hand-picked Iranian officers (two from the police, and two from G-2) to Britain in late October 1950 for one year of anti-Communist training. Their expenses were paid by the Iranian government, but knowledge about what these officers were doing was even concealed from the Iranian Embassy in London.[118] Sir Francis Shepherd noted to Sir Michael Wright that 'on return they would be capable of setting up a competent unit for dealing with subversive activity'.[119] He also noted that:

> we have already provided them [the Iranians], at their request, with an expert to advise the General Staff on these matters [anti-Communist measures], and he is now busily and successfully at work … The responsibility for watching and checking Tudeh activities is also shared by the Police, and here again we are helping by arranging for two police officers (and two army officers) to undergo a course of training in the United Kingdom. These two measures should go far to keep the Persian Government fully aware of the insidious nature of Communist methods and of ways of dealing with them.[120]

Nevertheless, the Iranians' effective anti-Communist measures did not last long. Razmara was assassinated on 7 March 1951, two days after he refused to nationalise the Anglo-Iranian Oil Company in the face of pressure from the National Front, led by Dr Mohammad Mossadeq. This abrupt end to Razmara's premiership was a clear setback for anti-Communist measures in Iran. In addition, the appointment of John Briance, presumably the security adviser to Razmara, did not last long either. And once Briance's post had been withdrawn by 1952, any intelligence on internal political matters 'practically dried up'.[121]

Just before Razmara was assassinated, there had been a series of propaganda campaigns by the left-wing press, such as 'cartoons' showing Razmara's and the Shah's close and secret association with 'the Union Jack'.[122] After his assassination, *Pravda*, one of the main Soviet arms for propaganda, also seized the opportunity to damage British influence in Iran, stating that the Razmara's assassin was largely influenced by 'imperialist' – British and American – plots, though its reason for stating this was obscure.[123] By June 1952, correspondence of the Foreign Office indicates that the Iranian armed forces had also been penetrated by the Tudeh Party.[124] The available evidence suggests that neither further security training of the Iranians nor the appointment of a new security adviser took place at least until the mid-1950s.[125]

The Iraqi Connection and Concerns about American Influence

Iraq had maintained a strong anti-Communist stance from the 1920s until 1958. However, there was growing concern in Whitehall about the regional influence of the United States, whose participation in strengthening the Iraqi Police in anti-Communist measures troubled British policymakers and prompted the appointment of a security/police adviser to the Iraqi government. Before 1953, Britain essentially regarded Iraq as a British province and had been wary about cooperating with the Americans in security building. Close connections between MI5 and the CID of the Iraqi Police formed the foundation of British–Iraqi security cooperation and, in the early 1950s, this was further enhanced by regional foreign and defence policies until the focus of British strategy shifted from Egypt to Iraq.[126]

Given this robust security cooperation, it is no surprise that Iraq was not on the AC (O)'s priority list of countries in need of anti-Communist measures in the early 1950s. The JIC estimated that there were only approximately 2,000 active members of the ICP in 1950, far lower than in Lebanon and Iran.[127] Since the outlawing of the ICP in January 1947, its members had been severely suppressed with its most influential leaders all imprisoned or executed.[128] Their foe, the Iraqi CID, was regarded as the 'most efficient' anti-Communist force in the region and maintained a strong liaison with MI5, which was noted to be 'probably closer than anywhere else in the Middle East'.[129] When Sir Henry Mack, the British Ambassador in Baghdad, was asked by the AC (O) in October 1950 to report any recommendations for strengthening legislative and administrative measures against Communists, he was content with the measures adopted by the Iraqi authorities, and wrote to Ernest Bevin:

> In my opinion these laws and administrative measures have proved an effective check on communist activity and influence in Iraq ... The Iraqi Criminal Investigation Department, which owes much to the tradition established by British officers who served in it up till 1947, is by Middle Eastern standards a fairly efficient organization. Doubtless it could be improved if British officers were reintroduced, but the political difficulties in the way of this are very great, and moreover to find a suitable man would not be easy. Even if these difficulties were overcome there would be a risk of prejudicing the present close relation between the Criminal Investigation Department and the representative of the [Security Service].[130]

This situation and British attitudes towards the cooperative Iraqi CID would, nevertheless, change in 1953, with a growing Communist influence in the country and, more importantly, a growing American interest in Iraqi affairs.

Despite the ICP's small membership, underground Communist activities persisted in Iraq, and in October 1953 the Iraqi Minister of the Interior, Said Qazzaz, approached the British Embassy in Baghdad and asked for assistance in reorganising the Iraqi Police and the CID. Whitehall was alarmed to learn that Said Qazzaz was also prepared to engage the Americans, who were able to provide support free of charge through the Truman Administration's Point Four Program, providing financial aid for development.[131] Sir John Troutbeck, the British Ambassador in Baghdad, warned the Foreign Office that this was not only 'the thin edge of the wedge of American penetration in what has been our province', but would also lead to the dislocation of the Iraqi CID and Police, with 'results potentially disastrous to the security of the whole country'.[132] Troutbeck has been noted as a typical

British official: anti-American and distrusting American oil policy in the region.[133] However, it was not only he who opposed American interference in Iraq on this matter, but others too. The Iraqi move was also flagged by Roger Lees, MI5's representative in Baghdad, serving in the guise of the Assistant Air Attaché to the British Embassy in Baghdad,[134] who commented that it would be 'a great pity if the reorganisation of the Iraqi police were to fall into the hands of the Americans'.[135] Moreover, Sir Hugh Stephenson, Chairman of the JIC (ME), also raised his concerns about this matter, stating that 'from an intelligence point of view and in our concern with Communism, we are largely dependent in Iraq on our CID liaison'.[136]

The British not only had to provide the advisers free of charge if they were to compete with the Americans, but they also had to avoid financial and political complications in the Iraqi Parliament. Anti-British sentiment in Iraqi politics added to a growing concern that the Iraqis were leaning towards the Americans. This preceded Eden's aforementioned approval of financial resources (£25,000 a year) for training foreign security forces. While waiting for a formal request from the Iraqi government, there was a clear increase in British concern over American influence in Iraq. In a telegram, Troutbeck commented from Baghdad that:

> An American might well come as a temporary visitor . . . under the cover of 'Security Adviser to the American Embassy' or something similar rather than as an employee of the Iraq Government . . . The most effective way therefore of preventing the appointment of an American is for us to evince a more active desire to help the Iraqi Minister of the Interior on the issue . . . Otherwise, an American adviser – or at least a temporary adviser – may be here before we know it. There are various signs that the Americans are prepared to move rapidly to redeem their diminished prestige here at our expense.[137]

Despite the insignificance of Communist activities in Iraq, the Foreign Office came to the conclusion that 'if we do not provide free assistance, there is a very strong probability that the Americans can and will', and above all, that the maintenance of order and stability in Iraq was 'essential for our oil and other interests'.[138] Indeed, around this time, while the United States agreed that Iraq was 'entirely within Britain's political sphere', the US Ambassador Burton Berry sought to 'exert a more positive role in guiding Iraq's future planning'.[139]

The Foreign Office decided to forestall the appointment of an American security adviser to the Iraqi Police and go ahead before the budget was settled, asking the Treasury to provide funds for the security adviser. This meant that a British adviser would be sent to Iraq free of charge.[140] Meanwhile, the Foreign Office searched for potential security/police advisers, enquiring to the Home and Colonial Offices about suitable candidates for the post. All enquiries to the Home Office were consistently turned down without any positive recommendations, and the case of Iraq proved no exception.[141]

The hunt by the Foreign Office thus relied on the Colonial Office, which recommended suitable candidates from the colonial police. Although MI5 only had an advisory capacity in this process, the Foreign Office sometimes appeared to expect MI5 to play a more active role.[142] When Said Qazzaz made the initial approach in October 1953, MI5's representative, Roger Lees (1951–3), was due to be replaced. Sir John Troutbeck suggested to the Foreign Office that a successor to Lees should be able to advise the Iraqis on the reorganisation of the CID. In this way, he hoped, the Iraqi requirements would be met 'without any extra burden on either their or H.M. Government's budget'.[143]

However, MI5 already had its own chosen candidate as Lees's successor in Baghdad, who had served in the 'British Police on Special Branch duties' and was thus competent to advise on anti-Communist work, but who had 'no special qualifications for advising on the organisation of the CID or criminal work'.[144] The MI5 officer being lined up appeared to be Norman Himsworth.[145] Upon his departure, however, Roger Lees made arrangements with Said Qazzaz that his successor would take a more active role in advising the CID 'unofficially on anti-communist work', and reported that 'the head of the CID has been instructed accordingly'.[146]

Both MI5's and MI6's suggestion to the Foreign Office for

the two posts in Iraq was their favourite candidate, Sir George Jenkin, about whom H. P. Goodwyn of MI5, liaising with the Foreign Office, commented that 'a man of his calibre would best suit all purpose' and 'could do both jobs'.[147] Following interviews with the candidates conducted by Paul Falla, head of the Levant Department of the Foreign Office, with the help of Lloyd Thomas, an expert from the Home Office, the Foreign Office decided to send, not two, but only one adviser to Iraq due to financial limitations. The chosen candidate was not Sir George Jenkin but Duncan MacIntosh, the retiring Commissioner of Police in Hong Kong (1946–52). The Colonial Office described Jenkin as 'rather too much of a specialist to take the lead of a general mission on Police re-organisation'.[148] In addition, Jenkin was 'somewhat highly-strung, shy and reserved', whereas MacIntosh was considered to have a 'blend of astuteness and friendliness', which would 'earn the confidence, and goodwill of the Iraqi authorities'. Above all, MacIntosh was regarded as a 'first-class all-rounder', who thus could manage not only the CID but also the police post.[149]

Although his appointment was delayed due to the dissolution of the Iraqi Parliament and general elections in Iraq, MacIntosh finally arrived in Baghdad in October 1954 after the thirteenth government was formed under the premiership of Nuri el-Said. Said Qazzaz remained as the Minister of the Interior and was still 'eager for MacIntosh's cooperation in his campaign against the Communists'.[150] Sir Robin Hooper, Counsellor at the British Embassy in Baghdad, observed two months after his appointment that MacIntosh was liked by the Iraqis and was making progress in the Iraqi Police and the CID:

> his advice is being sought and readily taken. He has made far-reaching recommendations for the re-organisation of the C.I.D. and the uniformed branches of the Police Force, including . . . the creation of a Special Branch and integrated reporting of political and subversive activities between the various districts . . . [and] there is a marked desire among junior officers of the Police Force to better themselves now that they see that the Government is taking steps to reform and improve the Police Force, which has for so many years remained virtually stagnant.[151]

MacIntosh's post ended when the Iraqi Revolution occurred in July 1958.

Until the 1958 revolution, Iraq offered anti-Communist training facilities and courses designed for Middle Eastern security officers. The AC (O) had used Iraq, Britain's closest ally in the region and the most adamant anti-Communist regime, to encourage other Middle Eastern authorities to take 'legislative and administrative action to combat Communist activities' through the sharing of Iraqi experience in anti-Communist measures.[152] Iraqi police officers also acted as Commandant of the Police Training School in Mukalla, Aden, until 1958.[153] Iraq was a bastion of British security influence in the region and supposedly a model to inspire others. Like Lebanon and France, Iraq also formed a quiet battle ground to keep the upper hand over the Americans. Unfortunately for Britain, though, the cooperation was cut short.

Jordan's Arab Legion and the 'Anti-Communist Triangle'

The Jordanian case was unique in the region as the Arab Legion, the chief external and internal security force of the country, was commanded by a British officer, General Sir John Bagot Glubb, until March 1956. Under this special arrangement, British personnel were also involved in training the Arab Legion and developing Jordanian military intelligence.[154] As Jordan is a relatively small country, where difficult terrain limits areas suitable for habitation, Communist activities were almost non-existent there. In 1950, the JIC estimated that members of the Jordanian Communist Party numbered fewer than fifty.[155] While the AC (O) rightly considered the Communist problem in Jordan to be far less significant than elsewhere, this assessment differed from that of the Jordanian government. Since late 1950, Jordanian police officers constantly attended 'special training' courses in anti-Communist measures in Britain, and the Jordanian government requested that Britain share any information on Communist activities.[156]

At Jordan's request, Colonel Sir Patrick Coghill, the wartime head of the British Security Mission in Lebanon (1941–5), was appointed Security/Police Adviser to Jordan in April 1952. He coordinated anti-Communist measures and helped with the reorganisation of the CID and Arab Legion.[157] His formal title was Director-General of Intelligence of the Arab Legion (1952–6) but he was also known as the Head of the Jordanian CID.[158] Jordan had no diplomatic relations with the Soviet Union or other Eastern bloc countries, and technically nationals of those countries were not allowed to enter Jordan. Colonel Coghill was responsible for internal security concerning the movements of foreign nationals and subversive activities in the country. He also closely monitored the Free Officers movement within the Arab Legion.[159]

Despite Communist activities being nearly non-existent in Jordan, subversion did include Egyptian and Saudi activity, which Coghill deemed 'the worst' in the country.[160] In late 1955, the Egyptians were propagating hostile attacks on King Hussein of Jordan as one of the 'imperialists' and 'colonisers' in the region, and were also trying to provoke the Israelis by organising the infiltration of sabotage groups, disguised as Jordanians, from Jordan into Israel. Likewise, the Saudis were bribing the Jordanians, including the royal family, politicians and newspapers, to weaken the Hashemite influence.[161] These activities, perceived as subversive, were indeed in part instigated by Soviet and Egyptian propaganda, particularly their call to arms against 'imperial powers', and they presented a potential danger to be exploited by local Communists.[162]

In his capacity as the Director-General of Intelligence, Coghill reorganised the Jordanian Police, within which he also headed the CID, and sent a number of Jordanian police officers to Britain for training in counter-subversion.[163] It is noteworthy that Coghill sent his senior (Jordanian) officers for security/police training not only in Britain but also in another Middle Eastern country, Libya. In the post-war period, Libya hosted an 'advanced' police school, which Coghill described as 'extremely efficient', run by a retired superintendent of the British Metropolitan Police, Arthur Giles, who had also served in the Palestine Police before 1948.[164] On the practical side, Coghill's (Jordanian) officers often found it difficult to understand the meaning of courses in Britain owing to poor English. The Jordanian legal system was also principally based on the code of Napoleon, inherited from the Ottoman Empire, the whole approach and procedure in the courts of which was different from the British system.[165] In addition, Coghill also wished to avoid sending his officers to Egypt or Iraq for training as both states had their own designs on the internal affairs of Jordan. For these reasons, security/police training in Libya, where training was conducted by a British ex-police officer in Arabic, was ideal for Coghill's purpose.[166] A mixture of local security officers from different Arab countries attended the course.[167]

Colonel Coghill's work with his Arab counterparts was one of the most important factors in developing Britain's regional security liaison. He collaborated closely with Farid Chehab, Head of the Sûreté Générale, and Bahjat Attiyah, Director of the Iraqi CID, by exchanging information on anti-Communist and anti-subversive matters in the region. Based on his personal relationship, firstly with Farid Chehab and later with Bahjat Attiyah, liaison between Lebanon, Iraq and Jordan became gradually institutionalised and known in Coghill's own words as the 'Anti-Communist Triangle'.[168] This security liaison involved intelligence sharing on subversive activities not only in Lebanon, Iraq and Jordan, but also elsewhere, most of which were instigated by Egypt and Syria.[169]

Their security cooperation also included a 'specially strict' surveillance request on the leading figure in anti-British activities in the region, Haji Amin al-Husseini, the ex-Grand Mufti of Jerusalem, whom Colonel Coghill called 'the most evil power in Palestine Arab Nationalism'.[170] Coghill's role in anti-Communist work was appreciated not only by the Jordanians but also by the Iraqis. Before Duncan MacIntosh took up his post of Security/Police Adviser in Baghdad, Said Qazzaz, the Iraqi Minister for Interior, insisted that he 'should break his outward journey at Amman to discuss his work with Coghill'.[171] It was no exaggeration when Colonel Coghill described the presence of the Arab Legion as 'one of the principal key-stones' in providing stability to Middle Eastern security as a whole.[172]

One of the most important contributions of the Jordan–Lebanon–Iraq 'Anti-Communist Triangle' was perhaps its coordination of anti-Communist measures with neighbouring Arab states by establishing closer liaison between the regional security services. One aspect of this regional initiative came to the fore in 1954 as the foundation for covert cooperation in 'the fight against Communism and Zionism' under the Arab League, with participants from Egypt, Lebanon, Jordan, Iraq and other countries.[173] The united anti-Communist campaign led to the discovery of several underground Communist cells in the region.[174] Behind this regional collaboration, the AC (O) acted as a facilitator, seeking to enhance the anti-Communist measures of Middle Eastern governments by 'means of improving liaison and the exchange of information' between the relevant governments.[175] In addition to Iraq, Britain's closest ally in the region, the Lebanese Sûreté Générale, was also chosen to lead the initiative.[176] A senior official at the Foreign Office noted that Farid Chehab appreciated 'the need for and the value of liaison between themselves and their counterparts in other Arab states' and that the Lebanese initiative 'would be less likely to arouse suspicion' than if it came from any other Arab state.[177] The cooperation between the Jordan–Lebanon–Iraq 'Anti-Communist Triangle' even extended beyond the Arab states, Turkey and Iran from the mid-1950s onwards.[178]

There were, however, certainly limitations to Coghill's anti-Communist measures. That Coghill's position was filled by a British officer had often been a cause of political confrontation between the Jordanian government and political opposition groups.[179] Eventually, the Jordanian Police were separated from the Arab Legion, and placed under the Ministry of the Interior from July 1956. King Hussein initiated this move in response to a recommendation by the Jordanian Cabinet Committee, and also due to public pressure to separate civilian and military functions.[180] Before the separation of the Jordanian Police was brought into effect, Coghill's post as the Director-General of Intelligence of the Arab Legion abruptly ended as Sir John Bagot Glubb was dismissed from the Arab Legion in March 1956.

Despite the volatile political climate in Jordan, especially over its connection with Britain, the Jordanian government remarkably requested a British security adviser to its Police some three years after the dismissal of Colonel Coghill. Duncan MacIntosh, who had been the Security/Police Adviser to the Iraqi Police and the

Iraqi CID, escaped from the Iraqi Revolution and was appointed as the Police Adviser in Jordan in October 1958.[181]

A letter by Sir Roderick Parkes, British Ambassador in Amman (1962–6), indicates that, despite opposition by 'dyed-in-the-wool' traditionalists and conservatives, as Police Adviser (1958–62) MacIntosh achieved his aim of reorganising the Jordanian security services 'on an independent, logical and modern basis' using his experience in Hong Kong as his principal model. In addition, the CID's public security functions were separated out to form a new department responsible for 'all internal security matters outside the province of the uniformed police', including sections dealing with Communists and liaising with foreign services. This department was established and later named the 'General Intelligence Department [Dairat al-Mukhabarat al-Ammah]' in accordance with Act 24 of 1964.[182] Sir Roderick Parkes commented on MacIntosh's achievement in a letter:

> I cannot finish this letter without warm tribute to MacIntosh. His health has suffered recently, yet the energy, single-mindedness of purpose and wisdom with which he has carried out a singularly difficult assignment have impressed me deeply. He is due to go at the end of January, when his six-month contract comes to an end. All those Jordanians who have been in touch which him will be sorry at his departure. I shall share their feelings.[183]

Indeed, even after MacIntosh's retirement from the post, training of Jordanian police officers as a part of anti-Communist measures continued.[184] In addition, the British anti-Communist policy in Jordan allowed the Americans to participate in the internal affairs of Jordan from the mid-1950s onwards, and, since then, the United States has enjoyed its own influence over the Jordanian government.[185]

Conclusion

British concerns about Middle Eastern security dovetailed with the demands of Middle Eastern governments for British advice on anti-Communist measures. However, Britain did not have a security/police adviser in every Middle Eastern country. Placing one in Syria, for example, was considered, but the country was too unstable for such a liaison to be established.[186] Owing to the flow of illegal Jewish (and possible Communist) immigrants from the Eastern bloc into the newly established state of Israel, MI5 also contemplated liaison with the Israeli authorities in 1951, but there is no archival evidence to suggest that MI5 put this into practice.[187] In addition, Britain maintained a close connection with the Egyptians through the representative of MI5 on anti-Communist matters until the early 1950s: there was no need to place a security/police adviser there.

Placing security/police officers in the heart of Middle Eastern governments was advantageous for Britain: the local security services, including police forces, were unique assets for intelligence and security purposes, and security liaison with them was invaluable in at least two ways. Firstly, as Communist movements were illegal in the region, intelligence collection on them was carried out by the local security services, with physical surveillance of the suspects and premises, probably even utilising the power to tap telephones and intercept other communications. Security liaison with regional police forces meant that Britain was able to access intelligence on Communist activities in the region, including police records, which would otherwise have been inaccessible. Secondly, the training of the security services was seen as the best way of containing the spread of Communism in the region. In addition to the training of the security services, officials deemed placing security/police advisers the best way to influence the conduct of anti-Communist measures by Middle Eastern states.

The main problem with these relationships for Britain was that they were based on a non-institutionalised agreement in a hostile environment, where anti-British sentiment was commonplace, and thus an institutionalised arrangement was impossible for Middle Eastern leaders who were risking their political careers by associating so closely with Britain. As a result, although some personal connections were maintained, the posts of British security/police advisers were abruptly ended in the face of a crisis.

3 The Defence of the Realm in the Middle East[1]

In the minds of many people, it [the British Secret Service] has become a dark legend, an organisation of fantastic power, whose tentacles extend everywhere. The reality was a little different. Nobody will deny the power and ability of the Secret Service, but it is a long way from being the 'all-seeing eye' of popular legend. What keeps the British Secret Service functioning is simply money, and the irresistible temptation which money represents to rogues and traitors.

Anwar El Sadat[2]

Introduction

British intelligence services and their activities were mysterious to many. One organisation which remains particularly mysterious was SIME, MI5's regional headquarters run from Egypt during and after the Second World War. Little is known about its activities, relationship with MI6, or its liaison with local authorities.[3] This chapter explores these issues before demonstrating what the story of SIME's closure in 1958 reveals about the shift in Whitehall's conduct of the Cold War. With the prospect of war against the Soviet Union reduced, SIME became obsolete in the eyes of military planners. This chapter shows that having increasingly become an instrument of the Cold War, the role of SIME was not to defend broadly against anti-British movements, but rather to focus narrowly on Communism. It further argues that the fragile nature of post-war intelligence liaison, when local populations became increasingly hostile to the British military presence, limited SIME's activities and effectiveness.

SIME in the Second World War

A former British Army officer, who served under the Middle East Command during the war, once described SIME as 'MI5 behaving rather like MI6 and doing it better'.[4] This is rather misleading because SIME was never the regional headquarters of MI5 during the war: it was staffed and administered by the British Army and operated entirely under the direction of the General Headquarters of the Middle East (GHQ/ME). The exception was the Defence Security Officer (DSO) in Cairo, Colonel (later Brigadier) Raymond J. Maunsell, an Army officer on the MI5 payroll.[5] SIME's connections with MI5 developed on an ad hoc basis throughout the war, often driven by SIME requiring technical advice on counter-espionage in the region. As the war progressed and the 'double-cross' deception operations developed, MI5 sent SIME instructions to enhance its security practices, necessary given its counter-espionage functions.[6] Thus, MI5's direct commitment to regional security did not precede the post-war reorganisation of the British intelligence community, through which its overseas commitments expanded substantially.

SIME was a very successful organisation during the war. The Middle East at that time consisted of a diverse collection of Crown colonies, protectorates, mandated territories and neutral countries, where the provision for maintaining internal security differed significantly. The complexity of maintaining regional security over these territories fostered the organisational development of SIME and led to an increase in its activities. While SIME originally started in December 1939 as a spin-off from the DSO in Cairo, it expanded rapidly in size and territory covered. At the height of the war in 1941, SIME was staffed by ninety officers and a hundred others, mostly from the Army.[7] A number of military officers served as DSOs across the region to liaise with local authorities and to advise on internal security in territories covering the Balkans, the Middle East and North Africa, including Greece, Turkey, Cyprus, Palestine, Syria/Lebanon, Iraq, Iran, Transjordan, Tripolitania, Cyrenaica, Egypt, the Canal Zone, Eritrea and Aden.[8] An example of

Britain's proactive security measures through SIME can be found in the context of Egypt, where the DSO in Cairo closely cooperated with the Egyptian security forces such as the Cairo City Police. Anglo-Egyptian joint security cooperation in fact resulted in the rounding up of Abwehr agents in what was known as Operation Condor.[9]

The wartime conditions also made it necessary for Britain to exercise executive powers backed by military support. Some reluctant local governments were indeed threatened with military measures, with notable examples including the Anglo-Soviet invasion of Iran and the overthrow of the anti-British Prime Minister of Iraq, Rashid Ali, in 1941.[10] Security measures taken by local governments included the detention of enemy agents and suspects likely to spy for the Axis Powers or turn to sabotage; the security examination of new arrivals in the region from neutral or enemy-occupied territory; and border control conducted with the field security force of the military police.[11] For security purposes, detention camps were established in Syria, Lebanon, Palestine, Cyprus and Egypt, strictly under the control of the Middle East Command, under whose direction SIME operated. It was a busy time and by November 1944, a total of thirty-two German intelligence officers who had parachuted into the region were detained, whilst 1,719 'fifth columnists', who might have acted in favour of the enemy powers, were interned.[12] In the first six months of 1944, 11,171 refugees and travellers were examined, excluding all the Jewish refugees who were examined by either the Palestine Police or SIME.[13]

SIME only functioned as the regional centre for collation and dissemination of security intelligence. Apart from a special section which controlled double-agents against the Axis Powers, SIME never ran its own agents for use as intelligence sources nor conducted counter-intelligence operations especially in the post-war period.[14] SIME instead had two main sources of intelligence on which it was entirely dependent: MI6 and the outstation DSOs. As enemy agents mostly crossed the borders from neutral countries such as Turkey,[15] SIME needed the close cooperation of the regional headquarters of MI6, also known as the Inter-Services Liaison Department (ISLD). Historians note that a close relationship between SIME and ISLD was naturally maintained due to the 'excellent personal relations between the officials concerned'.[16] In addition, SIME shared with ISLD intercepted materials from enemy wireless communications, technically termed ISOS (Intelligence Section, Oliver Strachey) materials – Oliver Strachey was responsible for solving, decrypting and circulating German intelligence messages at the Government Code & Cipher School (GC&CS); these decrypts were named after Strachey and issued as the ISOS series.[17] These decrypts of Abwehr hand-ciphered messages proved vital for SIME's counter-espionage work during the war especially in the context of 'double-cross' operations against the Axis Powers.[18]

The main functions of the DSOs were not only to advise local authorities on any measures necessary to enhance internal security, but also to collect intelligence from local security services, in most cases the police, through liaison. For instance, intelligence obtained by the DSO in Cairo, Colonel Raymond Maunsell (later the first Head of SIME, 1939–44), included copies of 'full surveillance reports on suspects both of European and Arab/Egyptian origin' from a Special Section of the Cairo Police and the Ministry of the Interior, which compiled a list of suspects earmarked for arrest and internment on the outbreak of war. In addition, under the supervision of DSO Cairo, British–Egyptian censorship provided Colonel Maunsell with the opportunity to examine a special 'dirty tricks' section concerned with 'secret censorship' of both private and diplomatic mail.[19]

SIME and Post-War Imperial Defence in the Middle East

The post-war conditions in which SIME operated were entirely different from the wartime period. Except for Cyprus, Aden, the Palestine Mandate and Arabian/Persian Gulf, the Middle East predominantly consisted of independent countries. Intelligence organisations that had thrived in the region during wartime thus had to be dismantled, returning prime responsibility to MI6.[20] The first casualty of the post-war reorganisation was the Combined Intelligence Centre Iraq/Iran (CICI), a comparable organisation to SIME under the control of the Royal Air Force (RAF). CICI's networks were taken over by MI6.[21] Despite working predominantly within foreign territories, SIME was nevertheless preserved. While key executive positions (the Head and Deputy Head of SIME) and strategically important outstations (Egypt, Iraq and the Palestine Mandate) were held and maintained by MI5 officers, SIME was not a civilian but a military organisation, the majority of staff being seconded from the Army, Navy and RAF on an ad hoc basis.[22] The purpose of maintaining SIME into peacetime was purely to serve the needs of the Chiefs of Staff.

As MI5 had become *in loco parentis* towards SIME owing to the closeness of their relationship during the war,[23] the Chiefs of Staff logically assumed that SIME would pass into the hands of MI5, whose commitment in the region was understood as the 'fourth defence force'.[24] In addition, the outgoing Commander-in-Chief Middle East Command – General Sir Bernard Paget, the key decision maker regarding the fate of post-war SIME – noted that an effective intelligence system in the region should be 'one organisation for security, one for political intelligence and one for military intelligence, i.e. MI5, MI6 and MI [Military Intelligence]'.[25] Dissatisfied with the recent transition of its networks in Iran from CICI to MI6, he preferred to preserve SIME and also welcomed SIME 'becoming part of a larger Imperial Security Organisation' under the authority of MI5.[26]

The post-war SIME did not, however, resemble its wartime brilliance. When Sir Dick White, Deputy Director of B (counter-espionage) Division of MI5 and later both the Director-General of MI5 and Chief of MI6, visited the region, he was 'not at all impressed by the general organisation of SIME' as, since the end of the war, it had mostly been staffed by junior officers, who had no knowledge about intelligence and security. However, White had to accept the need of the Chiefs of Staff to preserve SIME and for it to be administered by MI5, noting that a new separate security organisation to maintain a British military presence in the region would be 'inadvisable'.[27] A formal recommendation was made through the JIC (ME) and approved by the JIC in London and the British Defence Co-ordination Committee in the Middle East (BDCC/ME).[28] Thus, in September 1946, SIME finally came under the authority of MI5, and SIME was the regional headquarters of MI5 thereafter.

As the regional headquarters of MI5, SIME functioned similarly to MI5 at home but had different commitments. Like the wartime SIME, it was responsible for the collation and dissemination of security intelligence relating to counter-espionage and counter-subversion, which might have had implications for British authorities throughout the region. Its intelligence customers included the Army Commander-in-Chief Middle East; the Naval Commander-in-Chief Mediterranean; the Royal Air Force Commander-in-Chief Middle East; the Naval Commander-in-Chief Eastern Fleet; and British Ambassadors, Ministers, High Commissioners and Governors.[29] In his memoir, Brigadier William Magan, Head of SIME (1947–51), notes the responsibility of SIME:

> My task consisted in knowing in as much detail as possible the threats to the area as a whole and in ensuring that we had the means, the knowledge and the understanding to counter them. To that end it was my responsibility to pass to MI5 the information of which they needed to be informed, and to feed to local authorities the information of which they needed to be aware, [and a]lso to advise the individual territories on their security organisation and practices. In many of the territories we had our own SIME representatives to liaise with and advise the local authorities.[30]

More importantly, the difference between SIME and MI5 was that, although MI5 enjoyed no commitments to a particular department, SIME was 'an integral part of the military machine' in the Middle East.[31] It was in fact distinctively associated with the military forces and planning in the region and had its own commitments to the post-war strategy of the Chiefs of Staff.[32]

However, operating in peacetime did influence SIME's work. Activities were scaled back and the number of SIME personnel kept to a minimum: capped at twenty-five staff of all ranks under the inter-service agreement reached before the end of the war.[33] Although the territorial coverage remained equal to that under BDCC/ME Command, the number of its outstations – in other words, the physical presence of DSOs – was reduced to a few strategically key stations such as Egypt, Iraq, the Palestine Mandate and Cyprus.[34] The purpose of maintaining its own representatives at these outstations was to liaise with local security services, especially on advice about security measures in the event of war. If war did break out, however, SIME's staff was to increase by at least 50 per cent through secondments from the War Office.[35] Moreover, in the event of war, when British military forces were to reoccupy those countries in the region with which Britain had a defence treaty, SIME was expected to 'keep its links going wherever possible, [so] that Middle East Command should have a proper security organisation at its back'.[36]

SIME faced difficulties operating on foreign soil, but these arose predominantly in securing cooperation from other departments of the British government. This was particularly true in the case of Iraq, where the RAF's wartime CICI had been forced to close down and was replaced by a new Army-oriented SIME outstation. When one of the 'best' MI5 officers, John ('Jack') Percival Morton, former officer of the Indian Police, the Delhi Intelligence Bureau (DIB), was despatched from London under cover of Assistant Air Attaché to establish his DSO office within the British Embassy in Baghdad in 1947, he had to cope with opposition from RAF staff serving there.[37] As the RAF maintained its own headquarters at Habbaniya, a major regional airbase, Iraq was considered RAF territory and Morton's association with the Army-oriented SIME made him 'rather friendless'.[38] Owing to this lack of cooperation, the DSO's records of the Registry, all necessary for Morton's security work, were kept fifty miles away in Habbaniya due to the 'lack of suitable and secure accommodation in Baghdad'.[39] The reason for Morton's physical presence in Baghdad was to maintain the close connection with the Iraqi CID.[40]

In addition, Morton's DSO cover was publicly blown by Douglas Laird Busk, the Counsellor at the British Embassy in Baghdad, who was 'cynical about intelligence'.[41] The main reason for this uneasy relationship with the British Embassy in Baghdad was perhaps that Morton was seen as an intelligence officer comparable with the wartime CICI operative, who had been responsible not only for internal security, but also tribal and political intelligence. During the war, the local CICI operatives, named Area Liaison Officers (ALOs), had operated to collect 'raw material' from their several stations in Iraq, but had caused trouble for the diplomats in their political dealings with the Iraqis who 'increasingly' resented the ALOs' presence.[42] The issue was resolved only after an investigation by Sir Edward Bridges, Permanent Secretary to the Treasury and head of the civil service (1945–56), who understood Morton's liaison work and 'the intelligence value' he received from his Iraqi counterparts.[43] Owing to the importance of 'the special strategic position' of the region, an interdepartmental meeting chaired by Bridges agreed that 'the work of SIME was essential and should continue'.[44]

The Relationship between SIME and MI6

It is commonly understood that MI5 and MI6 had since 1931 (if only in principle) operated under the so-called 'three-mile limit' rule, whereby MI6 'should confine itself to operations at least 3 miles away from British territory, and that the domestic agencies [i.e. MI5] should operate only within this limit'.[45] The Attlee Directive of 1948 redefined the jurisdictions of the services for the complex era of post-war decolonisation and gave MI5 authority for imperial security throughout the British Empire.[46] Nevertheless, the Middle East was an exception and SIME had no specific role or directive. It operated on an ad hoc basis, governed by the broadly defined SIME Charter, which stated: 'SIME will maintain close relations with MI6.'[47]

Tension existed between MI5 and MI6 over the post-war role of SIME and their jurisdiction over the Middle East.[48] In order to avoid duplication of work, an agreement over the division of labour was reached in 1950 through Dick White of MI5 and Jack Easton of MI6, which was referred to as the 'White/Easton Agreement'.[49] From 1950 onwards, MI6 took charge of the field of counter-espionage in the region, with an MI6 officer heading the counter-espionage division of SIME, often referred to as the Joint Intelligence Division (JID), which was composed of both MI5 and MI6 officers on secondment.[50] A similar arrangement was also made with a sister organisation of SIME in the Far East, Security Intelligence Far East (SIFE).[51] Thus, while intelligence on any espionage activities of foreign states was dealt with by MI6, intelligence on any subversive activities in the region was chiefly handled by MI5. SIME was responsible for the final collation of security intelligence (any intelligence on espionage, sabotage and subversion) as the regional headquarters of MI5.

Unlike the politics at their headquarters in London, the working relationship between the services on the ground seems to have been less problematic. Sir Bernard Burrows, Head of FO's Eastern Department, who had assumed both MI5 and MI6 in the region were in a 'struggle for power', was surprised to find out that their working relationship was 'very much more friendly'.[52] The reason for the good relationship was that while SIME formed the regional hub of security intelligence, MI6 was an intelligence collector. Moreover, because the headquarters of SIME was housed within (sequentially) the Army headquarters in Cairo (1939–46), Fayid, in the Canal Zone of Egypt (1946–53), and Cyprus (1954–8), it cooperated closely with the British military in the region. SIME officers, including the representatives of MI5 working in the guise of DSOs, mostly used the cover of military ranks.[53] MI6 was, on the other hand, operating with civilian cover mostly associated with the Foreign Office, though occasionally with the Ministry of Defence. The regional headquarters of MI6 in the post-war period was in Beirut, operating under the cover name of the Combined Research and Planning Office (CRPO), with which SIME worked well.[54]

SIME and CRPO enjoyed an effective relationship because their organisational differences and activities, and the way in which they collected intelligence, were mutually beneficial, not competitive. This was due to the division of overt and covert means of intelligence collection in the region. MI5's networks consisted entirely of 'overt' SLOs, whose presence was declared to the host governments and was thus accepted by their local counterparts, mostly the local or secret police. MI6, on the other hand, was a covert intelligence network in principle, operating without the knowledge of the host governments.[55] This special arrangement gave MI5 access to particular, and otherwise unobtainable, intelligence. Indeed, as the formation of Communist Parties was illegal in most Middle Eastern states, any activities associated with them were handled by the local police. Thus, MI5's special overt liaison, especially its 'close and useful relations' with 'the local police', was praised by the local MI6 representative as a 'considerable help' with regard to its own intelligence requirements.[56] Guy Liddell recorded in his diaries that the demarcation between MI5 and MI6 in the post-war period was in fact not geographical but functional.[57]

In return, MI6's covert networks in the region provided SIME with intelligence otherwise unobtainable from its local counterparts through DSOs. Unsurprisingly, this was a sensitive issue as there was a tacit understanding amongst the intelligence and security services that while liaison was maintained, they would not be spying on each other. Once the existence of covert activities by MI6 became known to local authorities, the British, rightly or wrongly, explained that they were operating in host countries under the 'third country rule', whereby MI6 stations were 'supposed to target neighbouring states, rather than the host nation'.[58] In his memoir, Kim Philby also testifies in relation to his role as Head of Station in Turkey that 'They [the Turkish intelligence/security organisations] knew of us, and tolerated our activity, on the understanding that it was directed solely against the Soviet Union and the Balkans, not against Turkey.'[59]

MI6 therefore operated in line with SIME requirements to collect security intelligence – in other words, intelligence on subversive activities – in the region.[60] In the late 1940s, for instance, when Kim Philby was in Istanbul, he was asked by William Magan, Head of SIME, to provide another officer from MI6 to fill the vacuum in Eastern Turkey.[61] Moreover, while the DSO in Baghdad, Jack Morton of MI5, was closely cooperating with the Iraqi CID as an overt contact, Magan also requested an MI6 representative to be posted in Northern Iraq, where the Kurdish tribes were a cause for concern for SIME.[62] This reflects the fact that MI5 and MI6 officers were often working in the same country.[63] The main sources of intelligence for SIME in the post-war period thus remained both MI6 and the local authorities.[64]

Limitations in Intelligence Collection and Counter-Subversion

The strength of SIME was that, unlike MI6, it collated intelligence from all available sources and served as an intelligence assessment body. In doing so, it did not always agree with other British authorities. One such instance occurred when anti-British riots broke out in Egypt in early 1952, and SIME refuted the British Embassy in Cairo's views that they must have been plotted by either the Soviet Union or Communists. SIME argued that 'no acceptable evidence has been produced in support of them'. SIME's source was 'a senior official in the Special Section of the [Egyptian] Ministry of the Interior', and the information provided by him was checked against all available intelligence.[65]

Although SIME managed to maintain the quality of intelligence reports on regional security, it faced limitations in intelligence collection in the post-war period. Despite the close cooperation on counter-espionage between SIME and MI6, the quality of intelligence obtained by MI6 seems to have been less than satisfactory. According to Guy Liddell, intelligence from MI6 in the region was 'practically valueless', and MI6 was 'clearly employing a number of agents who were MAUVE' (a codename for Russian émigrés who were unreliable and unverified).[66] Anthony Cavendish also claims that the sources of MI6 on the Soviet Union were mostly MAUVE and that MI6 obtained no valuable intelligence from them in the early 1950s.[67] To make matters worse, MI6 suffered from a fatal defect: Kim Philby, a Soviet mole, was placed at its heart as Head of R5 (counter-espionage), the Head of Station in Istanbul, and later in the United States to liaise with the Americans.[68] An example of his disruption of MI6's work was the Volkov affair of 1946, in which Philby was personally involved in disrupting a defection by Konstantin Volkov, an NKGB officer stationed in Turkey, who was sent back to Moscow due to Philby's intervention.[69] Meanwhile, Donald Maclean, a Soviet mole within the Foreign Office, was present at the British Embassy in Cairo as Head of Chancery (1948–50), to which DSO Cairo was also attached. According to Major A. W. Sansom, the

Security Officer at the Embassy, Maclean certainly enjoyed his privileged position as he 'openly went home with a brief-case stuffed with secret material whenever he pleased'.[70]

SIME had a problem with intelligence collection not only from MI6, but also from local authorities liaising with DSOs. As the relationships were not institutionalised under diplomatic regulations or treaty, intelligence collection and exchange was very delicate. MI5's intimate relationship in the late 1940s and early 1950s with its Egyptian counterparts illustrates this point. With thirty years of personal experience of Egypt and extensive inside knowledge of the Egyptian Police, Colonel Geoffrey Jenkins, the DSO Cairo (1943–8), enjoyed 'excellent relations' and was able to obtain 'much useful intelligence' through his liaison.[71] The intelligence obtained by Jenkins included, for instance, documentary evidence of secret negotiations between the Wafd Party, a nationalist political party in Egypt, and the Russians suggesting 'future collaboration'.[72] However, Alex Kellar of MI5 described the relationship between Colonel Jenkins and his Egyptian counterpart thus:

> While admitting that the Egyptian police as such are unlikely to pass information to Jenkins that may harm Egyptian interests ... their liaison with Jenkins on Communist, Russian and Jewish matters has nevertheless been, and should increasingly be, of considerable value to us. Egyptians of the present ruling classes, and their counter-parts in the rest of the Arab countries, hate the Zionists and fear the Russians and the increasing influence and strength of the Communists within their frontiers. We can therefore always be certain of their willingness, while they remain in power, to exchange intelligence with us on all these topics.[73]

Sir Alistair Horne, a former SIME officer, also recalls that whilst the Egyptian Police provided intelligence to SIME on 'Communist activities', SIME supplied the Egyptians with information on 'hashish-traffickers'.[74]

In addition to the Cairo Police, Colonel Jenkins maintained a 'close and friendly' relationship with the Under-Secretary of State at the Ministry of the Interior, and with the Director-General of

Public Security throughout the war. Once new appointments were made after the war, Jenkins had to convince the Egyptians of the *raison d'être* of the intelligence liaison and rebuild mutual trust with the Egyptians. For instance, a new but sceptical Director-General of Public Security questioned the extent of Jenkins's intelligence activities in Cairo, concerned that he was 'seeking intelligence about Egyptian politics', particularly about the activities of anti-British figures. Jenkins's first task was to win 'the goodwill' of the new Director-General of Public Security.[75]

This indicates that the extent to which SIME was able to obtain intelligence through its own sources (MI6 and DSOs) and to warn its intelligence customers in the region was indeed limited. The Egyptian coup of 1952 demonstrated these limitations. Despite the DSO Cairo being in close contact with his Egyptian counterparts during the turmoil of early 1952, SIME had no intelligence forewarning of the Free Officers coup. There was no source within the Free Officers movement.[76] The 1958 Iraqi Revolution offers a similar example. Despite SIME being acutely aware of disaffection within the Iraqi Army from the early 1950s, information which had been passed from the Head of SIME to his Iraqi counterparts in the CID of the Iraqi Police,[77] no prior warning of the coup was provided.[78]

In a similar vein, there were also severe limitations on SIME's counter-subversive activities in the post-war Middle East. During the war, SIME had enjoyed executive and law enforcement powers to undertake security measures in each country. However, Britain no longer enjoyed such powers over the local authorities in the post-war era and SIME therefore struggled to obtain cooperation from local actors, many of whom had changed since the war. Rising anti-British sentiment in the post-war years made SIME's task even more difficult. Sir John Shaw, Director of the OS (Overseas) Division of MI5, for instance, informed the JIC that the Egyptian Police, SIME's closest ally in the late 1940s and early 1950s, gradually became 'hostile' and SIME received 'no help' from 1952 onwards.[79] Unlike at home, where the role of MI5 was to defend its own government against subversion, SIME was not necessarily conducting counter-subversion for the benefit of local governments. William Magan once explained to his successor,

Colonel (later Brigadier) Robin 'Tin Eye' Stephens (1951–3),[80] that:

> Security Intelligence presents a difficulty because it cannot be exactly defined for SIME purposes. You have only to consider the impossibility of drawing a line by definition between an Arab political party and an Arab subversive organisation to see the problem. A broad definition of Security Intelligence, however, gives rise to that part of the intelligence division of the organisation which concerns itself with subversive individuals and bodies – 'subversive' also, of course, cannot be exactly defined.[81]

The complexity of the demarcation line between subversive and anti-British elements caused confusion even among MI5 officers. With nationalist disturbances and street riots breaking out across the Middle East, Colonel Stephens requested MI5 Head Office to send more officers to the region as 'links' to local authorities in places where MI5 was not represented.[82] Head Office, however, considered the request unnecessary and turned it down.[83]

Nonetheless, Stephens had successfully generated a discussion about MI5's commitments to safeguarding British interests overseas. William Magan, former Head of SIME, was at the centre of the discussion having recently returned from the Middle East to take up a position at MI5 Head Office.[84] Magan was soon promoted by Sir Dick White in 1953 to Director of E Branch (the overseas department in charge of external affairs, liaising with all colonial, Commonwealth and friendly foreign countries) and remained in executive positions for fifteen years until his retirement.[85]

According to Magan, maintaining law and order – including the suppression of disturbances, riots and terrorist activities, even when directed by a political organisation – was outside MI5's remit and should be dealt with by the relevant local authorities. The police were responsible for maintaining law and order but it also made sense for the armed forces to keep their own link with the local authorities as they might be deployed 'in aid of the civil power'. Magan also expected local authorities and military forces to take charge of 'purely local indigenous subversive political persons, movements, parties and organizations' in British territory. MI5 should only be informed if these organisations were categorised as 'conspiratorially political subversive', and/or if they had the 'possibility of outside influence, such as contact with a hostile foreign power'.[86] Referring to the roles and responsibilities of SIME, Magan further commented that:

> our resources, whether at home or overseas, are inadequate for a one hundred per cent fulfilment of our tasks. This is an inherent feature of all defence forces. We must, therefore, follow the age old military principle of concentrating on the main objective. I have thus always held the view that the wise thing is to stop the holes of the big rats properly even if this meant ignoring the little rats, and risking the odd nip from them.[87]

'The big rats' referred to by Magan were the Russians and Communist movements; he considered anti-British movements and disturbances as 'little rats'. This meant that SIME, as the regional headquarters of MI5, was supposed to be concerned with 'conspiratorially political subversive' activities, mostly those associated with external threats such as International Communism and the Soviet Union. This indicates that SIME was geared more towards the Cold War.

The Primacy of Cold War Concerns over Anti-British Nationalist Movements

Magan's approach to MI5's responsibilities in British territories overseas indicates that its main post-war concern was the Soviet Union and the Cold War. However, MI5 also had to deal with the new challenge of Zionist extremists and terrorism and had to learn quickly about how best to manage its overseas commitments.[88] During the transition from war to peacetime, SIME was mostly ill-equipped to cope with the flow of 'illegal' Jewish immigration and with countering Jewish terrorist activities in Palestine. With the prime responsibility for internal security in the Palestine

Mandate resting with the Palestine CID, which had the intelligence and executive powers necessary to deal with the situation,[89] SIME's chief concern was the infiltration of Soviet agents into the region amidst the flow of illegal Jewish immigrants.[90] Despite a shortage of staff, SIME also looked for any opportunity to penetrate the KGB in the Middle East.[91] SIME was in fact right to be worried about Soviet penetration here as the KGB sought to exploit the situation by, as Soviet documents reveal, ensuring 'that large numbers of its agents were included in the ranks of the Soviet Jews allowed to leave for Israel'.[92]

Having taken over SIME from the Army as *in loco parentis*, one of the ways in which MI5 sought to improve SIME's security measures was to institute its own standard practice of record-keeping at SIME's Registry.[93] There was a gradual but clear shift in SIME record-keeping by the early 1950s, and SIME and its outstations (DSOs) collected and collated intelligence according to specific principles. The SIME Central Registry stored all information on identifiable officers and proven or suspected agents of foreign intelligence and security services, regardless of nationality; and the DSOs were instructed to record all information on identifiable Communists, Communist sympathisers, as well as nationalists at their own Registries.[94]

In 1953, SIME only had four outstations: Cairo, the Canal Zone, Cyprus and Baghdad. The largest outstation was still DSO Cairo, which also had the largest Registry, containing an estimated 50,000 card-indexes, covering 40,000 individuals.[95] DSO Baghdad was the second largest, and its Registry contained 33,000 cards on about 20,000 individuals. Having inherited records from the wartime organisation, CICI, Roger Lees of MI5, DSO in Baghdad, noted that a large number of people were carded on 'tenuous grounds or for reasons which are now no longer of interest to us [MI5]', but he stored 'all persons of security interest', about 12,000 of whom were 'communists or communist suspects'.[96] The DSO in the Canal Zone operated on a much smaller scale and was mainly responsible for protecting the presence of the British Army there. Its records held 'approximately 2,050 cards', mostly referring to 'nationalists and "thugs"'.[97] The DSO in Cyprus stored approximately 10,000 cards: 5,500 on Communists or Communist sympathisers, 'about 1,500 cards connected with nationalists' and 3,000 more on suspects.[98]

It is notable that while keeping records on 'subversive' elements for their own security purposes, the prime concern of SIME, and thus MI5, was their direct connection to the Soviet Union and the spread of Communist movements in the region. A declassified MI5 file on the Iraqi counterpart of the Muslim Brotherhood, the Jamiyat al Adab al Islamiya, also known as the Moslem Ethical Society (MES), shows that SIME recognised the full subversive potential of the MES as a strong anti-British force and as a 'nationalist movement', but one whose fate was largely dependent on whether the local authorities were able to resist it.[99] While the MES was militant and subversive in character and notably anti-British, the DSO Baghdad, Jack Morton of MI5, nevertheless judged that the MES was of 'little security interest' to SIME as it was a religious and theological group. SIME's prime concern was whether any leading members of the MES were in contact with Soviets who might exploit them; or whether the MES could emerge as 'an effective barrier against Communism'.[100]

Prime Importance: War Planning

Prioritising records on Communists rather than nationalists shows that all post-war activities associated with MI5, and indeed SIME, were subordinate to British government policy. As noted in Chapter 1, the central components of this policy were the Defence Transition Committee (DTC) and the 1948 Government War Book.[101] Without exception, the War Book was the key driving policy for MI5's activities in the Middle East. SIME was particularly important in this given that the integrity of the Middle East was essential for British war-making, and the Chiefs of Staff envisaged the possibility of a Soviet invasion of the region.[102] For this reason, SIME Headquarters and its outstations were all attached to British military bases and, under instruction, SIME and DSOs prepared security measures and their own 'arrest lists' in each country for 'the event of war, or other emergency' taken from their own Registries.[103] The lists consisted of subversive individuals and organisations deemed the most likely to engage in subversive activities to disrupt allied war efforts against the Soviet Union. They were particularly designed to grant the DSOs 'information sufficient to neutralise them, for which purpose it will normally be adequate to be able to identify their principal directing personalities'.[104] Amongst all other activities, the preparation of arrest lists of those who would be detained in the event of war or an emergency was an 'important SIME commitment' in post-war imperial strategy in the Middle East.[105]

Implementing these security measures was, however, not an easy task. This was primarily because the territorial coverage of the BDCC/ME Command consisted of mostly foreign countries, with the exception of Cyprus and later the Aden Colony. Since these security measures inevitably required the cooperation of local authorities, an effective security liaison was essential. Iraq offers a glimpse of this process, where the DSO Baghdad became the main outstation of SIME in the 1950s after the decline of Anglo-Egyptian relations.[106] The association between the MI5 representative and the Iraqi CID, led by Colonel Bahjat Beg Attiyah, originated from the establishment of the DSO Baghdad in 1947.[107]

Their close relationship necessitated intelligence sharing on certain topics. For instance, following the round-up of some 160 ICP members, including those of the Executive Committee, in 1949, the Iraqi CID duly passed intelligence on the linkage between the ICP and the Russians to Philip Bicknell Ray of MI5, the DSO in Baghdad (1949–51). Detailed reports over 300 pages long on ICP composition, members and their activities, made by Philip Ray for MI5 Head Office and the Foreign Office, show that the Iraqi CID interrogated the leading ICP members and obtained confessions to their having direct connections with the Russian Legation in Iraq. ICP members had received financial support and propaganda materials, named the 'Al Qa'ida Press', from the Legation; the latter were also shared with members of the Tudeh Party.[108] It was also discovered that the Russians had made contact with the ICP through a small group of Armenians and that the ICP had also intended to spread agitation among minority circles such as the Kurds.[109]

The relationship between the representative of MI5 and the Iraqi CID grew even closer in the 1950s as a result of the joint war planning. According to Guy Liddell, the relationship between the DSO Baghdad, Philip Ray, and his counterpart, the Director of the Iraqi CID, Bahjat Attiyah, was 'extremely close', and Bahjat Attiyah had a 'tremendous respect for all the advice and help which Ray had given him'.[110] The BDCC/ME instructed Ray, through the Air Officer Commanding (AOC) Iraq Command, to discuss arrangements with the Iraqi authorities for 'the preparation of lists of security suspects to be arrested on the outbreak of war'. His approach was dependent on 'the general deterioration in the international situation' rather than war planning against the Soviet Union as envisaged by the Chiefs of Staff.[111] As instructed, he also cooperated with Bahjat Attiyah on a war plan covering travel control, censorship, interrogation and the protection of vulnerabilities, leading to the combination of the arrest lists of both parties.[112] The number of suspects who were destined to be arrested for interrogation in 'special' camps at the outset of war was estimated at 2,000 in the first stage, and would consist mostly of those who were associated with the ICP and Soviet Union. Any underground Communist members and suspects, or other persons likely to engage in subversive activities, were destined to be detained and interrogated automatically by the Iraqi CID under the existing legal framework.[113]

The security measures in place in the event of a war in Iraq expanded towards the mid-1950s and extended beyond mere intelligence liaison. As these measures required the highest level of cooperation, Sir John Troutbeck approached the Iraqi Prime Minister, Nuri al-Said, in March 1952 regarding the security plans for war. Agreeing to the suggestion in principle, Nuri al-Said preferred using the police as opposed to the armed forces to 'concoct the planning on the Iraqi side', mainly due to volatile Iraqi sentiments towards the West, particularly Britain. He worried that the disclosure of war planning would cause 'a serious political storm' in which his government would be accused of 'dragging the country into war on the side of the Western Powers'.[114] He decided to delegate the task to Alwan Hussain, known as Alwan

Pasha, Director-General of Police, who would later hand the task over to Bahjat Attiyah. On the British side, Sir John Troutbeck nominated Roger Lees of MI5, DSO Baghdad (1951–3), the successor to Philip Ray.[115]

After an initial discussion between Roger Lees and Bahjat Attiyah on the security planning to implement the Iraqi Prime Minister's orders, Lees reported that:

> After several meetings [with Bahjat Attiyah] and after examining old files covering the last war to see whether any aspects of the planning were covered then, which could be adapted for our present needs, it became apparent to me that a completely fresh approach in our present planning would be necessary. I therefore met both Alwan Pasha and Bahjat Beg and it was agreed that I should draw up a detailed scheme for their consideration.[116]

While keeping an updated combined arrest list, the security plan, contemplated by DSO Baghdad and the Iraqi CID, was for 'the laying of the foundations of sound security under peace-time conditions, on which efficient war-time measures could be immediately introduced on the outbreak of hostilities'. For this purpose, the Director of the Iraqi CID, Bahjat Attiyah, was given training by the British in 'protective security matters' during his visit to London in June 1952.[117] Bahjat Attiyah also visited Guy Liddell during his stay in Britain.[118]

In addition, after examining Lees's proposed scheme, Alwan Pasha gave orders to set up a 'special planning section' under cover of the Iraqi CID. This small and compartmentalised section was headed by Colonel Yusef Peters, Commandant of Police, aided by two Assistant Commandants.[119] Colonel Peters was also given 'detailed instruction' on the security measures in Baghdad, 'paying particular attention to the oil industry'. During his visit in May 1953 to Basra, Kirkuk and Khanaqun, where the major oil refineries were situated, Colonel Peters was accompanied by 'a British officer', presumably DSO Baghdad, Roger Lees, and detailed advice was given on 'protective security matters to the managers of oil companies and other important installations'. These security measures included the coverage of 'the oil producing, refining and storage centres, public utility installations, such as water and electricity, and certain Government departments'.[120]

The security planning between Roger Lees and Bahjat Attiyah was carried out in 'great secrecy'. It continued even after the resignation of Nuri al-Said in July 1952, and without the knowledge of subsequent Prime Ministers, Ministers of the Interior or Ministers of Defence.[121] As a result of this close liaison with the Iraqis, Roger Lees submitted the security plan to the Local Security Board. It was also approved by Sir John Troutbeck.[122] In the event of war, the Iraqis agreed on the provision of a small group of British interrogators to the detention camp where all suspects on the combined arrest lists would be detained, and, more importantly, the provision of British representatives to the central censorship headquarters, controlling postal and telecommunication censorship throughout Iraq.[123] Sir Hugh Stephenson, Chairman of JIC in the Middle East, was 'extremely gratified' to learn of such substantial progress despite the 'difficulties inherent in the unstable political state in the country'.[124] As already discussed in Chapter 2, it was in this context that Britain was reluctant to allow the Americans to appoint their own security advisers to the Iraqi Police and the CID. The security plan was constantly reviewed as to whether it was still 'valid and workable' until at least 1955.[125]

In addition to SIME, MI6 was also operating in the region under the direction of the 1948 Government War Book. The limited literature on MI6 suggests that it incorporated the wartime sabotage organisation, Special Operations Executive (SOE), in the post-war reorganisation of the British intelligence community in the late 1940s,[126] and, based on the lessons of the war, largely those of SOE, the Directorate of War Planning (D/WP), later renamed the Special Political Action (SPA) Section, was formed in MI6 to establish stay-behind networks in foreign countries.[127] Recently declassified files of the PUSD confirm that from the late 1940s, MI6 engaged in war planning.[128] In 1952 the Chiefs of Staff tasked MI6 to create a stay-behind network in independent foreign countries of the Middle East.[129] Regardless of regional governments' intentions to cooperate in the event of war, the British pressed ahead with war planning, which included establishing stay-behind networks in Egypt[130] – one of which was established in the early 1950s, headed by James Swinburn.[131] In 1956, after the Egyptian government, which had been aware of the Swinburn network since 1953, became more hostile to Britain, the stay-behind network was rounded up, although John McGlashan, an MI6 officer who had been involved in plotting to assassinate Nasser, was successfully smuggled out of Egypt.[132]

SIME Wound Up: A Shift in Conducting the Cold War

SIME was closed down in 1958.[133] With the advent of thermo-nuclear weapons, it gradually became apparent to British policy-makers by the mid-1950s that a war with conventionally armed forces against the Soviet Union seemed unlikely and that the large military presence in the region was thus less important. Britain's defence policy became more focused on European defence and the British Army of the Rhine (BAOR) at the expense of committing military forces to the Middle East at the outbreak of war.[134] This gradual shift to reducing conventional defences, often termed 'East of Suez', was at the heart of the 1957 White Paper.[135] This was the context in which General Sir Gerald Templer conducted his review of intelligence organisations overseas, including the colonies.[136] SIME was only one of many other imperial or quasi-imperial intelligence organisations being wound up during the same period.[137] During that period, the British government re-examined the balance between civilian and military uses of intelligence and the JIC was moved to the Cabinet Office in 1957 accordingly.[138] The closure of SIME should therefore be understood in the wider context of British decolonisation and, more importantly, the Cold War, towards which competing approaches existed within Whitehall.

The process of winding down SIME had already begun when Sir Dick White assumed the position of Director-General of MI5 in late 1953. The number of personnel was substantially reduced and the three supervisory posts (Head of SIME, Deputy Head, and Head of the Counter-Intelligence Section) were merged into one post.[139] SIME was then staffed with thirteen officers and twenty-five female staff.[140] While senior MI5 officers complained that the Head of SIME was 'bound to be handicapped in fulfilling his advisory responsibilities to the BDCC (ME)', Sir Dick White also abolished the counter-espionage section, the JID, headed by an MI6 officer, in late 1955.[141] In his mind, SIME had unnecessary burdens, and White sought to reduce it to a 'security advisory role'.[142] Despite maintaining a good relationship between SIME and MI6, Sir Dick White was also concerned about MI6's activities in the field of counter-espionage for which MI5 was officially responsible.

These reforms extended beyond the Middle East to other places where the JIDs of the regional headquarters of MI5, headed by MI6 officers, were 'geared almost as much to the broader objects of MI6'.[143] This was a reference to MI6's 'cold war' activities, associated with clandestine activities including covert operations, often referred to as 'special political action' or 'disruptive action' in the British lexicon.[144] According to William Magan, White was 'worried about the extent to which the JID may be involved in steering MI6 stations and concerned in "cold war" activities'.[145] The problem for MI5 was that the 'cold war' activities of MI6 were often a cause for concern regarding their maintenance of a good liaison relationship with local authorities who were not informed of such clandestine activities. In March 1955, SIME only had a total of twelve staff (five officers and seven female staff), and was outnumbered by MI6, the strength of which was four times larger than that of SIME (with a total of fifty-six staff at all ranks: twelve officers, plus two in SIME, twenty-seven secretaries and fifteen operators).[146]

Not only was MI5 concerned about the activities of MI6 in its territory, but there was also a shift under way in thinking about the conduct of the Cold War. More precisely, as suggested in Chapter 1, there was a growing concern within Whitehall at the way in which the Chiefs of Staff were involved in the conduct of the Cold War. Since the end of the Second World War, the Chiefs of Staff had been one of the key decision makers regarding the conduct of the Cold War and in directing the activities of the intelligence and security services, including the clandestine operations of MI6. As a result, any attempt at directing intelligence-related activities overseas, especially in foreign territories, by the Chiefs of Staff was often considered as interference in matters which were 'essentially the business of the Foreign Secretary'.[147]

Sir Ivone Kirkpatrick, the Permanent Under-Secretary of the Foreign Office, was concerned with 'the inflated size' of intelligence staff at regional headquarters, particularly those who were associated with the military planning of the Chiefs of Staff, which he regarded as unnecessary.[148] Furthermore, Sir Norman Brook, the Cabinet Secretary, also considered 'large regional intelligence organisations [as] being outmoded',[149] whilst Sir Patrick Dean, Chairman of the JIC, noted 'some duplication' between London and the Middle East in 'the collation of intelligence' and suggested that 'it would be better if this was done in London'.[150] Sir Dick White added that the work being done by SIME 'could be done as easily from the UK'.[151]

Of course, the closure of SIME in 1958 does not necessarily mean that MI6's activities were also reduced accordingly. As Sir Dick White left MI5 to succeed Sir John Sinclair as 'C' of MI6 in 1956, he found it difficult to rein in the 'cold war' activities of MI6, especially in the Middle East. These activities were led by so-called robber barons, senior MI6 officials who extensively engaged in special operations designed to change world affairs by clandestine means.[152] Christopher Andrew notes that MI6 was 'drawn into increasingly unrealistic plans to bolster Britain's declining influence in the Middle East by covert action'.[153] Jack Easton, Deputy 'C', warned the newly appointed 'C', Dick White, 'I've had to stop a lot of operations in the Middle East. Too many are suspiciously unsafe.'[154] There was indeed a series of attempts by MI6 to overthrow Nasser in the course of the Suez Crisis in 1956.[155] According to Mohamed Heikal, George K. Young, the Vice-Chief of MI6, said to his American counterpart, James Eichelberger of the CIA, '"[MI6 will] do a Mossadeq" with Nasser.'[156] MI6 also contemplated using nerve gas to assassinate Nasser.[157]

MI6 was not of course acting alone, but these operations were directed by the British government. Above all, it was Prime Minister Anthony Eden who wanted Nasser 'destroyed'.[158] At the working level, Douglas Dodds-Parker, the Parliamentary

Under-Secretary of State and the Chairman of the Overseas Planning Committee, formed a special committee with Sir Charles Hambro, a former chief of the wartime SOE, to suggest any clandestine actions against Egypt and Nasser.[159] By mid-August 1956, Dodds-Parker was already contemplating Britain's strategic position in the Middle East on the assumption of Britain's relationship with a new Egyptian government after Nasser.[160] There was also an attempt to overthrow Nasser led by Conservative backbenchers, such as Julian Amery, also a former SOE officer.[161] Observing these British attempts to change the situation in their favour, Miles Copeland, a former CIA expert in the Middle East, writes that 'the British weren't reacting at all like seasoned, cold-blooded gameplayers', and had no real thinking of 'which Egyptian officers or civilians might constitute a new government if Nasser were to be eliminated'.[162] Nevertheless, these attempts failed, and Nasser's popularity grew significantly after the Suez Crisis.

Owing to the inaccessibility of MI6's archives, the question of how Sir Dick White saw the closure of SIME in 1958 from his new position at MI6, and how he reconciled the balance between security/counter-intelligence on the one side and 'cold war' activities on the other, remains open. Available evidence makes clear, however, that these activities were still favoured by civilian policymakers at the time, as well as politicians such as Harold Macmillan.[163]

Conclusion

The role of intelligence and security services is subordinate to government policy. SIME was above all an instrument of the Cold War and operated as 'an integral part of the military machine' in the Middle East under the direction of the Chiefs of Staff. Indeed, war planning drove SIME's activities. The story of SIME in the post-war period is also revealing regarding the nature of intelligence liaison between the British intelligence services and their Middle Eastern counterparts. It was based on mutual benefit but was strictly confined to one particular subject of common interest: Communist movements.

Despite close cooperation, especially in the field of anti-Communist security measures, the biggest difficulty faced by SIME was the maintenance of an effective liaison with local authorities in a volatile and politically hostile environment which was often detrimental to intelligence liaison. In spite of these difficulties, SIME and the DSOs maintained their relationship with local authorities and worked with them on developing security measures in the event of war. It is noteworthy that local authorities maintained knowledge of these security measures, including compiling the arrest lists, despite the closure of SIME.

Towards the mid-1950s, MI5 grew increasingly concerned about MI6's activities in its territory. While both services worked closely together on counter-intelligence in the region, MI5 feared that clandestine operations conducted by MI6 would potentially undermine its own relationships with local authorities, which had been built on mutual trust. Policymakers in London failed to recognise this practical but important concern, and these incompatible counter-subversive measures, security liaison and special political actions were still carried out in the region under the direction of government policy.

4 Prerequisites of Intelligence Cooperation

The three CENTO Regional countries are governed by dictatorships ... Their Intelligence Services have no continuing tradition of semi-independent non-political action ... The senior officers depend for their appointments and for funds on their ability to keep in favour of a very small ruling minority. They are thus intensely involved in politics, both internal and foreign ... This is a disadvantage; but it cannot be helped.

Alex Kellar[1]

In my personal view the Iranians individually are security conscious and are probably well able to take care of their own secrets; but the protection of common secrets is another matter. Here the slothfulness, venality and love for intrigue and personal animosities of the average Iranian, as well as his unwillingness to assume responsibility, are all hazards along the road to good security.

Roger Lees[2]

Introduction

Webs of intelligence networks existed at different levels all across the Middle East. As mentioned in the earlier chapters, the British cooperated with local security services, trained local officers, and implemented security measures against Communists through local security forces. These arrangements were not systematic and thus were made on an ad hoc basis. At the same time, local authorities also cooperated with each other at various levels. These intelligence networks at local initiatives were also sporadic and operated on an ad hoc and personal basis between officers at a senior level. As noted in Chapter 1, the British considered a regional Cold War defence treaty, the Baghdad Pact, later renamed CENTO, as the best means to preserve their foreign and defence interests in the region, as well as to counter Communist movements. They also attempted to institutionalise intelligence cooperation, but were plagued by difficulties from the outset. As the above quotations indicate, the British found certain characteristics of Middle Eastern intelligence and security practices incompatible with their own approaches.

This chapter explores the nature of the intelligence/security liaison between Britain and Middle Eastern states, including both necessary preconditions and obstacles. The intelligence liaison in the region had two dimensions. Firstly, since any form of cooperation required a secure organisation, the British strove to improve the security of systems before actual intelligence cooperation began. A by-product of this British effort was the formation of the Iranian National Intelligence and Security Organisation, known as SAVAK, in 1957. Owing to the lax security of systems in the Pact, Britain was also the most reluctant to share its own intelligence with the Pact members and sought to exchange intelligence on a bilateral basis. Secondly, intelligence liaison in the region was based on different political systems: democratic and non-democratic regimes, the latter of which were dominated by the presence of strong security services.

Prelude to the Security Cooperation under the Baghdad Pact

Intelligence cooperation across national borders was essential for maintaining internal security in the Middle East. Michael Howard, the military historian who authored *British Intelligence in the Second World War, vol. 5*, has described the nature of wartime security work in the region as 'an intelligence officer's paradise and a security officer's hell'.[3] As the Middle East was virtually borderless from a security perspective, the geographical conditions inevitably made the local authorities work together with their neighbours for internal security. Middle Eastern policymakers were also eager to have their intelligence and security services liaise with their neighbouring counterparts. Their eagerness mainly came from their assumptions that political developments and crises were orchestrated by external powers.[4] These conspiratorial views were exacerbated by the nature of Middle Eastern politics in which political assassinations, plots and intrigues were chronic, and any crisis in one country alarmed policymakers in another country. So, working with a good neighbour in an alliance or an ad hoc arrangement against their common enemy was a natural move for Middle Eastern policymakers.

The Baghdad Pact came into existence in 1956, when the desires of the Iraqi and Turkish governments to establish their positions in the region converged with the interests of both Britain and the United States.[5] The Baghdad Pact was not only a Cold War defence treaty against the Communist bloc, but also an alliance for the maintenance of internal security within the Pact area. The regional member states were above all eager to tackle subversive activities in their countries. High-level policies were not the only contributing factor in the formation of the Baghdad Pact; there was also a security dimension at work. As briefly discussed in Chapter 2, before the establishment of security cooperation under the Baghdad Pact, the 'Anti-Communist Triangle' alliance, namely Jordan, Lebanon and Iraq, had collaborated on subversive activities in the region since the early 1950s.[6] This security cooperation was gradually but informally institutionalised following Coghill's appointment in Jordan in 1952 and grew out of a realisation amongst the Triangle countries that subversive activities in each country were directly connected with, or indirectly instigated by, external actors such as the Soviet Union, Egypt, Syria or Saudi Arabia.[7] The three members of the 'Anti-Communist Triangle' attempted to involve the Syrian government under Adeeb al-Shishakli in anti-subversive measures in early 1953 as it was believed that most subversive activities in Lebanon, Jordan and Iraq were originating from Syria. After attempting for over a year, however, they decided to abandon this plan as the Syrians were 'far too unreliable'.[8]

This also indicates that the nature of Middle Eastern relationships was not monolithic, but highly complex. While Middle Eastern governments sought to cooperate on their common interests, they were hampered by conflicts of interest and politics. Although the Arab League existed, there was no effective cooperation between the member states. It is not surprising that when the Egyptian leader, Colonel Gamal Abdul Nasser, sought to establish a form of intelligence and security cooperation, 'an Anti-Communist Bureau in Cairo', other states swiftly voiced opposition.[9] Before sending their own delegations to Nasser's Cairo conference, Coghill, Chehab and Attiyah had met together in Beirut to 'hammer out the line to take to ensure the failure of the conference to set up such a Bureau'. They feared that establishing such an organisation under Nasser's enterprise would 'only increase the power of Egypt'.[10] Coghill recorded in his diaries that, 'thanks to the blunt rudeness of the Syrian delegate', the Egyptians failed to establish their own Anti-Communist Bureau.[11]

While Nasser still sought to exercise his influence over the Syrians, Coghill, Chehab and Attiyah successfully expanded their opposition with a multilateral secret discussion held in Baghdad in January 1956. The three met with the Heads of the Turkish and Iranian Security Services to discuss and exchange intelligence on subversive activities in the region.[12] While there had been bilateral talks on the subject between most of these countries, this was the first multilateral discussion between the Arab and non-Arab security services in the region.[13] Before this meeting, Coghill, Chehab and Attiyah had conducted a preliminary conference together streamlining how they would make the meeting successful to gain 'mutual confidence in one's opposite number' by showing a united front against subversive activities in the region, which was, Coghill noted, 'the only way of making this sort of liaison work'.[14]

There was a similar ongoing arrangement around the same period under the Baghdad Pact. At the inaugural meeting of the Pact Council held in Baghdad on 21 and 22 November 1955, the Iraqi Foreign Minister raised the dangers of Communist infiltration in the Middle East, particularly in Syria.[15] The idea of forming 'joint anti-subversion machinery' under the Pact was then discussed.[16] Harold Macmillan, then Foreign Secretary, suggested establishing multilateral intelligence and security cooperation. He also proposed that Britain 'make available technical advice on Communist subversion' to the members drawing on its experience in the Far East, where Britain had also been involved in a similar arrangement under SEATO.[17] Iran was also concerned about the spread of subversive activities, despite its more robust counter-measures after the 1953 coup, given its problems with the communistic Tudeh Party.[18] The Iranian Ambassador in Baghdad, who represented Iran for the Baghdad Pact, was willing to learn 'practical measures for combating Communist subversion' from more experienced countries such as Britain.[19]

Based on the policy laid out by the Baghdad Pact Council meeting, a discussion to form 'joint anti-subversion machinery' between the regional counterparts, later known as the Liaison and Counter-Subversion Committees, was then followed by the meeting of the Security Committee, where the representatives of the security services of the signatories came together for the first time. Directed under the policy suggested by Macmillan, Philip Kirby-Green, Head of SIME (1955–8) and Britain's representative at the committee meeting, gave a detailed proposal to form such an anti-Communist committee at the meeting. Kirby-Green's proposal was supported by Britain's closest ally, Bahjat Beg Attiyah; A. M. S. Ahmad, a Pakistani counterpart; and an American 'observer'.[20]

The Liaison and Counter-Subversion Committees were formally established after agreement was reached by the Council of Deputies of the Baghdad Pact on 25 January 1956. These committees under the Pact were intended for collaboration in anti-Communist measures between the signatories and the US 'observer'. [21] The purposes of the Liaison Committee were to 'facilitate exchange of information relating to Communist subversive activities and Soviet bloc espionage' and 'recommend ways and means by which security services can best discharge their tasks'. The Liaison Committee also aimed to 'facilitate and encourage bilateral liaison and practical cooperation between the security services'.[22] Throughout the period between 1956 and 1963, with some exceptional cases, the meetings were routinely held twice a year.

Multilateral intelligence cooperation ran parallel to the 'informal' security cooperation on subversive activities that had been initiated by the regional security services around the same period. At the first meeting of the Liaison Committee in April 1956, a copy of the 'convention' outlining the cooperation, and signed by the members of the so-called 'Club', was submitted by the Turkish delegate as a foundation for future anti-Communist liaison. It was later, however, withdrawn in favour of one submitted by the British government, which was seen as a more experienced ally in this field.[23] In fact, the regional counter-subversive machinery began to be institutionalised on British initiatives.

British Concern about the Security of the Baghdad Pact

At the inaugural meeting of the Baghdad Pact, a by-product of the discussions was the creation of the Security Committee, often referred to as the 'Security Organisation' in Foreign Office correspondence.[24] The Security Committee was formed under and directed by the Secretary-General of the Baghdad Pact.[25] The purpose of the Security Committee was to ensure proper standards of protective security for the Baghdad Pact, including the maintenance of information security (classification of documents and physical access to classified records) and vetting procedures under the security regulations of the Pact.[26] The Security Committee routinely conducted security inspections of the registries of the signatory powers, where classified CENTO documents were handled and held, and recommended improvements in protective security for each country.[27] Setting security standards was particularly important for multilateral intelligence liaison as information security was a prerequisite for the efficacy of the alliance. Britain had its own approach to intelligence, especially when it came to intelligence cooperation. For the British, the security of systems was the most important prerequisite to making intelligence cooperation effective. However, this approach was not shared by the regional counterparts.

Protective security was the domain of MI5. Philip Kirby-Green, the regional representative of MI5, was chosen to attend the first meeting of the Security Committee in December 1955 to discuss security practices with his counterparts in Baghdad.[28] At his first meeting, Kirby-Green learned that there was no comparable protective security in the member states, and was also asked by his counterparts to draw on Britain's experiences in NATO and SEATO to provide security training to them.[29] After the meeting, Kirby-Green warned the Ministry of Defence that, owing to 'no adequate security' and 'no proper vetting procedure' in some regional member states, 'any information passed to other deputies and planners may be in Moscow in a matter of days'.[30] With an urgent request by the Foreign Office, MI5 was instructed to improve the standards of protective security in the Baghdad Pact. Michael Clayton of MI5, an expert in protective security, was then despatched to Baghdad on 17 January 1956.[31] Clayton remained as Deputy Security Officer of the Security Committee until the end of 1957, providing training in protective security to member states.

Philip Kirby-Green estimated that it would take at least six months to get a minimum standard of security within the Baghdad Pact.[32] This proved deeply optimistic. Despite a series of lectures on protective security by Clayton over two years during his tenure as the Deputy Security Officer, and despite a range of British protective security mechanisms (including security regulations, vetting procedures and physical access to classified documents), there was not much improvement in the protective security regime. Concerned with the state of security at the Registry of the Pact headquarters, Sir Michael Wright reported to the Foreign Office in November 1956 that there was 'little appreciation of how to classify documents correctly' amongst non-British civilian staff, and classified documents were 'frequently lost' and handled inadequately.[33] Despite some improvement in protective security at the CENTO headquarters, the state of security of the individual member states remained far below the minimum standard when Clayton ended his stint as the Deputy Security Officer at the Pact headquarters towards the end of 1957.[34]

In 1961, when James Robertson of MI5 inspected the state of security of all regional alliances, including NATO, SEATO and CENTO, he observed that the representatives of the CENTO Security Committee had little 'support forthcoming from [their] superiors', and also that recommendations for improving security in the signatories were 'hardly carried out', except for 'inspections of CENTO registries in member countries'.[35] After a year's attempt at improving the protective security of the Pact, Britain decided to abolish the Security Committee in 1963 as the chief organisation to maintain the security of the Pact, and instead proposed that the Liaison Committee, which was dominated by the highest ranking of intelligence and security officials of the member states, take over this task. After a series of lengthy discussions with the signatory powers, the proposal was eventually accepted and from 1963 onwards, the Security Committee became the Security Sub-Committee under the Liaison Committee of the Pact.[36]

A combination of several factors appears to have prevented the improvement of the Pact's protective security. First and foremost, the regional Pact members neglected the importance of security measures – they were overwhelmingly concerned with countering subversive elements in their countries. Sir Roger Hollis, the Director-General of MI5, reported at a 1960 JIC meeting that the regional members were 'concentrating unduly on the threat' against the internal security of their countries, while, Hollis thought, 'they should give greater attention to [protective] security'.[37] Moreover, in addition to the lack of security awareness amongst the regional members, Philip Kirby-Green also identified at his first encounter with his regional counterparts that some members had no understanding of the difference between security, counter-intelligence and counter-subversion.[38]

Secondly, there was also a structural issue at the levels of both CENTO and regional members. Unlike the Liaison Committee, where very senior officers of the security services responsible for the internal security in their countries were represented, the Security Committee was composed of middle-ranking security officers of the member states who were seconded to the Pact headquarters in Baghdad (1955–8) and Ankara (from 1959 onwards). As a result, the regional representatives to the Security Committee were considered 'international civil servants' by their own governments and thus 'cut off' from direct contact with those governments.[39] There was also a problem at the national level. The problem was that, even if these representatives were in close contact with their national governments, there were 'no effective' security authorities in their countries 'with whom they could correspond and from whom they could obtain such briefs'.[40] As a result, it was thought that it would be better for the Liaison Committee, comprising of the highest ranks of the security services, to take over the duty of protective security in the Pact.

The third problem was departmental infighting over internal security in the regional countries. This was the main reason that Britain insisted that the Shah of Iran establish the national security organisation, later known as SAVAK, and provided training in protective security to the Iranians. However, even after SAVAK nominally assumed full responsibility for internal security from the military in 1957, a conflict of jurisdiction with the military was reported in August 1961, when the security organisation of the military still sought to represent Iran at the Liaison Committee of the Pact.[41] These kinds of problems were also common among the regional members. In the case of Iraq, which hosted the headquarters of the Pact until 1958, there had been antagonistic relationships between the police and the military. As a result, the CID, which was part of the police and responsible for the internal security of the country, was unable to inspect the security of the military, which might have contributed to the failure of the Iraqi government to forestall the coup by a small group of Iraqi Army officers in July 1958.[42] While Turkey and Pakistan were considered to have better security, the responsibility of the military for internal security in these countries was still a concern for the British.[43]

The available evidence suggests that Britain was right to be concerned about the security of the multilateral intelligence liaison. Classified information was leaking to Egypt from the Iraqis,[44] whilst another member state leaked material to the Soviets. According to a KGB defector, Ilya Dzhirkvelov, a conversation between Turkish diplomats led to the discovery of a KGB officer in

Azerbaijan, A. Guseinov, who was about to defect to the West in Turkey in late 1955. The conversation had been recorded through a listening device planted in the Turkish Embassy in Moscow. Similar to the defection attempt by Konstantin Volkov in 1946, which was intercepted by Kim Philby, Guseinov provided fruitful information on Soviet activities in the Middle East. According to Dzhirkvelov, Guseinov was carried to Moscow semi-conscious on a stretcher by a special KGB team. Guseinov's wife, who was the main conspirator in the plan to defect to the West, leapt from a third-floor window and killed herself.[45]

Although Britain had more experience in protective security than other members, it too had defects in its own security. Kim Philby, despite his treachery being suspected by MI5, was still under the patronage of MI6 as a journalist and stayed in Beirut from 1956 until his defection in 1963.[46] Emir Farid Chehab, Head of the Lebanese Sûreté Générale, who was puzzled by the behaviour of his British colleagues and could not understand how Philby had been allowed to escape, noted that the Sûreté 'could so easily have arranged a small accident' to arrest Philby.[47] In addition, George Blake of MI6, another Soviet mole, who was at the time compromising secrets of Britain's NATO allies, also stayed in Beirut.[48] Moreover, records from the Soviet archives smuggled out of Russia reveal that the British Embassy in Beirut was also penetrated by the KGB through a Lebanese maid and bugging devices for a number of years in the later period.[49]

The British Contribution to the Establishment of SAVAK

According to the existing historiography, the Iranian national security and intelligence service, SAVAK, was established in 1957 under the auspices of the CIA and Mossad.[50] Britain's involvement in this process is little discussed. Indeed, scholarly attention to Britain's continuous interest in Iran in the post-Mossaddegh era diminishes once the United States became interested in Iranian affairs. However, it is worth pointing out that Britain had long regarded Iran as within its sphere of influence. While Operation BOOT/TPAJAX to overthrow Mossaddegh was a joint venture with the Americans, the development of the events leading up to the coup from 1951 until August 1953 clearly shows that the coup was chiefly initiated by the British, and that the American involvement came from British, and Iranian, necessity – the logistics, the money and the oil.[51] Continuing to maintain influence in Iran, Britain deemed a national security service essential. Mansur Rafizadeh, a former SAVAK officer, clearly states in his memoir that SAVAK was created on 'the joint advice of the CIA, British intelligence service, and Mossad'.[52] Supporting this testimony, the available documentation attests that Britain was instrumental in establishing SAVAK, arising from its concerns with the state of protective security in Iran, which would affect the efficacy of multilateral intelligence liaison under the Baghdad Pact as a whole.

Philip Kirby-Green identified Iran as the weakest link in protective security at the first meeting of the Security Committee in 1955.[53] While Michael Clayton was in Baghdad to provide courses on security practices, he was also tasked with assessing the standards of security in Iran, as well as the necessity of the Iranian government to establish an organisation 'officially charged with full responsibility for enforcing security'. Roger Hollis, then Deputy Director-General of MI5, also assured Clayton that MI5 was willing to accommodate a 'limited number of senior Iranian security officials' for training in Britain if necessary.[54] Clayton was then told by General Hadjazi, the Iranian representative on the Deputy Military Committee of the Baghdad Pact, that Iran had 'no security organisation' at all.[55]

Despite an American Military Mission having been stationed in Iran since the early 1950s and tasked with 'the production of an adequate security system', the state of security in Iran remained inadequate. Although there had been three organisations responsible for security (the aforementioned 'G-2', the counter-espionage organisation of the Iranian armed forces; the Special Branch of the Iranian Police; and the Military Governors), none of these organisations had any responsibility for protective security in civilian departments, including the Ministry of Foreign Affairs. Discussing the matter with his Iranian colleagues in Baghdad, Clayton soon reported back to Hollis:

I judge that knowledge of protective security practice is limited to the army only ... There is certainly no national security authority as we know it, and no system of interdepartmental security co-ordination ... I agree that the first essential is to establish [a] national security authority, but consider that unless we advise on how this should be done and additionally give detailed instruction on methods to implement details of regulations, the prospect of any reasonable degree of security in Iran in the foreseeable future is very remote.[56]

The matter was also discussed in Baghdad between Sir Michael Wright, the British Ambassador in Baghdad, and Francis Marten, a diplomat at the British Embassy in Tehran. They agreed that training a few Iranians in Britain was 'not enough', and instead suggested the Foreign Office 'despatch a fully qualified officer to Tehran from London' to advise the Iranians on improving their security matters. Sir Michael Wright concluded that 'unless some such arrangement is made, the prospect of a fundamental improvement in Iranian security standards, on which the ability of the Baghdad Pact to undertake serious planning of sensitive matters depends, is remote'.[57]

Training the Iranians in protective security in either London or Tehran was, however, not sufficient to solve the security problems in the forthcoming meetings of the Baghdad Pact. To solve this short-term problem, the Iranian government was urged to set up an interdepartmental organisation responsible for coordinating the activities of the various intelligence and security organisations in the country. As a result, the Iranian Chiefs of Staff established a new joint staff of the armed forces, named J-2, which was also given responsibility for national security matters.[58] However, under the security regulations of the Pact, it was also essential for Iran to have a 'national security authority' responsible for the security of Baghdad Pact classified information.[59]

The matter was then referred to the British Ambassador in Tehran, Sir Roger Stevens (1954–8), who responded to the request from the Foreign Office that he would 'take [the] next suitable opportunity to impress on the Shah the importance of security' and to 'ask him about Iranian plans for establishing a "national security authority"'.[60] It was noted that 'the Iranians should be persuaded to settle the identity of their national security authority without delay'.[61] Consequently, and as requested by the Iranian government through the Baghdad Pact, MI5 despatched Roger Lees, formerly DSO in Baghdad (1951–3), to Tehran in May 1956 to advise the Shah on enhancing the state of security in Iran.[62] In addition to his career in the Middle East – where he had served in Egypt as a SIME officer, assisting the Head of SIME, William Magan, until 1950 – and in addition to his role in Baghdad, which was highly praised in Whitehall, Lees was considered well qualified for the task following his long career in the Indian Police (over twenty years until 1948), with a supervisory role in the Special Branch (Patna).[63]

Lees visited Tehran twice during the period between 1956 and 1957 in which the Iranian national security and intelligence organisation was being established. During his first, three-month visit to Tehran in 1956, Lees, in the guise of the First Secretary at the British Embassy, was personally assigned by the Shah himself to give security advice to General Haj-Ali Kia, the Chief of Military Intelligence. At the time, the J-2 was temporarily responsible for supervising the implementation of the security regulations of the Baghdad Pact.[64] Once SAVAK was established and had assumed responsibility for the internal security of Iran, taking over from the J-2, Roger Lees was then assigned to advise the first Head of SAVAK, General Teymour Bakhtiar (1957–61), and to train the SAVAK officers in protective security.[65]

From the outset, Roger Lees's objective was to 'train the Iranians in the proper implementation of the Baghdad Pact Security Regulations'.[66] His role in Tehran was thus primarily limited to providing the Iranians with an effective security system in the country through his advice and the training of senior Iranian officers in protective security. During his first visit, he supervised the establishment of a Registry system and trained the Iranians in handling classified documents and vetting procedures, and also drafted a set of 'national security regulations'. All of his recommendations and drafts were approved by the Shah himself and implemented accordingly.[67]

During his second, six-month visit to Tehran, his primary task was to ensure that the newly established SAVAK would meet the security requirements of the Baghdad Pact, including arrangements for the protection of classified documents, which were constantly inspected by the members of the Security Committee of the Baghdad Pact.[68] Meanwhile, Iranian female staff at the Registry of SAVAK were trained in London in protective security.[69] Roger Lees gave his report to the Head Office of MI5 on the assessment of his overall achievement at the end of his visit in 1957. However, he was rather sceptical about the prospects for protective security in Iran, and dogmatically noted the Iranian national characteristics – 'the slothfulness, venality and love for intrigue and personal animosities of the average Iranian, as well as his unwillingness to assume responsibility' – that would all be 'hazards along the road to good security'.[70]

During the same period, the CIA was also in Tehran to provide training to SAVAK officers – not in protective security but in foreign intelligence collection, counter-intelligence and intelligence analysis.[71] Mansur Rafizadeh, a former SAVAK officer, also noted that, unlike the CIA and Mossad, both of which were actively involved in interfering with SAVAK's operations, by 'consent of the three foreign [American, Israeli and British] intelligence groups, Britain had no active involvement' in SAVAK's operational aspects.[72] Britain became more actively involved in the internal affairs of Iran after losing its closest ally in the 1958 Iraqi Revolution. However, at the time of the establishment of SAVAK, the British contribution mainly came from the need to raise Iranian security standards to meet the security arrangements of the Pact and assign the responsibilities necessary to establish sufficient national security in Iran.[73]

The Liaison Committee of the Baghdad Pact

The Liaison Committee was one example of high-level intelligence and security cooperation amongst members in the Pact area. While Britain and the United States normally sent senior officials (of MI5 and the CIA, respectively) to the committee meetings, the regional countries were represented by the heads of the intelligence and security services. The Liaison Committee focused more on Soviet subversive activities than espionage.

From the mid-1950s onwards, the security services of the signatory powers probed activities associated more specifically with the Soviet Intelligence Service in the region. The aforementioned Ilya Dzhirkvelov states in his memoirs that a new department was established in the First Chief Directorate of the KGB at the beginning of 1955 to spy on the Soviet Union's 'frontiers', including Turkey, Iran, Afghanistan, India and China.[74] Amongst them, Turkey was the main target as it was a member of NATO and maintained close contacts with the Americans and British. Dzhirkvelov was personally involved in organising a network of agents in Turkey from 1955 onwards.[75] During the period between the 1950s and 1960s, the Soviet Union sought to exploit anti-colonial sentiment in the region, such as radical Arab Nationalism, so as to eliminate Western influence. Moscow still regarded Communist Parties as the instrument to best advance its cause, despite anti-Communist sentiment throughout the area.[76]

Available records suggest that members of the Liaison Committee might have cottoned on to the Soviet offensive through CENTO intelligence sharing. In May 1957, the Turkish representative reported on the methods and techniques employed by the Soviets, demonstrating that from at least 1956 the Soviet Union targeted ethnic minorities in Turkey for both espionage and subversion purposes. They included the use of a former young Nazi officer, named Wilfried Herbrecht, and an Armenian-born reserve officer of the Turkish military service, named Arman Vartanian, to obtain information on NATO defence plans and the cryptographic system used in NATO communications.[77] In addition, Herbrecht also confessed to the Turkish authorities that the Soviets instructed him to contact a group of Kurds to instigate subversion against the Turkish government for Kurdish independence.[78]

One of the advantages of intelligence sharing under the Pact was that members shared their knowledge of Communist activities, which enabled the member states to obtain a better picture of the threats posed by International Communism in the region.

These discussions were highly important not only to the British, but also to the security services of the regional powers as their ability to counter internal threats was essential for the stability of each government. The subjects of their information exchange included, for instance, the strength and activities of the Communist Parties; propaganda broadcasts by various radio stations of the Eastern bloc countries aimed at instigating subversive activities in the Pact area; and any scheduled Communist-sponsored international meetings.[79] The information exchanged between the member states also included a list of known Communist members in the region. This was considered more important after the withdrawal of Iraq from the Baghdad Pact; thereafter the members of the ICP operated freely and became more active in the region.[80] In addition, as international organisations and groups were regarded as sources of Communist subversion, a 'watch list' containing forthcoming Communist and non-Communist meetings or events was regularly exchanged for relevant authorities to 'take action' against it.[81] Moreover, their discussions also extended to counter-measures by the respective governments that had proved effective against Communist activities. The consensus amongst the regional member states regarding 'effective' measures against any Communists and their sympathisers was 'heavy penalties in accordance with the Criminal Code'.[82]

Apart from the RAF bases in Habbaniya, Iraq, and also those in Cyprus, Britain faced no direct threat to its security in the Pact area. However, unlike the Americans, who were mostly a passive participant as an 'observer' (at least until 1959), MI5 actively contributed to discussions about the methods and techniques of Communist bloc espionage and subversion, and Communist activities.[83] Alex Kellar of MI5, who chaired the Liaison Committee in January 1961 on a routine basis, used his chairmanship to include a report on 'communist penetration of the labour movement' in the Pact area, and 'the student problem', covering the 'causes and nature' of unrest among students in the 'Afro-Asian area'.[84] In addition, as Chairman of the NATO Special Committee, Kellar also made available classified NATO documents to his counterparts, who were keen on finding out more about 'Soviet Bloc intelligence operations' against regions outside the Pact and the way in which other security services were coping with 'their own student communities within and without their countries and in and around the CENTO area and Europe'.[85] As the Chairman of both NATO's and CENTO's Committees, Kellar also decided to exchange security reports between the CENTO Liaison and NATO Special Committees on the grounds, as he noted, that 'what was sauce for the goose was sauce for the gander', meaning that the intelligence exchange would be valuable to both parties.[86] The regional members welcomed Kellar's suggestions.[87]

Despite the advantages of cooperation on anti-subversive measures in the Pact area, there was an inherent problem with regional intelligence and security liaison under the Liaison Committee. Although the regional members maintained their anti-Communist stance throughout the period, their focus on subversive activities often extended to non-Communist activities, which caused difficulties in coordinating anti-Communist measures. While a collective effort for anti-Communist measures was mostly conducted in the form of propaganda under the Counter-Subversion Committee, the difficulty of coordination was also apparent at the Liaison Committee, where the threat assessment reports from each representative were shared and a consensus on the threats was sought between the committee members.[88]

There was a peculiar aspect to CENTO's Liaison Committee, which Alex Kellar noticed as the Chairman of his first meeting in 1961. Kellar pointed out that their discussions were 'more of the kind that one would expect from a political committee', and that the intelligence assessments submitted by his regional counterparts 'trespass[ed] much too much on the preserves of the political experts'.[89] The implication of this peculiarity was that intelligence assessments by the regional members were heavily influenced by the policy of their own governments. Since the senior intelligence officers present at the Liaison Committee were committed to defending the existence of a very small ruling minority, who also appointed them, they were 'intensely involved in politics, both internal and foreign' – heavily politicised and 'endemic' – to make sure of their regime security. Kellar found this disadvantageous for intelligence cooperation in the Pact, but also noted that, due to the inherent nature of the cooperation, 'it cannot be helped'.[90]

The difficulty of reaching a consensus on internal threats amongst the member states also came from the limitations in intelligence sharing. Despite their security cooperation at the highest level, the Liaison Committee was a place for sharing intelligence-based assessments between the Pact members. The problem with the limitations in intelligence sharing was the fact that the protection of intelligence sources was a prerequisite for any liaison, especially multilateral cooperation. As any intelligence services had responsibilities for the security of their own sources, the only solution for multilateral intelligence liaison, according to John Bruce Lockhart, the Deputy Chief of MI6 (1961–6), was thus to only share intelligence in 'a collated form where it would be impossible to identify the source'.[91] This, however, often made it difficult for other members to verify a claim made by a member based on their intelligence-based assessments.

The problem was apparent from the early period of the Baghdad Pact. At the meeting of the Liaison Committee in May 1957, the Pakistani delegate frequently referred to the activities of the Indian Communist Party supporting subversive activities in Kashmir. The assessment by MI5 confirmed that there was indeed a threat from the Indian Communist Party in the form of propaganda attacking Pakistan's self-proclaimed 'neutralism', and that the situation in Kashmir also presented a 'substantial threat to member countries particularly Pakistan'. However, there was no supporting evidence that these subversive activities in Kashmir had a direct link to the Indian Communist Party.[92] The heart of the problem lay in the inaccessibility of the sources. A report from the Head of SIME to the Head Office of MI5 recorded:

> here is clearly a limit to the degree to which I can over-ride the DIB [Director of the Intelligence Bureau: Pakistani Security Service] when, complying with the roles of the Liaison Committee, they produce their own National Assessment. Equally, there is a limit to which I could challenge their evidence, although it was clear that some of

their statements were somewhat dubious and others highly exaggerated, but when outrightly challenged, SADULLA [Director of the Intelligence Bureau] always claimed to have evidence on record to support his arguments.[93]

The Pakistanis' claim that 'Indian subversion against Pakistan was, in fact, Communist inspired' was considered by the Foreign Office as a technique to widen the mandate of the Liaison Committee, as they had used the same technique earlier in the SEATO Committee.[94]

These kinds of local and regional problems were not only present in the Pakistani case. All the regional members, the Iraqis, Turkish and Iranians, were preoccupied with countering their own national subversive elements. The difficulty was then to have an agreed assessment on the nature of subversive activities in the region. As a result, the coverage of the Liaison Committee was widened from 'Communist' to 'Communist-inspired' threats from 1957 onwards.[95] Non-Communist threats, including Nasserite subversive activities, were also included in the category of 'subversive' threats to the Pact in 1962.[96] This was mainly due to the fact that local governments viewed non-Communist threats as being equally as subversive as Communist threats in the region, and also that non-Communist threats threatened the existence of the pro-Western member states, which was 'directly in the interests of Communism'.[97] A report on the meeting of the Liaison Committee in 1964 recorded that 'the main subjects that had been expected to cause difficulty were the respective preoccupations of Turkey with Cyprus, of Iran with the UAR [Egypt], and of Pakistan with India and Afghanistan'.[98] The preoccupations of the regional members with their local or regional problems continued throughout the period.

The Limited Contributions to the Liaison Committee

Unlike the other members, who were willing to cooperate on subversive activities in the region, Britain was in fact the most reluctant to give full assessments to the member states, especially in the early years of the Baghdad Pact. H. P. Goodwyn of MI5 once noted to the PUSD of the Foreign Office that:

> hitherto we have not provided any comprehensive paper on subversion in the Baghdad Pact area. Rather we have confined ourselves to snippets of information on individual matters. H/SIME [Head of SIME, Philip Kirby-Green] has pointed out that on the last occasion the US Observer contributed something a good deal more elaborate than anything we have produced and he, H/SIME, has observed that it is for consideration whether we (as a matter of fact 'we' involves mainly your friends [MI6]) should produce a paper something like it ourselves.[99]

Two factors explain Britain's reluctance to make its own contribution to intelligence sharing at the Liaison Committee: security and ability.

As discussed above, the Pact suffered from lax protective security. The protection of intelligence sources was a prerequisite for any intelligence liaison. Thus, any intelligence shared with the member states took the form of intelligence-based assessments, carefully concealing the identities of intelligence sources, rather than *raw* or *single-source* intelligence. Britain was mostly concerned that sensitive information might leak to unintended recipients through intelligence sharing with the Pact members. John Bruce Lockhart of MI6 notes that 'if you have nine nations together swopping secrets and you include details about sources, the security risk of revealing those sources is multiplied by nine, or even nine-plus'.[100]

Britain considered using a more secure bilateral intelligence liaison with individual members on certain topics instead of intelligence sharing with all its counterparts in the multilateral form of the Liaison Committee.[101] This bilateral intelligence exchange, sometimes one-way traffic, was mostly conducted through other channels than the Liaison Committee. One such channel was the Counter-Subversion Office (CSO), a permanent working body at the headquarters of the Pact for counter-propaganda purposes; the members were mostly seconded from the security services.[102] Using this channel, a report on Communist activities in Syria was passed to the Turkish representative by the British counterpart, as the Turks had a 'thirst' for finding out more about 'the Syrian situation'.[103] On a different occasion, the Turks supplied intelligence to the British demonstrating that 'Communism in Turkey is directed by exiles in Paris.'[104]

The second factor is Britain's (in)ability to contribute its own intelligence to the Liaison Committee. MI5's concerns about its lack of contribution to the Liaison Committee meetings may have come from the nature of its relationship with its regional counterparts. Since it was largely dependent on mutual trust, gaining credibility from the member states as a liaison partner was a cause for concern for MI5 as the British delegate. MI6 officers were also operating a covert network in the region – mostly without the knowledge of the local authorities – and the exposure of these activities risked undermining the mutual trust of MI5's liaison with the local authorities. Thus, the extent to which intelligence could be shared with the Pact members was indeed a very delicate concern – the identities of the agents controlled by MI6, and also its activities, had to be carefully concealed before sharing any intelligence. Available evidence suggests, for instance, that while MI5 maintained liaison with SAVAK, MI6 conducted espionage in Iran and had its own agents within the Tudeh Party. SAVAK was suspicious about British activities in Iran.[105]

Of course, MI6 was not MI5's only intelligence source. Government Communications Headquarters (GCHQ) was, and still is, Britain's largest and most fruitful intelligence organisation. Britain maintained listening stations at RAF Habbaniya, Iraq, until 1958, and at the Army headquarters in Cyprus throughout the period.[106] RAF Canberra aircraft modified for signals intelligence (SIGINT) interception/collection were flying from RAF Habbaniya and actively collecting wireless communications close to the Soviet border.[107] A former RAF officer also recollects that he flew from Habbaniya with a group of 'technicians', who had university degrees in Russian, listening in on 'Russian wireless traffic', and that the recorded and interpreted materials were sent to the British Embassy in Baghdad.[108] In addition, despite the reduction in manpower and the retreat of regional headquarters overseas to Britain in the mid-1950s, including SIME, a JIC report recorded that 'no transfer of SIGINT effort from the ME [Middle East] to the UK could be made without reducing the efficiency of the service to Middle East consumers'.[109] Nevertheless, these SIGINT operations were essentially for military purposes, and lacked much value for assessing internal security within the Pact area.

SIME was also involved in other SIGINT operations in the region. During the Second World War, Sir Dick White noted that SIGINT was indeed 'the biggest source of intelligence' for detecting Axis agents engaged in espionage and subversive activities in the region.[110] In his memoirs, Sir Alistair Horne writes that the headquarters of SIME, attached to the headquarters of the British Army in the region, housed its own signals interception unit. He notes that:

> The heavily protected SIME villa was like a tabernacle within the temple of GHQ; and within SIME, where none dared tread or even ask what went on, was a small holy of holies, manned by strange signals personnel and topped by a tangle of aerials. That was in fact the very heart of British intelligence, where all the intercept work of SIGINT (signals intelligence) went on – of which none of us normal mortals had an inkling until three decades later, when the story of Ultra and Enigma came to be revealed.[111]

Further evidence suggests that Britain's efforts were targeted at not only the Soviet Union but also Middle Eastern states. In his memoirs, Peter Wright, a former MI5 officer, notes that his efforts to bug the Egyptian Embassy in London, with technical support from the Post Office, enabled GCHQ to decrypt the Egyptians' Hagelin code machine.[112] This combined MI5 and GCHQ operation, he claims, 'enabled us to read the Egyptian cipher in the London Embassy throughout the Suez Crisis'.[113] Britain was indeed able to read Egyptian communications during the crisis – the Foreign Secretary, Selwyn Lloyd, congratulated Sir Eric Jones, the Director of GCHQ, on his organisation's success in breaking the Egyptian cipher during the Suez Crisis.[114] In addition, David Easter claims that GCHQ was able to trace the connections between Nasser and subversive activities in the late

1950s, which were directed against pro-British governments in the region, such as Lebanon, Jordan and Iraq.[115] Moreover, the American counterpart of GCHQ, the National Security Agency (NSA), which worked intimately with GCHQ, also targeted Middle Eastern states.[116]

Furthermore, declassified materials from the Second World War show that the GC&CS, the predecessor to GCHQ, competently decrypted the diplomatic communications of most Middle Eastern states, including the Pact members, such as Turkey, Iraq and Iran.[117] This fact indicates that GCHQ may possibly have continuously, or even intermittently, been reading the communications of the Pact members in the post-war period. In this context, intelligence sharing on a certain topic with its Middle Eastern counterparts might also have revealed Britain's intelligence gathering capabilities and compromised its sources. Therefore, British contributions to the liaison had to be carefully tailored.

There remains, nevertheless, the question of the extent to which Britain was able to contribute fruitful intelligence assessments on subversive activities in the region to its counterparts. During this period, it is clear that MI6 had limited sources of intelligence and so was unable to make much contribution to MI5's assessments. There are four main reasons for this. Firstly, MI6 was responsible for counter-espionage in the region, not counter-subversion as agreed with SIME in 1951. Secondly, British intelligence as a whole was largely dependent on local authorities for information on Communist activities. Thirdly, MI6 had only very 'few Arabists' to understand the nature of the Middle East throughout the 1950s. Lastly, but not least, instead of collecting intelligence, MI6 was occupied with conducting clandestine political operations in the region, including an assassination plot against Nasser.[118] In order to overcome this intelligence deficiency, John Bruce Lockhart, the Deputy Chief of MI6, held a three-day conference in the summer of 1960, to which all MI6 heads of station in the region were 'summoned' to discuss 'how to penetrate the Nasserite movement [subversive activities in the region]'.[119]

The issue is also true for SIGINT: it is questionable how useful

SIGINT was for identifying subversive threats in the region. Indeed, the subversive activities of radical Arab Nationalism, associated with Nasser, were certainly a concern for the British during the period. However, it is important to note that, as is discussed in detail in Chapter 5, Nasser's subversive activities were not considered as serious a threat as Communist activities until the early 1960s by the Pact – they were certainly a subversive threat to the regional members but not to the Pact as a whole, the target of which was exclusively set as Communist activities during the period between 1956 and 1962. In addition, when the security services studied Communist activities in the region and radical Arab Nationalist movements associated with Nasser in 1960, the members of the Liaison Committee clearly distinguished between the two threats.[120] It is thus doubtful whether Britain's SIGINT could make much of a contribution to the picture and intentions of underground Communist movements in the Pact area especially during the period between 1956 and 1963.

This point also raises the question of the value of SIGINT as a useful source on Communist activities in the region. It is known that in the immediate post-war period, SIGINT was a critical source for exposing a web of Soviet espionage networks (with American Communists) in the United States and elsewhere (codenamed VENONA).[121] However, no documentary evidence suggests that VENONA had any impact on the Middle Eastern context.[122] Moreover, there was no evidence to suggest that Communists in the region were using wireless communication, a medium that could potentially be intercepted by GCHQ, at least, during the period.

Most importantly, evidence indicates that owing to the nature of the Middle East, where Communist activities were prohibited by local authorities, direct contact between Russians and Communists in the region were rare. Even if the contact had been made by landline or post, for instance, the first organisations to intercept the communication by either wiretapping or censorship would have been those of the local authorities – the local police but not GCHQ. Furthermore, the techniques and methods for contacting local Communists employed by the Russians – using selected Communist members or minorities, such as the

Armenians and the Kurds, as intermediaries – were exposed by the interrogation of ICP members by the Iraqi CID.[123]

In this context, it is questionable whether Britain had much intelligence on subversive activities in the region beyond the capacity of MI5 during the period, especially in the early years of the Baghdad Pact. Britain may have been largely dependent on the intelligence assessments submitted by the members of the Liaison Committee. Nevertheless, documentary evidence suggests that after the withdrawal of Iraq from the Baghdad Pact, Britain had several sources of information on the internal affairs of Iraq, including the activities of the ICP.[124] In his biography of Sir Dick White, Tom Bower notes that, 'despite the antagonism of the Kassem [Qasim] regime', Britain's old relationship with the Iraqis, including the police, the armed forces and businessmen, allowed MI6 to 'penetrate government agencies'.[125]

Conclusion

Richard Jasse interpreted the Baghdad Pact as a form of British colonialism – it was essentially run by British imperial interests to maintain Britain's influence in the region.[126] To some degree, Jasse's interpretation is accurate: Harold Macmillan's offer to the regional members to train them in the techniques and methods of Britain's anti-Communist measures was indeed intended to prevent the spread of Communist activities in the region, and was equally meant to serve British interests in maintaining influence over the pro-British governments in the region. Nevertheless, despite Macmillan's desire, intelligence cooperation under the Baghdad Pact was not smooth. This was mainly owing to the security, or otherwise, of the Pact – Britain considered that sharing classified intelligence with the regional members was unsafe. A by-product of this lax security was the establishment of SAVAK in 1957. The security concern was not only about the Iranians, however. Throughout the period between 1956 and 1963, Britain sought to improve the security of the Pact members. The extent to which the state of CENTO security improved after 1963 is a matter of speculation; however, it seems most unlikely that the state of security improved substantially soon after 1963.

Differences between Britain and its Middle Eastern counterparts also hampered liaison. The security services of the regional members were loyal to their own governments and thus strongly committed to suppressing subversive activities in their countries by any means necessary. The Communist threat was not monolithic, nor clear-cut. Britain (and the United States) was mostly concerned about the spread of Communist activities in the region, but regional members' concerns were wider – they were not exclusively about Communist activities, but included other 'Communist-inspired' threats. The difference in perceptions between Britain (and the United States) on the one hand and Middle Eastern states on the other demonstrates the dynamics of the Pact.

5 Conflicting Interests in Anti-Communist Measures

CENTO was a disappointment to the regional members, all of them ... We [US and Britain] took a, very, I'd say, fairly rigid line, that the CENTO organization was intended to deal with a communist threat, and basically a Soviet Communist threat obviously. Whereas Iran would have liked us very much in public statements, the communiqués, or actual activities to use the organization against Iraq [after Iraq had left] ... The Pakistanis wanted us to use the organisation against India in some fashion or other.

Charles Naas[1]

Our main concern at the start of the meeting was that the Asian members [i.e. the regional members] would tend to interpret counter-subversion as simply an excuse to discuss and develop operations by their own police and security services ... [comprising] Generals and Colonels, who took rather a physical view of counter-subversion, and no one even remotely connected with information work as we know it.

Sir Leonard Figg[2]

Introduction

According to historian Daniel Pipes, Middle Eastern leaders had a 'conspiracy mentality' when interpreting regional affairs.[3] This was compounded by threats of internal subversion, often fanned by propaganda. Accordingly, many Middle Eastern leaders believed that anti-governmental activities were all instigated and propagated by external enemies. As we have seen, regional security services held diverging views on internal security from their British counterparts. This rift was most noticeable during discussions of the Counter-Subversion Committee and most destructive in anti-Communist propaganda.

This chapter explores the nature of the threats that Middle Eastern governments encountered; how Britain and the local authorities used propaganda as an anti-Communist measure under the Baghdad Pact; and the extent to which local authorities understood and conducted anti-Communist measures in their countries. It shows that although all members considered Communist movements the main threat, limitations in the Pact's collective efforts existed. These mainly stemmed from its dynamics: while Britain and the United States considered the Pact as an alliance against the Soviet Union or International Communism, the regional members were more concerned about local or regional problems. This problem was reinforced by the fact that the Counter-Subversion Committee of the Baghdad Pact, the highest policymaking committee for propaganda, consisted of the heads of the security services of the regional states, which also handled counter-subversive propaganda campaigns in their respective countries.[4]

The Threat from Propaganda

The significance of propaganda in shaping regional affairs should not be underestimated. Baruch Hazan's classic study on the techniques of Soviet propaganda in the region makes clear that Moscow had been the chief instigator in calling the local population to arms against 'imperialists' and 'reactionary' – or pro-Western – governments in the region since the late 1940s.[5] Despite some differences among the Middle Eastern governments in their anti-Communist stances, all local security services were engaged in anti-Communist measures, including arresting Communists and confiscating subversive publications and equipment.

Middle Eastern security services struggled to counter the spread of subversive publications. In the case of Lebanon, for instance, a British diplomat noted that an illegal publication, *Akhbar*, was believed to have a circulation of 'about 10,000 copies a day', which for a country the size of Lebanon was 'very large'.[6] These subversive publications served as the main platform for Communist activists to agitate local populations and turn against their own governments. In addition, some materials were smuggled into countries from outside whilst activists also moved beyond their borders. This made life all the more difficult for local security services.[7] Moreover, the presses printing these illegal publications were often reported to be located either in the Soviet Union or in the Soviet Embassy itself, against which the local security services were unable to take action.[8]

Communist publications were not only the threat. Extraterritorial radio broadcasts were often more subversive and even threatened the very existence of local authorities, especially ones associated with the West. Fear of internal subversion amongst Middle Eastern leaders was also fostered by the rise of radical Arab Nationalist movements in the region from the mid-1950s, associated with the Egyptian leader, Colonel Gamal Abdul Nasser. It is important to note that, while any relationship between the Soviet and Egyptian threats preoccupied British thinking, and has subsequently been debated by historians, regional governments of the Baghdad Pact, or even Lebanon and Jordan, gave it little thought.

For the regional governments, the techniques and methods used either by Communists, through the Soviets, or by Nasser were the same – discrediting the legitimacy of governments, and ruling elites, that were associated with the West. These propaganda campaigns were subversive and anti-governmental in nature. Colonel Sir Patrick Coghill, the Director-General of Intelligence of the Arab Legion (1952–6), once noted that, in addition to Communists, 'the worst' subversive activity he had to deal with in fact came from Egypt and Saudi Arabia:

They [Egyptians] are entirely unscrupulous ... [T]hey broadcast a stream of vitriolic abuse of Nuri Said in Hebrew. So much for Arab brotherly love. For months recently they have been trying to organise sabotage gangs to operate from Jordan into Israel, in order to compromise this country. Their local M.A. [Military Attaché] is the mainspring of this. For all the time I have been here – nearly four years – Egypt has flooded the Press and Air of the Middle East with bitterly hostile attacks on 'Imperialists' and 'Colonizers' ... Saudi Arabia is working hand in glove with Egypt ... – [through] lavish bribes on a fabulous scale which include or included subsidies to the Jordan royal family – Cabinet Ministers, Deputies and newspapers, one and all on their pay-roll. Their principal objects of dislike are the members of the Hashemite family ... So all is directed at weakening Hashemite influence.[9]

Communist and radical Arab Nationalist propaganda was a clear threat to local authorities. Egypt, later the United Arab Republic (UAR), and the Soviet Union continually targeted their populations with calls for revolution. As noted by Baruch Hazan, the association of the Baghdad Pact with Britain and the United States 'created a community of interests' between Nasser's Egypt and the Soviet Union as a target for propaganda.[10] The Iraqi Prime Minister, Nuri al-Said, also felt that the existence of the Hashemite dynasty of Iraq was threatened by propaganda from Moscow, Cairo and Damascus.[11] From the mid-1950s, the problem only worsened as non-Communist forces, chiefly radical Arab Nationalists, grew increasingly hostile to the local authorities.

The Egyptian government led by the Free Officers, first General Muhammad Nagib and later Colonel Nasser, harnessed the power of propaganda to consolidate their position after the coup in 1952. In doing so, they were assisted by a small group of CIA officers, including Kim Roosevelt, Miles Copeland and James Eichelberger.[12] Similar to Communist activities, Nasser also sought to generate internal subversion, or 'revolution' in Nasser's words.[13] Yaacov Caroz notes that Nasser 'considered subversion to be a legitimate means of achieving his objectives'.[14] By the time the Baghdad Pact was formed in 1955, Nasser had recognised the power of propaganda and considered it his only weapon against 'imperialists', that is, the British, and, above all, pro-imperialist Middle Eastern governments, such as the Hashemite dynasty, Iraq, Jordan and pro-Western Lebanon.[15] Prime Minister Anthony Eden says in his memoirs that there was evidence that

Nasser was preparing 'to mount revolutions of young officers' in various countries in the region.[16]

According to Mohamed Heikal, Nasser's closest confidant, Nasser understood that the power of words through radio was the only way to make the masses become the 'weapon of the Arab Revolution' beyond the borders of Egypt.[17] This was particularly true in the cases of Lebanon and Jordan, where Egyptian newspapers were banned and the Egyptian embassies were under surveillance by local security services.[18] As Nasser's popularity grew, the reactionary pro-British regimes, including even Iran, felt increasingly threatened by internal subversion.[19] The power of radio also became an important symbol of emerging nationalism throughout the region, and Cairo Radio's popular programme 'The Voice of the Arabs' played a role in fostering Algeria's revolutionary movements as well.[20] Diplomatic correspondence in July 1957 records that King Hussein of Jordan was being attacked by 'hostile Egyptian propaganda' through an Egyptian-backed 'clandestine radio station' named 'Radio Free Jordan', and the Egyptians were 'trying to recruit Jordanians' for revolution.[21] Similarly, another radio station situated outside Iraq, named 'Radio Free Iraq', was calling on Iraqis to revolt against the government led by Nuri al-Said.[22] Sir Sam Falle, the Oriental Counsellor at the British Embassy in Baghdad (1957–61), believes that the Iraqi Revolution in 1958 was clearly instigated by Egypt's propaganda through 'The Voice of the Arabs', and notes that 'its virulence and incitement to violence were horrifying'.[23] Wilbur Crane Eveland, his American counterpart, also writes that the Iraqi Revolution resulted from a series of propaganda efforts emanating through 'Nasser's radio'.[24] As the popularity of Nasser grew across the region via the power of propaganda, George K. Young, the Vice-Chief of MI6, complained to his American counterparts that the CIA 'created a monster in Nasser'.[25]

In addition to the Cairo Radio broadcasts, Egyptian Military Attachés also acted as vehicles of revolution in the region.[26] They conducted subversive activities, such as supplying arms and explosives to politically motivated locals for use against their own governments. Documentary evidence shows that Egyptian Military Attachés were expelled from countries such as Iraq,

Lebanon, Libya, Ethiopia and Saudi Arabia between 1956 and 1957.[27] This reached the most senior levels of British intelligence. In August 1958, the JIC reported that Nasserite 'influential opponents' of regimes such as Jordan and Lebanon had been provided with 'weapons and explosives for use in promoting disorder and, if necessary, to overthrow the established government by revolution'.[28]

Emir Farid Chehab, the Head of the Lebanese Sûreté Générale, believed that Nasser was merely serving the interests of the Soviet Union.[29] He feared that Lebanese independence was increasingly threatened by internal subversion, especially as Nasser's popularity grew and the Syrians allied with Egypt. His most secret source, the wiretapping of the Egyptian Embassy and local politicians, revealed that the Egyptian Ambassador and Military Attachés in Lebanon were instigating subversive activities and even supplying arms and explosives to local politicians and politically motivated activists against the Lebanese President, Camille Nimir Chamoun.[30]

Britain also viewed Egyptian teachers throughout the region as subversive propagandists.[31] The Overseas Planning Committee tasked MI6, MI5 and the IRD to counteract their activities in the Arabian/Persian Gulf States in March 1956, noting that 'we should do whatever is possible to counteract Egyptian influence, especially the influence of Egyptian teachers'.[32] Despite these efforts, MI6 reported in 1958 that the number of Egyptian teachers throughout the region had actually increased from about 300 before the Egyptian coup of 1952 to 3,000 in 1958, and that there was 'evidence' obtained from various countries, such as Lebanon, the Arabian/Persian Gulf States and Jordan, that the Egyptian government used 'Egyptian teachers' for both espionage and subversion. Senior Cold War planners back in London concluded that this 'large and well-placed body of propagandists abroad' presented 'a grave threat to the future stability of the countries in which they are working, and to the Middle East as a whole'.[33]

From the perspective of the regional members, regardless of their political affiliations, these threats were substantial and often spread across borders. Although they took the 'revolutionary tendency' of Communist-inspired threats seriously,[34] it was 'The

Voice of the Arabs', a non-Communist threat, which was most vocal in calls for revolutions in the region – and which local leaders most feared.[35] Nevertheless, countering these threats with propaganda under the single authority of the Baghdad Pact proved complex. This was mainly due to a lack of consensus at the policy level as to whether non-Communist activities constituted a subversive threat. As the perceptions of these substantial threats differed between Britain and the United States on one hand, and the regional members on the other, this was a significant cause of frustration for the regional states who insisted that these non-Communist activities posed an existential threat to their regimes.

British Propaganda Policy in the Middle East

Britain's main arm of fighting the Cold War was the Foreign Office's propaganda apparatus, the IRD. This was, as one historian put it, 'Britain's secret Cold War weapon'.[36] James Vaughan notes that by the mid-1950s, 'significant evidence' suggested the IRD was 'extremely successful in establishing high-level contacts within Middle Eastern governments' who were willing to cooperate with the British on anti-Communist propaganda and accepted its materials for use in their anti-Communist policy.[37] In this context, the formation of the Baghdad Pact was an additional boost for British anti-Communist propaganda. Once the Counter-Subversion Committee of the Baghdad Pact was established in 1956, it provided Britain with the opportunity of obtaining additional resources as well as channels through which anti-Communist propaganda materials could be circulated.

Although anti-Communist propaganda campaigns were conducted by the regional countries, the significance of the Baghdad Pact in this context cannot be underestimated. It proved highly advantageous for Britain. Firstly, British involvement in anti-Communist efforts in the region ostensibly became invisible. The Middle East had become a hotbed of anti-British sentiment, and British membership of the Baghdad Pact was the source of exploitation by Cairo Radio and Radio Moscow. While Britain maintained the initiative in anti-Communist propaganda campaigns by giving guidance and direction, the regional governments assumed the front line of anti-Communist propaganda in the Pact area. An IRD officer noted that had the public found out about 'British-made programmes', it would have been 'politically embarrassing' not only to Britain but also to the local authorities.[38] As a result, the regional governments carefully concealed the source of the propaganda materials that came from the British.

Secondly, owing to their inexperience in anti-Communist measures and especially in propaganda, the regional members welcomed British experience and expertise. Britain's role was thus to provide the regional members with technical support including training and materials for broadcasting and publications. The relationship of the Pact members was characterised as such that the regional governments were dependent on the 'British skill' and 'American material resources' for their own counter-subversive propaganda campaigns.[39] This was mutually beneficial for Britain and the regional members, as John Speares, First Secretary at the British Embassy in Baghdad, noted regarding the Iranian case:

> Even if our policemen [the regional representatives of the Baghdad Pact] lack propaganda expertise, they have at least in this case issued some Western material under a Middle East dateline, and this seems important. Although the regular local propaganda services are more experienced they may also be more sophisticated and therefore less open to our influence ... these police channels even if they are inexpert and incomplete are at least open to us ... General Kia [the Iranian representative, Head of Military Intelligence] has, incidentally, already indicated willingness to accept a training and advisory survey of information services.[40]

This training role served British interests well. By providing the regional members – especially the oil producing countries, Iran and Iraq – with support for anti-Communist measures, Britain hoped to gain the 'goodwill' of its regional partners, and thus ensure that they would remain in the sphere of Western influence.

Throughout the period, British propaganda efforts were directed against not only Communists but also Nasser. The British anti-Nasserite propaganda policy started in the mid-1950s, but it was during the 1956 Suez Crisis that Britain adopted outright anti-Nasserite propaganda campaigns through an interdepartmental committee comprising both the IRD and the military against the strongest anti-British voice, Cairo Radio.[41] By the eve of the Suez Crisis, the IRD was employed as an instrument of psychological warfare against Nasser.[42] Jack Rennie, Head of the IRD, was given a specific brief to lead IRD's Middle Eastern operations in an anti-Nasserite and anti-Arab Nationalism direction while Norman Reddaway, Rennie's deputy, was left in charge of the day-to-day anti-Communist work.[43]

These anti-Nasserite propaganda operations were conducted secretly and codenamed Transmission X.[44] They sought to 'rebut' Cairo Radio's anti-British propaganda in the Middle East, and 'to discredit Nasser and to expose Egyptian expansionism' by using 'unattributable propaganda'.[45] The themes for this propaganda included Nasser's future economic plan, which was portrayed as being ill-prepared for building the Aswan Dam; 'the dangers of Egypt's pan-Arab imperialist ambitions'; and 'Nasser's link with the Russians'.[46]

However, the activities associated with Transmission X were short-lived. Once the Hashemite dynasty of Iraq was swept away in the Revolution of 1958 and after British–Egyptian relations began to improve towards the end of 1958, the Foreign Office decided to redirect the IRD back to its original anti-Communist task of countering 'Communist-bloc propaganda'.[47] The change in direction came from a change in British policy towards Egypt. Soon after the Iraqi Revolution, Britain re-examined its national interests in the region, and decided to adopt a policy of 'disengagement': in other words, 'not taking sides in inter-Arab disputes'.[48] This meant that the British anti-Nasserite policy in the region also softened.

In order to maintain good relations with the Baghdad Pact members, who would be unlikely to welcome Britain's 'disengagement' policy, the British government decided that the Americans, who had had so far 'no wish to support or protect British interests' in the region, 'should be induced to join the new organisation'.[49] While British policy was being repositioned, the process of restoring British–Egyptian relations after the Suez Crisis also began in the first half of 1957, and an exchange of Ambassadors finally happened in February 1961.[50] The negotiations included delicate issues such as the release of the MI6 officers, James Swinburn and James Zarb, who had been captured during the Suez Crisis of 1956.[51]

The Macmillan Government had stepped up its broadcasting and publication campaigns in the region from 1957 – before Britain's anti-Nasserite propaganda policy was reset after the Iraqi Revolution. Compensating for cuts in defence spending, propaganda was recognised as being of prime importance, and the focus of British propaganda efforts shifted away from Europe, where 'BBC broadcasts [we]re doing little good'.[52] This decision was made on the basis of a committee chaired by the Chancellor of the Duchy of Lancaster, Charles Hill, which reviewed the performance of Britain's information services overseas throughout the world in 1957.[53] Before this review, Britain spent the most money on non-Communist Europe (26.1 per cent – a fourth of the total propaganda expenditure), with the Middle East in second place at 14.1 per cent.[54] After the review, the Middle East, where Harold Macmillan had felt that 'our propaganda' was 'not strong enough', was given the highest importance, followed by the Far East, Europe and the United States.[55]

The Macmillan government also oversaw a change in the general approach to propaganda in the Middle East – before outright anti-Nasserite propaganda campaigns were abandoned in 1959 – with cultural propaganda efforts put forth to forward British interests in the region.[56] In February 1957, a working party was formed under the chairmanship of William Alfred Wolverson, the Director of the Radio Services Department, General Post Office Headquarters (1955–60), to consider the possibility of 'a light programme of entertainment and news directed to Arab countries of the Middle East'. This soft approach to propaganda in the region was intended to attract 'the uneducated masses' in the region 'away from Radio Cairo'.[57] For this purpose, Sharq Al-Adna, a Foreign Office owned Arabic-broadcasting station in Cyprus, which had unsuccessfully conducted anti-Nasserite propaganda campaigns over the Suez Crisis, was handed over to the BBC.[58] Under its new ownership, Sharq Al-Adna started broadcasting 'bazaar' music throughout the region using a second medium-wave transmitter of 100 kilowatts.[59] According to Douglas Boyd, the new Sharq Al-Adna 'became the most consistently popular and credible Arabic-language radio service in the 1960s, 1970s, 1980s and 1990s transmitting in Arabic'.[60]

These various changes in the British propaganda policy towards the region did not, however, reflect the counter-subversive policy undertaken by the regional governments of the Baghdad Pact. Their collective propaganda efforts proved far more complex.

The Dynamics of the Baghdad Pact and the Committees

The Liaison and Counter-Subversion Committees of the Baghdad Pact were clearly tasked from the outset with tackling Communism in the region. Well aware of the potential danger of Communist movements, the regional governments maintained a strong anti-Communist stance and cooperated in anti-Communist propaganda via the Counter-Subversion Committee throughout the period between 1956 and 1963. The Iraqis were at the fore-front of such propaganda until their withdrawal from the Pact in 1958. After the Iraqi withdrawal, Sir Roger Stevens, the British Ambassador in Tehran (1954–8), noted that the Turks became 'by a long way' the leading force, with the Iranians 'second' and the Pakistanis 'a very poor third'.[61]

Beneath the Counter-Subversion Committee, which was the highest policymaking body for countering subversive propaganda efforts, sat a 'permanent executive arm' of counter-subversion, the Counter-Subversion Office (CSO). The CSO, consisting of representatives from each member, was placed under the administrative control of the Secretary-General of the Baghdad Pact and housed in the headquarters of the Pact in Baghdad (1956–8) and Ankara (1958–79).[62] Day-to-day contact amongst the Pact members took place though the CSO, which essentially coordinated counter-subversive measures between the member states and acted as a channel for disseminating propaganda materials.[63] A selection of IRD materials, especially anti-Communist publications, was shared through the CSO, whose members translated the texts into their own languages and then distributed them through their own national channels. These materials included a comparative study of Soviet aid to Israel and the Arab states;[64] stories exposing life in the Communist bloc;[65] and unpacking the ideas of Communism, in publications such as 'What Is Communism?'[66] The CSO members constantly visited Britain to attend training courses organised by the IRD.[67]

The CSO also studied the methods and techniques of Soviet disinformation activities, such as how the Soviet Union forged and disseminated documents throughout the press in the Pact area.[68] The CSO also facilitated closer bilateral relationships. D. C. Hopson of the Foreign Office noted that:

> because the CSO has to work on a basis of multi-lateral agreement its sphere of activity is necessarily limited. But meanwhile a great deal of bilateral co-operation in activities which can be called 'counter-subversive' is taking place on a routine, day-to-day basis between the Iranians and ourselves – and, in fact, between all the CENTO allies. For example, we are exchanging information about Communist activities, helping each other with the training of broadcasting staff, arranging educational, cultural and technical exchanges, etc. This distinction – between the CENTO allies on a bilateral basis and the relatively small but still useful contribution that can be made through the CSO on a multilateral basis – is very important.[69]

As a result of the CSO's work, for instance, there was an 'impressive increase' in anti-Communist material published in Turkey. During the first eight months of 1959, over 388 articles 'based on IRD materials' appeared in the Turkish press.[70]

Despite close cooperation on anti-Communist propaganda, as a multilateral organisation, CENTO was limited in its propaganda efforts. Similar to the Liaison Committee, the meetings of the Counter-Subversion Committee were mostly a site of political discussions, where little consensus existed amongst its members beyond the Communist threat in the region. For instance, the regional members were concerned by the activities of the Kurds, and their connection with the Soviet Union. When the Turks insisted that Kurdish nationals were suspected of being

Communists or at least communist-inspired, for instance, the British responded that this was 'nonsense'.[71] In addition, from the establishment of the Pact, Pakistan frequently raised its concerns about subversive activities in Kashmir and claimed that activities were supported and instigated by propaganda from the Indian Communist Party.[72] Once their claim was rejected, the Pakistanis appealed to revise the mandate of the Liaison and Counter-Subversion Committees to deal not only with Communists, but also with all subversion in the Pact area.[73]

The exclusion of a non-Communist or even Communist-inspired threat from the Pact's counter-subversion policy caused frustration among the regional members. As a result, and despite the Liaison Committee of the Pact having already agreed that Nasser was not a Communist puppet,[74] the regional members, especially the Turks and Iranians, wished to label Nasser 'a tool of Communist subversion'. In doing so, they hoped to conduct anti-Nasserite propaganda campaigns under the Pact.[75] The growing frustration was particularly seen after Iraq withdrew its membership in 1958, and Britain abandoned its anti-Nasserite policy shortly afterwards. Iran was the most concerned with this 'negative' approach as it still feared 'subversion' by neighbouring states, the Soviet Union, Egypt (through Cairo and Damascus Radio) and Iraq, until the early 1960s.[76] These concerns were frequently raised at the Counter-Subversion Committee by the Iranian representatives, General Teymour Bakhtiar (Head of SAVAK, 1957–61) and General Hassan Pakravan (Deputy Head of SAVAK, 1957–61).[77] The senior SAVAK officers complained that neither 'the British nor the Americans intended to make the Committee anything more than a talking shop'.[78]

Any decisions for collective propaganda campaigns were taken on the basis of consensus, and they were often vetoed by a Pact member. Although the members worked well on conducting anti-Communist measures in the region, their national interests clashed when their policies differed. As a result, the effectiveness of counter-subversive campaigns by propaganda was hampered by the dynamics of the Pact. Recollecting his time in Ankara (1964–7), Charles Naas, a former member of the US State Department's policy-planning staff, stated that CENTO was a 'disappointment' to the regional members. While the United States and Britain maintained a rigid anti-Communist stance, the regional members saw broader threats.[79] In this regard, as seen before, the Pact was broadly divided into two camps: the regional members on the one hand, and Britain and the United States on the other. The regional members' frustration was often directed at Britain and the United States.

The American attitudes towards the region merit brief attention here since the United States' involvement in the Pact sometimes obstructed propaganda efforts. Despite maintaining the official status of an 'observer', the United States in fact exercised influence on Pact policy through substantial financial and moral support to the regional members, enticing them to focus on anti-Communist activities. The United States firmly maintained that the scope of the CSO should be placed 'exclusively on meeting the Communist and Communist-inspired subversive threats' and nothing more.[80] Nevertheless, while maintaining its official neutral position, Washington pursued its own policy to contain radical Arab Nationalism by supporting Saudi Arabia as a challenger to Nasser's popularity in the region in the late 1950s until the end of the Eisenhower Doctrine in September 1960.[81]

The Americans' ambivalent attitude towards the region was, nevertheless, unsurprising since their departmental policies were often in conflict. Their indecisive and often non-existent national strategy, based on a short-sighted and ill-founded policy towards the region, has also been criticised.[82] For instance, Robert McClintock, the Ambassador of the United States to Lebanon (1958–61), who himself felt that it was 'a mistake to be anti-Nasser', informally spoke to his British counterpart, Sir Moore Crosthwaite, about a division of opinion regarding American attempts to undermine Nasser's popularity in the region.[83] The indecisive American attitude towards the region was also a cause of confusion to the Pact members and was frequently criticised by the regional members; for example, the Iranian delegate, General Teymour Bakhtiar of SAVAK, complained to his British counterpart that a representative from the Department of State and another from the CIA 'did not even agree with each other' over what constituted a 'subversive' threat in the region.[84]

As mentioned in the previous chapter, despite the dynamics of the Pact, CENTO functioned on the basis of a democratic principle: any decisions at either the Counter-Subversive Committee or the CSO were made collectively through a majority of the signatories. This principle gradually acted in the regional members' favour, and eventually, after long deliberation at a series of committee meetings, a request from the regional members was accepted. At a meeting of the Counter-Subversion Committee in Lahore in 1962, the term 'subversion' was finally broadened to include 'non-communist threats'.[85] This was mainly because non-Communist threats were equally as important as Communist threats in the region, and were threatening the existence of the pro-Western member states, which, in turn, was 'directly in the interests of Communism'.[86]

The Propaganda War

The dynamics of the Pact limited the efficacy of the cooperative propaganda efforts. This does not necessarily mean that the regional member states refrained from carrying out propaganda campaigns in their own countries. As the responsibility for conducting propaganda operations always remained in the hands of local authorities, the regional member states drew upon the techniques and CSO materials for their own purposes. For instance, while the British policy ordered a halt to the IRD's all-out anti-Nasserite campaigns towards the end of 1959, the regional member states did not follow the same practice.

In 1959, the IRD asked its outposts in the region to assess the extent to which the anti-Nasserite propaganda materials, so-called Transmission X, were still being disseminated in each country of the Middle East.[87] Given that the IRD had halted the supply of such materials to the region, nearly all Arab states, including Jordan and Lebanon, were no longer disseminating them.[88] However, the members of CENTO (then Turkey, Iran and Pakistan), where anti-Communist and Transmission X materials

were pooled at the headquarters, could – and did – still dissemi-
nate them. In doing so, they slightly tailored the material for their
own purposes, broadening the focus from not only anti-Nasserite but also to anti-Soviet Communism. The British Embassy
in Ankara estimated that 'up to 60 per cent' of Transmission X
material had been placed in the local press in Turkey, Iran and
Pakistan.[89]

At the centre of the propaganda war in the region, the most
influential broadcasting station was Cairo Radio. Amongst all the
regional players, Nuri al-Said, a long-standing Iraqi Prime Minister
who wished to see Iraq lead the Arab countries by unifying with
Syria, was willing to confront Nasser in a propaganda war.[90] In
order to counter subversive propaganda broadcasting from Radio
Moscow and Cairo Radio, the British helped to develop Iraqi
propaganda capabilities and Baghdad Radio was established in
1956.[91] Britain was also involved in developing the broadcasting programmes of Baghdad Radio, in line with the policy of the
Pact as 'a Moslem alliance to challenge the pan-Arab doctrines
sponsored by Egypt's Voice of the Arab broadcasts'.[92] These anti-
Communist propaganda efforts by Baghdad Radio were largely
targeted at 'all key moulders' of 'public opinion', especially in
the spheres of 'politics, commerce and labour, science, literature and education', by exposing 'Communist aims, tactics and
pretensions' through broadcasting and publicity media.[93] More
specifically, particular attention was given to 'youth, students,
intellectuals and leading academic figures'.[94]

Nevertheless, although Baghdad Radio was set up under the
Baghdad Pact, it was fully controlled by the Iraqis and became an
instrument of the propaganda war by Nuri al-Said against Nasser.
Baghdad Radio soon promoted Nuri as the leader not only in
Iraq, but also throughout the region, against Nasser's pan-Arab
Nationalism, with themes that included 'internal progress in Iraq'
and 'Iraq's role in international affairs'.[95] The Iraqi government
also appointed Yunis Bakri, the 'Arab "Lord Haw-Haw"', a
'mercenary prepared to abuse anyone if paid enough', to conduct
the propaganda war against Cairo Radio. Nasser broadcasted
through Cairo Radio that 'some of the nine clandestine radio stations' under the control of the Counter-Subversion Committee

of the Baghdad Pact were attacking him, implying that Baghdad Radio was propagated by the imperialists.[96]

As soon as it became apparent that the Iraqis were ready to wage a 'radio war' against Cairo, Britain decided to distance itself from the operational running of Baghdad Radio on the grounds that a radio war would only create political instability. Gordon Waterfield, Head of the BBC Eastern Services, working closely with the IRD, noted that there would be 'confusion in the Middle East air with one radio station fighting another', and 'British policy, as I understand it, is not to try to divide the Arab world, but to try to create understanding and cooperation among the Arab countries'.[97] Michael Hadow, Head of the Levant Department of the Foreign Office, also noted that 'we would not wish it to become branded in Arab eyes as an instrument of the Pact rather than an Iraqi national station'.[98] While there was no reason for not advising on the conduct of any operational matters, Michael Hadow limited British commitment to advising only on 'future planning' at the request of the Iraqi government, rather than on 'the programming side'. In this way, Hadow also envisaged that the Iraqis would be helped by more experienced regional members, such as the Pakistanis, who had also been involved in similar operations under SEATO.[99]

Nevertheless, Britain's regional partners could not compete with Nasser's influential and powerful anti-imperial rhetoric. According to official figures recorded by the IRD in 1961, 'The Voice of the Arabs', one of the most popular programmes extolling Nasser's concept of Arab Nationalism, was on the air for 156 hours per week and was broadcast throughout the Middle East and North Africa in twenty-three languages.[100] Cairo Radio steadily increased its capacity from 1953 and became the most powerful broadcasting station in the region with twelve medium-wave transmitters (including two 300 kilowatts and one 100 kilowatts) and eleven short-wave transmitters (among them, two 140 kilowatts and two 100 kilowatts). By comparison, Baghdad Radio, established under the Baghdad Pact, had only four 100-kilowatt transmitters.[101]

Growing anti-British sentiment and the rise of Arab Nationalism throughout the region, all of which moved in Nasser's favour, especially after the Suez Crisis, also acted to the anti-Nasserite governments' disadvantage. James Vaughan has observed that the development of regional affairs and crises in the mid- and late 1950s was a consequence of Nasser's propaganda war: the dismissal of Glubb Pasha; Jordan's abstention from joining the Baghdad Pact; the Jordanian and Lebanese Crises of 1958; and even the Iraqi Revolution.[102]

Dominance of Security Services

One of the difficulties faced by IRD officers cooperating with the Pact members was how to establish common ground on which to conduct their anti-Communist propaganda efforts. The representatives of the regional governments at the Counter-Subversion Committee were predominantly members of the security services: the Director of the Iraqi CID; Head of the Iranian G-2, later replaced by the Head of SAVAK; the Director-General of the Turkish National Security Service; and a senior official of the Ministry of Interior of Pakistan. On the other hand, Britain was represented by an IRD officer. The United States, which remained an 'observer' until 1959, was represented by either United States Information Service (USIS) or CIA officers. The composition of the CSO reflected that of the Counter-Subversion Committee. This domination by the regional security services often led to situations in which the British representative from the IRD was the subject of complaints for being too soft on counter-subversion efforts. Regional members accused the British of being less committed to the Pact's collective efforts.

This was particularly the case from the summer of 1956 onwards, when unrest and instability in Syria was a central cause of concern for all the regional members, who became more frustrated with the ineffectiveness of the Pact. General Behcet Turkmen, the Turkish representative (Director-General of the Turkish National Security Service), who chaired the Counter-Subversion Committee, demanded 'more drastic weapons' – setting up 'a sort of SOE' for conducting more aggressive operations in Syria. General Haj-Ali Kia, the Iranian representative, sought to give more authority to the Liaison Committee, which he chaired, to conduct clandestine operations against Syria on behalf of the Counter-Subversion Committee. The Pakistani and Iraqi representatives respectively endorsed proposals for creating a Pact intelligence service and also underlined 'the need for action in Syria'.[103] Nevertheless, the British representative vetoed the proposal on the grounds that it would lead to 'inefficiency and confusion', and was supported by the Americans, who at the time sought to maintain their neutral stance towards the region.[104] This sort of proposal was a recurrent theme in the discussions between the Pact members, and Britain constantly 'blocked' such proposals.[105]

This formed the context of Operation Straggle: based on the assertion that Iraq was 'the central point of British support and area stability', George K. Young, the Vice-Chief of MI6, explained to his American counterparts, the operation envisaged that Syria and King Saud, in that order, would be overthrown, and then Nasser would be eliminated.[106] Evidence suggests that the blueprint for overthrowing the Syrian government was laid out by George Young.[107] The master plan was entirely initiated and conducted by the regional players, and it was above all the Iraqis, Nuri al-Said and Abdul Ilah, the Crown Prince, who contemplated engineering a coup d'état in Syria – replacing the Communist Syrian government with the former Syrian leader, Colonel Adeeb al-Shishakli, and also invading Syria with Iraqi troops to force Syria into a 'union with Iraq'.[108] This was codenamed Operation X by the Iraqis.[109] The Turkish government endorsed the Iraqi plan and 'was ready to help'.[110] In this, the role of Britain, and also the United States, was then to provide financial and material support for the Iraqis, and to 'restrain' any Israeli actions against the Iraqi move.[111] However, as the Iraqi Revolution occurred, there could be no coup d'état as Nuri al-Said and Abdul Ilah had envisaged.

There was also a conceptual difference between the Pact members concerning counter-subversion. The term 'counter-subversion' was understood by the British, as information experts, as largely a passive activity – exposing and refuting subversive propaganda campaigns by the enemy. However, the regional members felt it ought to be 'more far-reaching and "forward"', including offensive counter-subversive measures.[112] The difference was rooted in their backgrounds and professions – from the viewpoint of security officers, counter-subversion often meant the elimination of existential threats. They were in 'the habit' of dealing with subversive elements 'by locking them up'.[113]

The extent to which the regional security services successfully contained the spread of Communist movements in their countries is noteworthy. A document released under the FOIA – a threat assessment prepared by MI5 in July 1958 on the indigenous Communist Parties in the Pact area and categorised as 'Top Secret' – indicated the effectiveness of the regional security services in anti-Communist measures in their countries. Despite the anxieties of the regional members, MI5 assessed that the Communist threat had been 'well contained' by the security services of the regional members. The leadership of the party had been forced into exile 'either in Europe or in such Middle Eastern countries' as were not actively hostile to Communism.[114] SAVAK continued to 'harry and disrupt' the Tudeh 'rump', which was 'split with dissension', and did not 'appear to obtain any effective direction from its exiled leaders'. Likewise, the ICP had been 'subject to increasing pressure' from the Iraqi CID, and appeared to 'find difficulty in maintaining its organisation'. As for the Turks and Pakistanis, MI5 reported that 'the problem does not exist in organised form in either Turkey or Pakistan'.[115] Although MI5's assessment was circulated to its Middle Eastern counterparts, the documentary evidence does not show how regional members responded or whether they felt less threatened as a result of the assessment.

The strong presence of the security services on the Pact committees also reflected the dominance of the security services in the internal affairs of the member countries. As these services regarded counter-subversion as their own domain, it followed that counter-subversion by propaganda must also be controlled by the same services. General Teymour Bakhtiar of SAVAK, for instance, noted that it was not an information expert, but only an intelligence or security expert, who 'could understand the problems of subversion thoroughly'.[116] He also attempted to shape the Counter-Subversion Committee as a 'psychological warfare headquarters'.[117]

This sort of strong security-minded thinking troubled the British representative, who believed that propaganda operations should be left out of the hands of intelligence and security officers. Ironically, the name of the committee, Counter-Subversion, encouraged the regional security services to participate in propaganda. As a result of the domination of the security services in the Pact countries, information and broadcasting experts were 'frightened off' or appeared 'not interested' in getting involved in anti-Communist propaganda measures.[118] Despite British efforts to the contrary, the information experts of these regional countries were excluded from anti-Communist propaganda measures.

The British representative made several attempts to make contact outside the security circle. For example, he contacted the Head of the Turkish Press Department of the Ministry of Foreign Affairs, who was regarded as 'well qualified on press relations and publicity matters, both in Turkey and abroad, particularly in the Arab States'. However, he had no success owing to the domination of the security officials in internal affairs, confident of their own abilities to handle all such matters.[119] Philip Adams, the Regional Information Officer in Beirut, noted to John Rennie, Head of the IRD, that:

> The views of delegates expressed at this restricted meeting have of course been known to us in general terms all along. They stem from the fact that the Asian [the regional member] countries have very little in the way of organised information services and from their more physical view than ours of what is meant by counter-subversion. I am afraid that this difference of approach is bound to continue so long as the Asian [regional] member governments are represented on the Counter-Subversion Committee by the heads or members of their security services.[120]

From the outset, the fear of the British representative was that the presence of the security services on the Counter-Subversion Committee would make it unlikely to produce effective plans for joint publicity in the sense that the British desired.[121]

Even as their propaganda skills and experience grew, there remained persistent frustration among the regional representatives who wished to develop the CSO into a '"psychological warfare" centre' operating against 'subversion from the USSR, the UAR, Afghanistan and even India'.[122] The representation of the security services on the Committee continued throughout the period of this study.

The Separatist Movement: The Question of the Kurds

In addition to the spread of Communism in the Pact area, the Kurdish independence separatist movement, the largest minority in the region, spread across Turkey, Iraq and Iran, was a major concern to these three states. A comment by Wilbur Crane Eveland, a personal adviser to Allen Dulles, the Director of the CIA, on Middle Eastern affairs, illustrates the different perceptions of the various governments, which were directed by their own policies:

> Iraqi Kurdish leader Mulla Mustafa al Barzani was then in Russia seeking Soviet support for an independent republic to unite his tribesmen with the Kurds in Iran and Turkey. To the Iraqi, Iranian, and Turkish governments, the possibility of Moscow's encouraging Kurdish and other tribal separationist movements represented a far greater danger than did the growth of local communist parties or the threat of an invasion of the Middle East by the Soviet Union. To the West, the area's oil was of primary importance; bolstering strong central governments to control the tribes was considered the best way to regain access to the oil fields.[123]

The Foreign Office was in fact fully aware of regional concerns about Soviet support for the Kurds from at least 1949, as the IRD monitored Kurdish broadcasts from inside the Soviet territories, which were directed primarily against the Iranian, Iraqi and Turkish governments.[124] In addition, the Iraqi government sought cooperation with the British, Turkish and Iranian governments on intelligence sharing on the Iraqi Kurdish leader, Mulla

Mustafa Barzani, who was exiled from Iraq and Iran after the Second World War and lived in the Soviet Union until 1958. The Foreign Office then made available to the Iraqis 'any information' which might affect security in Iraqi Kurdistan, provided this did 'not compromise top secret sources of information'.[125]

The British Embassy in Baghdad also suggested that the Foreign Office take action as, after a field trip to Kurdish areas, Sir Henry Mack noticed that the Kurds were generally 'radio-conscious', and were 'better informed about what was happening in Korea than about affairs in the next village and could only attribute this to their habit of radio-listening'.[126] The IRD also recognised this as a vulnerable point for Communist exploitation, and suggested broadcasting anti-Communist programmes in Kurdish through Britain's own Sharq Al-Adna station.[127] By late 1950, the Foreign Office was also aware that the Soviet Union was skilfully exploiting the Kurdish question as an anti-imperial weapon to damage the pro-British governments by giving its moral and material support for Kurdish independence. Barzani's connection with the Soviets was confirmed by the Americans.[128] While the radio programmes were broadcasted in the Kormanjo (northern Kurdish) dialect, and were thus 'unintelligible' to many Iranian and Iraqi Kurds, they skilfully highlighted the contrast of 'the oppression of Kurds by the Governments of Iran, Turkey and Iraq with the pleasure of being a Kurd in the Soviet Union'.[129]

Identifying this as a very delicate issue, the Foreign Office dropped the suggestions by Sir Henry Mack and the IRD and decided not to become actively involved.[130] This was mainly owing to the long-standing British policy in the region of supporting the Iraqi, Iranian and Turkish governments, all of which had actively been assimilating the Kurds in their countries, albeit to different degrees.[131] Between 1948 and 1963, British representatives in the region were encouraged not to bring unnecessary attention to the Iraqi, Iranian and Turkish governments unless there was any specific request from the regional governments on the grounds that they were 'extremely sensitive about the Kurdish minority'.[132] As a consequence of this policy, intelligence collection on the Kurds was also not prioritised, and the Foreign Office even apparently turned down a Kurdish volunteer who approached the British Embassy in Paris in 1950, wishing to enrol himself as an agent for MI6 and offering to travel to Soviet Azerbaijan to find out 'what Mustapha [Barzani] was up to'.[133] When the War Office requested information on Barzani in 1957, for instance, the Foreign Office held no information on him at all.[134] Any intelligence on him and his activities came mostly from liaison with the Iraqi, Iranian and Turkish governments, and from the United States through the Liaison Committee.[135]

While the subject of the Kurds was often raised by the regional members of the Baghdad Pact for consideration in connection with anti-Communist measures, the dynamics of the Pact prevented serious discussion of the issue. There were indeed not only political but logical reasons for the regional governments to claim a link between the Communists and the Kurds, and that the Kurds were working alongside the Soviet Union. Firstly, the intelligence collected by local security services proved that the Soviet Union was using minority groups, such as the Armenians and the Kurds, as a means to contact local Communist Parties. This connection became apparent from the interrogation of Iraqi Communists by the Iraqi CID in 1949, after which MI5 was also informed.[136] This Soviet method was also noted by the Lebanese Sûreté Générale.[137] In addition, as noted in Chapter 4, the intelligence shared at the Liaison Committee provided by the Turkish representative clearly indicated that the KGB incited the Kurds to subvert the Turkish central government.

Secondly, there were also committed Kurdish Communists in the region. The long-standing Syrian Communist leader, Khaled Bakhdash (1936–95), was a Kurd, and was closely observed by the Lebanese Sûreté Générale.[138] Despite their dismissive attitudes towards the Communist–Kurdish connection, the Foreign Office also followed Bakhdash's activities from 1952 as the leader of the SCP, and was aware of the Communist–Kurdish connection elsewhere.[139] In addition, the regional governments were aware that the Soviet Union actively supported the Kurds' efforts to achieve independence through propaganda, chiefly led by Mulla Mustafa Barzani.

Some accounts of clandestine activities of the Soviet Union have begun to appear in recent years. They now tell us that the Soviet

Union strategically supported post-colonial liberation movements in the 1950s onwards to win the Cold War.[140] In addition, Britain and France formed the main targets of the Soviet Union in its global grand strategy, both of which were heavily committed to maintaining their position against insurgents in their colonies and territories. The KGB Chairman, Aleksandr Shelepin (1958–61), was a chief instigator of this global grand strategy.[141] Vladislav Zubok has shown that Soviet policy supported radical Arab Nationalists to undermine Western influence in the Middle East.[142] More importantly, Mulla Mustafa Barzani (often called Mulla Mustafa by his colleagues), whose activities had been at the centre of concerns by Iraqi, Iranian, Turkish and even Syrian governments, was indeed a long-running KGB agent (codenamed RAIS) from the end of the Second World War.[143] According to Zubok, in July 1961, by which time Barzani had returned to Baghdad from his exile in Moscow after the Iraqi Revolution, Shelepin suggested to the Soviet Premier, Nikita Khrushchev, that 'old KGB connections' with Barzani, now the chairman of the Kurdish Democratic Party, be used to 'activate the movement of the Kurdish population of Iraq, Iran and Turkey for creation of an independent Kurdish' state.[144]

In the second half of the 1950s, when the stability in the region began to deteriorate, these three governments were more concerned about Mulla Barzani and his influence on the Kurds in their countries. During the Suez Crisis, the Iraqi Minister of the Interior, Said Qazzaz, was seriously alarmed by Nikita Khrushchev's speech (a probable bluff) over the Suez Crisis. The British Military Attaché in Baghdad noted that 'if the Iraqis were not showing themselves very active in support of the Egyptians – the Russians might send back Mulla Mustafa with some of his partisans and parachute them into Iraq'.[145] In addition, the change in the Iraqi government was proving to be the emerging threat in the region not only for political reasons but also owing to subversive activities, which were spreading into the neighbouring countries such as Turkey and Iran. Once Iraq had left the Baghdad Pact in 1958, new threats to the Pact area came from the Iraqi Communists, whose activities were tolerated by the new Iraqi government, including 'subversive Kurdish broadcasts from Radio Baghdad' directed at the Kurds in Iran and Turkey.[146]

A by-product of the multilateral intelligence cooperation under the Pact was bilateral cooperation between the regional members. In the wake of the Iraqi Revolution, when a rumour spread in the Foreign Office that the Iraqi Kurds were fighting the revolutionary government in Baghdad, the Turkish and Iranian governments sought to 'expropriate' Iraqi Kurdistan in order to keep the Kurds in their countries.[147] Once Mulla Barzani had returned from the Soviet Union to Baghdad after the Iraqi Revolution, there was an influx of refugees of anti-Barzani Kurdish tribes to both Turkey and Iran. The Turkish and Iranian governments agreed to set up a 'Turco-Iranian bureau' to work on the matter and to share any intelligence on Barzani's activities in Baghdad.[148] Counter-subversion efforts by the regional governments concerning the question of the Kurds are explored further in Chapter 6.

Limitations in Influencing Local Anti-Communist Propaganda Measures

After the loss of its strategic ally in the Iraqi Revolution, Britain became more proactive in intervening in the anti-Communist propaganda measures that local authorities might take. Britain found the Iranian government, the only remaining oil producing country under the Pact, particularly vulnerable to subversive broadcasting by Radio Moscow, and Iran was believed to be the main target of Soviet propaganda in the late 1950s.[149] Aware that they were ill-equipped to counter these threats, the Iranians were undoubtedly willing to receive British support.

Iranian propaganda efforts largely depended on the British and the CSO from the outset.[150] The Iranians primarily focused on two types of propaganda campaigns, agreed at the CSO and directed by the Counter-Subversion Committee. The first type sought to discredit the reputations of the Soviet Union and the Tudeh Party, exposing life under the Communist regime and also envisaging what life in Iran would be like under Communist rule.

The second type praised Iranian 'social well-being' and economic development with support from CENTO.[151] One of the methods of propagating these campaigns was broadcasting, and there were numerous transmitters in operation throughout Iran mainly intended for internal radio broadcasting, including propagating a factual account of 'Russian activities during the wartime occupation of Iran'.[152] In addition to broadcasting, publications – such as Boris Pasternak's novel *Doctor Zhivago* – were supplied by the IRD and translated through the CSO into Persian for the purpose of dissemination throughout Iran.[153]

After the announcement of its establishment in October 1956, SAVAK gradually expanded the focus of its security duty from military to civilian departments.[154] SAVAK assumed responsibility for conducting a range of political, economic and cultural anti-Communist campaigns in Iran between 1957 and 1963. One theme, on which the Iranians placed much importance, was the use of Islam against Communism. While the degree to which similar operations were conducted in their countries was different, the use of Islam and praise for the monarchy (as well as the government) became common practice across Pact anti-Communist propaganda campaigns. This theme was also propagated through Baghdad Radio as the Iraqis were 'very keen to keep up this positive aspect of the work'.[155]

An Iranian delegate, Professor Furuzanfar, who had taught at the Religious College of the University of Tehran and then worked for the Iranian government, reported on the progress of the ongoing programme to the Counter-Subversion Committee in June 1956:

> After our adherence to the Baghdad Pact . . . We decided . . . to establish a school where Marxist ideologies would be fought by means of religious faith . . . while educating men of religion we are at the same time trying to train young men faithful to the nation . . . Actually 320 students are receiving training in these courses. It is hoped that their number will increase to 1,000 by the end of this year . . . in the near future we shall be able to have our religious representatives and orators in all parts of our country.[156]

The main objective of the Iranian government for the use of Islam was indeed political. It was designed to train the 'efficient religious orators', through whom 'political, economic and cultural programmes' were relayed to the population 'in compliance with the directives of the central government'. Professor Furuzanfar emphasised that this was the only way to 'avoid the infiltration of harmful elements into the people and obstruct their way in their subversive activities'.[157]

Despite Iranian efforts to counter them, the threats of internal subversion – riots, disturbances and propaganda against the Iranian government and the Shah – were endemic. They protested against government policy and were often instigated by both Radio Moscow and Cairo Radio. Denis J. Speares, an IRD officer, residing as First Secretary of the British Embassy in Tehran (1958–60), after speaking with the Deputy Head of SAVAK, General Pakravan (1957–61), noted:

> A particular difficulty was that the Russians did not even have to attract people to their own cause in order to carry out their subversive aims; any unstable situation in the Middle East tended to react to their advantage, so that all they needed to do was to stir up trouble whenever an opportunity occurred (he [General Pakravan] particularly stressed the Kurdish problem as an example of a situation which could easily be exploited by the Russians).[158]

The frustration of SAVAK officers, who saw internal subversion being directed by external threats such as the Soviet Union or Egypt, often turned against the British and Americans. Consequently, as noted earlier, the Iranians frequently demanded the Pact set up a committee of counter-intelligence experts to act firmly against these external threats.[159]

As raised in the aforementioned MI5 threat assessment, SAVAK had been successfully containing the domestic Communist front, the Tudeh Party, since its establishment in 1956/7, but domestic unrest and disturbances were still common in the country. These subversive activities were not necessarily Communist-oriented, but they were directed against the Shah himself and their slogan was the same as that of the Tudeh Party. From the Iranians'

point of view, the British-led focus on anti-Communist measures was too narrow. This concern was frequently raised by
General Pakravan to the British.[160] A senior IRD officer, Norman
Reddaway, observed about the Iranian attitudes towards the
counter-subversion efforts of the Pact that:

> The Iranians . . . feel that the CSO, while useful as a source of train-
> ing, information and useful minor operations, hardly touches on their
> major problems. The Iranians worry about the many challenges to
> the Regime. Disaffected students, non-cooperative peasants, unen-
> thusiastic officials, critics of the Shah – these are the main preoccu-
> pations of the Iranians. They struggle on, recognising that the CSO
> can be marginally helpful by providing information about foreign
> subverters of students, hostile radios and front organisations and by
> getting for them the odd piece of favourable publicity, but they feel
> that the CSO's help is marginal and that the solution to their prob-
> lems lies elsewhere – they have no idea where. The Iranians are sad-
> dened but hardly surprised when the Americans and ourselves are coy
> about requests to analyse and do something about Nasser's anti-Shah
> propaganda.[161]

The IRD had recognised issues with Iran's anti-Communist measures by mid-1959. Peter Joy, an IRD officer in Ankara liaising
with the regional counterparts, visited Tehran in August 1959
and observed two main problems associated with the way in
which SAVAK conducted anti-Communist measures.

The first was that the Iranians' use of anti-Communist material,
which was combined with 'exaggerated eulogies of the Shah and
the regime', was causing the Iranian general public to identify
'anti-Communist comment solely with the regime and thus to dis-
count it in advance'.[162] As a result, the value of anti-Communist
measures, which were intended to influence and foster the antipa-
thy of the general public towards Communism, became meaning-
less. The second was the compartmentalisation of SAVAK into
external and internal functions.[163] While external liaison with
foreign intelligence, especially with the Pact members and the
CSO, was done by the external department, anti-Communist
measures including information control and propaganda were

conducted by the internal department.[164] A turf war between these departments made the matter even worse.[165] As a result, counter-subversion was above all chiefly managed by the internal department, which countered subversive elements against the Shah, and was applied to any opposition movements against him.

Security service domination of internal affairs continued to raise problems for the British. Although the Iranian government had the Department of Publications and Radio, SAVAK had substantial practical control of the national press and broadcasting as anti-Communist propaganda measures were considered a matter of national security.[166] As a result, SAVAK totally precluded any consultation with the Department of Publications and Radio on this matter.[167] SAVAK was 'a bottle-neck' in distributing and using anti-Communist materials, so the IRD decided to bypass SAVAK and to distribute its own material to the Department of Publications and Radio through the IRD officer in Tehran, Donald J. Makinson (1960–3).[168] Until August 1960, 'two thirds' of IRD materials were supplied to the Department of Publications and Radio without informing SAVAK.[169]

However, once this 'breach' of bypassing SAVAK was discovered, it caused strains in relationships between the British and the Iranians and between SAVAK and the Department of Publications and Radio.[170] After the 'breach', Donald J. Makinson had to devote most of his time in Tehran to repairing the relationship with SAVAK and to mediating with the Department of Publications and Radio.[171] Dealing with the member states on domestic counter-subversion was a delicate issue as they exclusively regarded it as their domain. Like other member states, while Iran was willing to learn methods and techniques from the British, it was averse to being instructed by outsiders on how it should approach its own problems. Peter Joy observed in 1960 that, on the issue of domestic anti-Communist counter-subversion, the regional member states saw only 'purely local and internal problems' that 'they would each prefer to deal with in their own way with the minimum of outside "interference"'.[172]

Britain was also severely limited in the extent to which it could help the Iranians in anti-Communist measures. Although operating jamming technology as a counter-measure against similar broadcasts in the colonies, Britain did not provide the Iranians with such technical support.[173] While the topic of jamming had been raised in Iran, the IRD made its position clear to Donald J. Makinson in 1962 that he should avoid any discussion of jamming with the Iranians.[174] Firstly, jamming could never technically be '100% effective'; and secondly, the costs incurred by jamming were 'enormously expensive'.[175] Most of all, the IRD's policy held that the practice of jamming was also 'an admission of weakness' and implied that the hostile radio being jammed was 'successful in its subversive aims'. Above all, it recorded that 'it goes against the principle of freedom of information, for which we stand'.[176]

Conclusion

The 'conspiracy mentality' of Middle Eastern leaders, as Daniel Pipes has termed it, grew out of their experiences of dealing with threats, and in turn fostered their views on the development of regional affairs. The cooperation in anti-Communist propaganda under the Pact was often perverse. This was mainly due to the Middle Eastern leaders and the British perceiving threats differently. Britain, as well as the US, sometimes had narrower targets than the regional members would have liked. A further difficulty stemmed from the way in which security services dominated regional members' home countries and frequently held views on security and intelligence that contrasted sharply with the policing and information-oriented approach of the British. This rift was most noticeable and most destructive in the Counter-Subversion Committee.

All members considered Communist movements as the main threat and they took it very seriously. However, Britain (and the United States) seems to have been more cautious in propaganda operations than its CENTO partners, owing to the different national interests of the Pact members. Inter-allied tensions in the field of propaganda restricted cooperation, just as they restricted intelligence sharing. As a result, Britain's efforts to maximise the effectiveness of the anti-Communist propaganda measures of the Pact members suffered since ultimate control was left in the hands of the local governments with their own propaganda and security objectives. In this regard, Britain's anti-Communist propaganda must inevitably be seen as a failure. Moreover, Britain's unsuccessful intervention in the Iranian case only reinforces this conclusion. The limitations of Britain's influence are discussed in the next chapter.

6 The Use and Abuse of State Power and the Limits of British Influence

I tried to give them a rough idea of what the Security Service was like and what it should do. I began by telling them that it should be wholly non-political and merely concerned with the security of the State, regardless of the Government in power; otherwise it could have no stability and no continuity. This did not, of course, mean that it was not entitled to investigate the activities of political parties which advocated the overthrow of the State by unconstitutional means. I realised from the expressions on their faces how unpractical they felt my suggestion was!

Captain Guy Liddell[1]

[S]cientific interrogation in the world's intelligence and security organizations has a limit, and wherever, because of a sensitive political situation, this method becomes somewhat ineffective, torture is resorted to in order to get speedy results or to create terror and fear. In normal circumstances, the aim of the interrogation is to extract information and so naturally the more scientific and thorough the methods the better! But in sensitive political situations where security is seen to be threatened, the interrogators' aim is not only at getting information, they also aim at breaking the suspect and creating panic in society.

General Hussein Fardust[2]

Introduction

Britain was heavily involved in Middle Eastern anti-Communist measures in various ways. It shared intelligence on Communist and Soviet subversive activities; provided training in preventive security, counter-intelligence and propaganda; and, through liaison officers, exercised influence over the local legislative and administrative measures. As noted in the previous chapters, however, the measures conducted by Middle Eastern governments differed from what the British had desired. This raises significant questions about British complicity in undemocratic and repressive activity including human rights abuses.

This chapter explores how far Britain was involved in anti-Communist measures conducted by Middle Eastern governments. It discusses the different approaches towards the training of colonial and Middle Eastern security services. It then examines the usefulness and limitations of intelligence liaison between British intelligence and its Middle Eastern counterparts in influencing regional policy. Finally, it examines Britain's attitudes towards the security measures conducted by Middle Eastern governments, often in violation of human rights.

Differences between Colonial and Middle Eastern Security Services

Intelligence historian Calder Walton argues that Britain successfully shaped local authorities' approaches to intelligence throughout the Empire. Techniques and methods were transported with the movement of MI5 officers from one colony to another.[3] Particular credit has been given to the successful 'formula' adopted by MI5 for dealing with colonial problems: exporting its own model of separating intelligence from law enforcement work to local security forces.[4] According to Walton, MI5 taught colonial security officers that there was a 'fundamental difference between policing and intelligence work', and that 'the two required completely different outlooks for officers'. Walton asserts that this was a 'central tenet' of the training courses.[5] In the words of Thomas Plate and Andrea Darvi, the intelligence function is 'the brain', and law enforcement is 'the body'.[6] The use and abuse of the police force as an instrument of political parties in power was also a discussion topic at a training course for senior colonial police officers. This was aimed at those serving in colonies where the police forces would fall under the control of a new local (indigenous) government after independence.[7]

A distinct characteristic of Middle Eastern states was that they were politically non-democratic in the Western sense, with domestic politics dominated by a strong security force, often labelled a secret political police.[8] Separating 'the brain' from 'the body' was therefore difficult. Despite some specific successes, Britain's track record of developing local security forces in the field of anti-Communist measures is questionable.

In Britain, the general principles of MI5 were defined by the Maxwell-Fyfe Directive in 1952, which served as MI5's charter until 1989 when it was superseded by the Security Service Act. Under the Directive, MI5 was to act in the interest of *'the Defence of the Realm as a whole'*.[9] It was 'essential' that MI5 'should be kept absolutely free from any political bias or influence' and 'no enquiry is to be carried out on behalf of any Government Department'.[10] To help achieve this, MI5 operations were entirely the responsibility of the Director-General of MI5, who was responsible to the Home Secretary. But MI5 was not part of the Home Office. In addition, the government could not direct whom MI5 would investigate. A former Director-General of MI5, Eliza Manningham-Buller, notes that this was 'an important safeguard against the politicisation of the Service's work'.[11]

Whether this principle was taught to, or understood by, Middle Eastern security officers is debatable. More importantly, while a new constitution could be introduced to safeguard the position of the police forces in the colonies before independence, this was not possible in foreign countries. The introduction and implementation of such a constitution instead rested entirely in the hands of foreign governments. When asked to organise anti-Communist training courses for foreign police officers at the Police College, Sir Frank Newsam, Permanent Under-Secretary of the Home Office, wrote back to Sir Gladwyn Jebb, the Chairman of the AC (O) Committee: 'I cannot help doubting whether a foreign police officer, however well indoctrinated in British police methods he might become after a course at the College, will be able to apply them in the very different circumstances of his own country.'[12] Sir

Frank Newsam was not a member of the AC (O) Committee, and his voice was ignored.

Despite being central in organising such anti-Communist training courses, MI5 was critical of providing training in anti-Communist measures especially for Middle Eastern security officers. After a meeting at MI5 Head Office in February 1951, Guy Liddell wrote in his diaries about the line MI5 should take with the AC (O) Committee about the training of foreign police officers:

> We wished to point out, first of all, that we were bound to look at the problem to some extent from the point of view of defence priorities. This caused us to feel that in the matter of building up foreign security organisations we should do more profitable work with the Western European countries, who thought, at least to some extent, on the same lines as ourselves.[13]

Nevertheless, amongst all foreign police forces, the AC (O) Committee prioritised the training of Middle Eastern security officers as the defence of the Middle East was given paramount importance by the British government in the early 1950s. MI5's views were also ignored by the AC (O) Committee.

In addition to disciplinary differences, there was also the fundamental issue of providing training to foreign police forces at all and this inevitably limited what MI5 could offer. A major difference between colonial and foreign police forces was that, above all, colonial police forces worked towards the internal security of the British Empire, and later the Commonwealth. However, as far as the training of foreign police forces was concerned, Guy Liddell noted that:

> in so far as attempting to teach [the Iranian officers] in London how to set up an efficient Security Service in their own country was concerned, it was to a large extent a waste of time; in fact MI5 did not stand to benefit at all directly; the only percentage lay with SIS who might acquire a certain amount of goodwill which would enable them to operate from bases in [Iran] . . . The only people we could teach profitably here were those from Western European countries whose

conditions were in some measure comparable to our own; we regard them as a first priority.[14]

This indicates that to MI5, or at least Guy Liddell's mind, the benefits of training foreign police forces would be virtually nil.

While the AC (O) Committee considered providing training to foreign police forces as one of the pillars of Britain's anti-Communist policy, this was a double-edged sword in practice. Providing training for foreign police forces also meant that Britain would enhance the counter-intelligence capabilities of foreign countries, which could potentially act against them. Guy Liddell noted that:

> I made it clear at the [AC (O) Committee] meeting that the training by MI5 in a general way could not last more than about four days, and in some cases not more than two days. It was necessary to take a realistic view of what the word 'training' meant. You could explain the general principles on which a security organisation worked, and in some branches you could give a certain amount of detail, but in other cases it was not possible to do so without running the risk of our own methods being used against us.[15]

This was indeed the deciding point on what kinds of training could be provided for foreign police forces – if a friendly country turned against Britain, the training would above all affect MI6's operations on foreign soil.[16] This was mainly the reason for Guy Liddell's reluctance to develop the anti-Communist capabilities of Middle Eastern security forces.

At the order of the Shah himself, General Hussein Fardust, a life-long friend of his, visited Britain at least three times during the period between the late 1950s and early 1960s to receive training for establishing an intelligence organisation to coordinate and supervise the activities of all intelligence and security services, including SAVAK.[17] General Fardust oversaw the development of the Iranian Intelligence Community from the late 1950s until 1979.[18] He was alone in the first and second visits and was escorted throughout his stay in Britain by MI6.[19] In the four-month training programme of his first visit in 1959, he wrote that he mainly learned the system and the functions of the JIC.[20] In the four-month training programme of his second visit in 1961, he received more practical training such as MI6 recruitment methods, counter-intelligence, and 'psychological war' aimed at 'weakening the enemy' and also 'influencing public opinion' through propaganda.[21] General Fardust felt that he had only been given what he needed to know, and noted that 'the British were always playing safe in their statements and did not talk in detail'.[22] More importantly, the training provided to him was not only aimed at enhancing the Iranian Intelligence Community, but also at influencing the domestic policies of the Shah.

The Usefulness and Limits of Intelligence Liaison and British Influence

An intelligence liaison with local authorities was essential if British policymakers sought to maintain their good relationship with them. Intelligence liaison was also the best means of obtaining invaluable information from local authorities. Sir Patrick Dean, then Chairman of both the AC (O) Committee and the JIC, once noted to the Foreign Secretary, Harold Macmillan, when explaining the functions and responsibilities of both MI6 and MI5 overseas, that an intelligence liaison with local authorities was 'one of the functions of the Security Service to obtain secret intelligence by its own means'.[23] This was particularly true in the case of the Middle East, where clandestine Communist movements were exclusively dealt with by the local security services. Good relations were particularly important as local security force insiders were often the sources of these assessments.[24]

There was, however, a downside to the over-reliance on intelligence liaisons with local authorities. As noted in Chapter 3, while Britain maintained good relationships, it gained no advance warning about the series of regional crises erupting at the time, such as the Egyptian coup in 1952 and the Iraqi coup in 1958.[25] Concerned that no warning was provided by MI6 about the Iraqi Revolution in 1958, Jonathan Bloch and Patrick Fitzgerald argue that:

MI6 had committed a classic intelligence error by recruiting agents among its allies rather than anti-British elements. General Daghestani [Dashistani], for example, was arrested not because he was an MI6 agent – which he was – but because he was a leading figure in the government.[26]

They make a fair point: there was indeed a tendency for British intelligence to focus on liaison with local authorities as a source of intelligence in the region.

This point, however, has to be taken further. More precisely, it is worth noting that, while MI6 was closely working with General Daghestani on special political action – the aforementioned Operation X, to overthrow the Syrian regime – MI5's liaison with the Iraqi CID inhibited MI6's traditional espionage role. This suggests that the lack of advance warning should not solely be blamed on British intelligence, but ultimately on the policy of the British government, which directed all intelligence activities at the time. Above all, since British foreign policy sought to sustain its relationships with local authorities, the intelligence requirement was to maintain a liaison relationship with them.

Intelligence liaisons were made on the basis of mutual trust. Even in institutionalised forms – such as the so-called Five Eyes, the intelligence cooperation of the Anglosphere nations (Britain, the United States, Canada, Australia and New Zealand) based on the UKUSA Agreement in 1946 – trust-building was crucial to cooperation. In order to establish such a relationship, the liaison had to be mutually advantageous. Britain also had to agree not to engage in espionage activities without the knowledge of the host country.[27] If such activities were exposed, trust in the intelligence liaison would be undermined.[28] According to Anthony Cavendish, for the purposes of maintaining a good liaison relationship, Sir Maurice Oldfield, as 'C', 'promised the Shah of Iran that while he was Chief, SIS [MI6] would not conduct any internal espionage against Iran'.[29]

This was also one of the main reasons for the closure of SIME's Counter-Intelligence Branch, JID. Sir Dick White became concerned about MI6's clandestine political activities, which could potentially undermine the credibility of MI5 representatives in the host countries.[30] Therefore, Britain in fact faced an inherent problem of maintaining good liaisons with its Middle Eastern counterparts: its intelligence necessarily came from the very same local authorities, and not from other local sources. This was the reason that no advance warning was provided by local authorities – who were also caught by surprise.

Intelligence services have activities that constitute two different but interwoven roles. The first is to collect intelligence from their agents, and the second is to exercise influence through their officers and agents, some of whom had a higher level of access than a British Ambassador.[31] In the context of the Middle East, Anthony Cavendish also claims that MI6 officers had more influence on the Shah of Iran than anyone else, including British Ambassadors and the Americans:

> The Shah asked that [Edward] de Haan [of MI6 (1954–7)] and subsequent Station Chiefs, such as Alexis Forter [of MI6 (1958–61)], report to him regularly, and the more competent of the MI6 representatives in Tehran soon *had more influence* with the Shah than the British Ambassadors, which proved an irritant to most Ambassadors [who lost their direct contact with the Shah] . . . The Shah was surrounded by sycophants and there were really only two people who could speak freely to him. One was the longstanding British SIS [MI6] officer in Tehran and the other was Assadollah Alam, a former Prime Minister.[32]

Other sources support the claim that the Shah had a good personal relationship with MI6 officers.[33] Richard Deacon claims that after the coup in 1953 Britain still had closer relations with the Shah 'on an intelligence level' than did the Americans, and that Maurice Oldfield, then Head of Station in Washington (1960–4), even 'helped' the Shah to 'accept American aid' when the Shah visited the United States to discuss military assistance in March 1962.[34]

This indicates in theory that a highly placed asset in a foreign government is able to exercise influence on the policymaking of that government on behalf of Britain. MI6 also had its own agent right next to the Shah himself, Sir Shapoor Reporter, a personal friend of the Shah, who was recruited by Monty Woodhouse when he was the MI6 Head of Station in Tehran in the early 1950s, before the 1953 coup.[35] According to General Fardust, Reporter was 'Britain's top spy', who was 'clearly superior to the Chief of the MI6 station in Iran' in being able to exercise British influence in the decision-making process of the Shah and other high-ranking Iranian officials.[36] Archival evidence also confirms the scope of his influence on behalf of Britain as an MI6 agent: the Ministry of Defence rated him as a 'close and trusted confidant of the Shah'.[37] Reporter's role seems to have been confined to sealing arms deals between Britain and Iran, rather than counter-subversive matters, and that, rather than being interested in preserving British interests in Iran, his motivation was mercenary. In the end, the Shah lost confidence in Reporter in the late 1970s after he found out that Reporter merely acted on a profit basis rather than as his close friend.[38]

Britain had far more influential figures in the Iraqi government throughout the period until 1958. Above all, the head of state, King Faisal II of Iraq, and the Crown Prince, King Faisal's uncle, Abd al-Ilah, who exercised substantial control over the administration of the Hashemite Kingdom of Iran, were pro-British.[39] In addition, the post-war Iraqi government was dominated by Nuri al-Said, who also appointed close colleagues to his Cabinet, such as Said Qazzaz, the Minister of the Interior. British intelligence also maintained close connections with its Iraqi counterparts, such as Bahjat Attiyah, the Director of the CID, later the Director-General of Security, and the aforementioned Deputy Chief of Staff, General Ghazi Daghistani.[40] After the 1958 Revolution, a total of 108 senior civilian and military officers, including Qazzaz, Attiyah, Daghistani, Fadhel Jamali, a former Prime Minister, and Yunis Bakri, the Iraqi broadcaster, were interned at Abu Ghraib and tried by Military Tribunal.[41]

These pro-British Iraqis were charged with corruption and 'conspiracy against the state', meaning that they were acting on behalf of the interests of foreign powers, namely Britain, and also conspiring in a plot to overthrow the Syrian government.[42] Amongst them, Said Qazzaz and Bahjat Attiyah were the first civilians to be hanged.[43] The death sentence of General Daghistani, who admitted Iraq's Operation X plot and its connection with MI6, was later commuted.[44] A retired member of the British intelligence community recalls that 'we had agents hanged in the main square in the late fifties'.[45] It is arguable whether these pro-British figures were actually British agents as they were mostly serving the Hashemite dynasty of Iraq under their own government. From Britain's point of view, however, they were invaluable assets through whom British interests could be preserved as they pursued their own domestic policies.

Yet evidence suggests that the value of liaison as a means of influence was questionable. British policy sought to maintain friendly governments in a region which was becoming increasingly anti-British. As Andrew Rathmell notes in his study of post-war Syria, because the Middle East had experienced a long colonial history for centuries, there was a tendency for 'political opponents commonly [to] accuse each other of being agents of a foreign power'.[46] This was apparent even before the Suez Crisis. While King Hussein of Jordan had a long-established relationship with Britain, he also often had to dissociate himself from the British, whose role in Jordan was 'the object of deep popular suspicion' in the eyes of the Jordanians.[47] Subsequently, King Hussein of Jordan dismissed Glubb Pasha from the command of the Arab Legion in March 1956, until which point Britain had enjoyed considerable influence over the defence and security policies of Jordan.[48]

Existence of the intelligence liaison between Britain and Middle Eastern governments was kept absolutely secret. From Britain's point of view, this was mostly for security reasons. As Ernest Bevin insisted several times, such liaisons would be vulnerable to penetration or might become the subject of a propaganda attack by the Soviet Union.[49] For the Middle Eastern governments, it was for exclusively political reasons. Middle Eastern policymakers with links to the West were vulnerable to being attacked by political opponents and risked forfeiting their careers, or even their lives, as in Iraq. As a result of anti-British sentiment throughout the region in the post-war period, intelligence liaisons had to be built on the basis of absolute secrecy, or some-times at personal discretion, in non-institutionalised forms. They remained on unstable foundations until the formation of the Baghdad Pact.

Although local authorities constantly asked Britain for advice on anti-Communist measures, Britain's image was far from posi-tive, even amongst Middle Eastern policymakers. This was espe-cially the case in Iran. As a result of Britain's collusion with the Americans to overthrow Mohammad Mossadeq in 1953, Britain was often seen as a conspiratorial force in international affairs. During the Suez Crisis, the Shah became 'deeply suspicious' of the British collusion with Israel against Nasser's Egypt, but Sir Roger Stevens, the British Ambassador in Tehran, who had no advance knowledge, repeatedly assured the Shah that 'there had been no prior collusion with the Israelis'.[50] In addition, when the Iraqi Revolution occurred, General Teymour Bakhtiar, the Head of SAVAK, publicly announced that 'the British had engineered the Iraqi *coup d'état*' and the new Iraqi government was 'the newly chosen instrument of the British'.[51]

Britain itself also seriously undermined its relationship with its allies. The Suez Crisis, in which Britain colluded with France, and above all, Israel, the enemy of the Arabs, to attack Egypt was a case in point. Although Middle Eastern governments maintained their existing intelligence liaisons with the British, the political costs were much greater in the long term – pro-British Middle Eastern governments found it more difficult to handle their domestic politics in the face of anti-British sentiment throughout the region. During and after the Suez Crisis, anti-British riots and demonstrations were forcefully put down by the police in Iraq, and, according to the official figure, at least twenty-five people were killed.[52] Iraq, Britain's closest ally, became particu-larly vulnerable to a barrage of hostile propaganda attacks both by Nasser and International (Soviet-sponsored) Communists. The US Ambassador in Baghdad, Waldemar Gallman, observed that, despite all the efforts which Nuri al-Said had put into enhancing the reputation of the Baghdad Pact against Nasser's Arab Nationalism, the Suez debacle 'came close to being Nuri's undoing'. Nuri 'felt that the British had let the Arab world down badly', and that 'Iraq was being forced into a position of opposition to the British'.[53] Not only was Iraqi policy towards Britain under attack, but so too was the credibility of the Baghdad Pact, questioned by the Iraqi opposition and attacked by Cairo Radio. Fadhel Jamali, a former Iraqi Prime Minister, recollected that Iraq 'was being undermined from within', contributing to the Iraqi Revolution.[54]

When subversive activities, riots and student demonstrations were commonplace in Iran during the late 1950s and early 1960s, Britain's plan was seemingly to influence local policy through General Fardust, one of the Shah's closest confidants. Britain designed specific training courses for him during his four-month stay in 1959. They consisted of three sessions, two of which mostly involved political education and were taught in Persian. The first, led by a 'Communist professional teacher', was all about Communism, including its social and economic system, whilst the second covered Iran's economy and was led by a 'British Iranologist' who was 'very critical of Iran's economic conditions' and believed that the Shah 'had to make some fundamental reforms otherwise his government could not remain in power for long'. The third session was concerned with intelligence matters and was taught in English through a translator.[55]

Once General Fardust returned home, he suggested some economic reforms to the Shah as instructed by the British Iranologist. However, the Shah rejected these outright and replied that the British Iranologist had 'nothing to do with our policies', and it was 'none of his business'.[56] According to General Fardust, the instruction given by the British expert on Iran's economic affairs 'ran exactly against' the Shah's 'White Revolution', a series of measures for reshaping the political, social and economic life of Iran, which was implemented in 1963, a few years later.[57] The initiation of the White Revolution was acutely opposed by some of Iran's clergy, including Ayatollah Khomeini, and has been said to be the beginning of the fall of the Shah in the course of his long battle with Khomeini.[58]

Iran was not the only ally to act against British wishes. Iraq did too. Despite receiving no advance warning, Britain was alert to the danger of a coup by the Iraqi Army prior to the 1958

Revolution. William Magan writes that, even during his tenure as Head of SIME, he had been acutely aware of the disaffection in the Army, and he duly passed his concerns on to Bahjat Attiyah, then Director of the Iraqi CID.[59] A JIC assessment made after the coup attests to Magan's recollection that his concerns had been already reported to London, presumably either by Duncan MacIntosh or the representative of MI5 in Baghdad.[60] But British intelligence was hindered by two things. The first was departmental infighting between the police and the army. The second was that, despite repeated warnings by their own chief of the secret police, Bahjat Attiyah, Iraqi ministers were completely blinkered by their anti-Communist concerns.[61]

In his memoirs, Sir Sam Falle, the Oriental Counsellor at the British Embassy in Baghdad (1957–61), dismisses the idea of Iraq as a 'British lackey' and states that:

> Nuri was very much his own man and nobody's stooge. The British Ambassador, Sir Michael Wright, was in Nuri's pocket, not the other way round. Wright had an immense and quite understandable respect for Nuri ... When I used to give Wright my political observations, he would counter with: 'But Nuri says ...' Occasionally and most reluctantly, at my most urgent prompting, Wright used to mention mildly to Nuri that there was a need for social and economic reforms and that it was important to curb the power of the tribal shaikhs. Unfortunately, Nuri took absolutely no notice; it might have been better if we had been able to exercise some influence.[62]

All of these limitations raise the question of whether Britain enjoyed any influence at all over the policy of Middle Eastern governments. Influence is intangible and incredibly difficult to assess at the best of times, and this is accentuated by the secret nature of the issues discussed here. Moreover, the degree of British influence depended on the sensitivity of the issue and the convergence of the mutual interests of both parties, which was constantly shifting with domestic and overseas events. However, the Shah's attitudes towards Britain's suggestion of Iran's domestic reforms, and Sir Sam Falle's point about Nuri's determination to pursue his own policies, demonstrate the limitations faced by British intelligence when attempting to exercise influence over the policy of the Middle Eastern governments. Middle Eastern governments were above all foreign governments – all decisions were in their hands and they acted at their own discretion.

Adherence to the Rules of Law: Use and Abuse of Secret Police

The practices associated with the secret police were not all illegal. Rather, most Middle Eastern states had passed laws defining Communist and subversive activities as illegal and authorising such practices to counter them. Security service activity was therefore mostly lawful under domestic penal codes or defence regulations. These often allowed suspects to be interned without trial and, in some cases, executed. However, the rule of law differed in each country, with some adopting more extreme measures than others. In the case of Iraq, under the Nuri al-Said Government from 1954, for instance, the Iraqi penal code covered subversive activities, including Peace Partisan and Democratic Youth activities, which were categorised in the same way as Communist activities. In addition, the introduction of the 'Association Law' in 1955 gave the Minister of the Interior extensive power over political groups and their gatherings. Waldemar Gallman, a former US Ambassador to Iraq, observed that under the Iraqi Association Law, 'any party would be completely dependent on the Minister's benevolence for its existence'.[63]

In addition to such differences in political systems, cultural underpinnings made the practices of Middle Eastern security services more akin to those of a secret police. For instance, Bahjat Attiyah, the long-standing head of the Iraqi CID, once explained to Guy Liddell about the adverse conditions for recruiting local agents in Iraq, on which Liddell noted that they were 'very different' from Britain. In Iraq, Attiyah said, 'the Police get no voluntary assistance whatever from the population', for whom 'the idea of doing something because it is in the national interest never enters their heads'. According to the Liddell Diaries:

[Attiyah] gave me an example of a murder committed in a café, when he and some friends were sitting in an adjoining house. He went round himself immediately and interrogated the proprietor, who pleaded that he had seen nothing. Even two men who had been sitting on the same bench as the murdered man pleaded the one that he was reading a newspaper at the time, and the other that he was thinking of something else and had only heard the report of the revolver! The only method of coping with a situation of this kind, Colonel Bahjat said, was to take some fifty people who were present in the café and put them all in jail. After some hours of confinement, people began to admit that they had seen something and eventually fifteen witnesses, corroborating each other's stories, were procured. This story, he said, would indicate how difficult it was to get informants; the only method is by using a personal or family connection and exploiting some situation where money is the primary factor. The average citizen in Iraq does not see any reason why he should court trouble by becoming an agent, and he further takes the view that it is contrary to the tenets of the Koran to act as a spy on his fellow men.[64]

Whether religion was another factor in preventing Muslims from becoming spies or informants for their own country is beyond the scope of this research,[65] but Iraq was not unique in this case. Jordan faced similar difficulties whereby the police did 'not get the co-operation of the public'.[66] Attiyah's story, and similar issues in Jordan, demonstrates the different conditions in which Middle Eastern security services had to operate, and why some secret police behaviour was seen as a necessary instrument for maintaining precarious internal security.

No comparable principles to the Maxwell-Fyfe Directive existed in the Middle East. Here intelligence and security services often served the interests of particular political groups or elites, who, in turn, used and abused their power. As a result, security services sometimes arrested political opponents simply on account of their being threats against the regime. When a group of Turkish military officers (both serving and retired) were arrested by the Turkish authorities in January 1958 on the grounds of a 'serious plot' against the government, Sir James Bowker, the British Ambassador in Ankara (1954–8), believed the affair to be 'simply another by-product of the general bitterness engendered by the elections'. He commented that the Turkish Prime Minister, Adnan Menderes, was 'determined to teach the army a sharp lesson about the desirability of keeping out of politics, or at least out of opposition politics'.[67] The Menderes Government was overthrown in 1960 and Adnan Menderes himself was hanged by the military government.

Abuse of the security services extended to Iran. It appears that Princess Ashraf, the Shah's sister, ordered SAVAK to 'eavesdrop' on her boyfriend's 'telephone conversations and closely watch his activities' for her own personal reasons.[68] The security services were also bedevilled by corruption. According to General Fardust, during his reign at SAVAK, General Bakhtiar accumulated 'a fortune' by confiscating properties from 'wealthy' bazaar tradesmen with fabricated files accusing them of 'being a Communist' and throwing them into jail.[69] Meanwhile in Jordan, corruption was not limited to the security services themselves, but also engulfed the ministers who directed them.[70]

In some monarchical states, the head of state controlled the security services, creating further problems from a Western perspective. Jack O'Connell, the CIA station chief in Jordan (1963–71), recalls that when he asked King Hussein of Jordan if he could see the head of the Jordanian Intelligence Service, King Hussein replied: 'I'm the head of the Intelligence Service.'[71] Similarly, Richard Helms, Director of the CIA (1966–73), recollected that the Shah of Iran himself was de facto 'the chief Iranian intelligence officer'.[72] As a result, the power of these security forces did not reside in the organisation itself but ultimately in the hands of the head of state and was therefore more likely to be politicised to support the policies of the monarch's own government.[73] In addition, the head of state often fired members of the security services who became too powerful. A notable case is General Bakhtiar, the first Head of SAVAK (1957–61), who was dismissed by the Shah in 1961 on the grounds of backing a plot against him and was exiled to Europe the following year.[74]

The unregulated extraordinary state power displayed in these cases often promoted the misconduct of counter-subversive measures and violations of fundamental human rights. After the fall of

Mohammad Moseddeq in 1953, the Iranian government became ever more unsympathetic to the Tudeh Party and conducted a security purge of Tudeh sympathisers within the administration and security apparatus, mainly among the army and police.[75] The purge was not well conducted: suspects were often treated inappropriately and even executed without firm incriminating evidence. Observing the situation, David Stewart of MI5, former Deputy Head of SIME specialising in Middle Eastern affairs, identified long-term underlying problems. He reported that:

> All the officers were young and a high proportion drawn from the technical, i.e. better educated, branches of the Armed Forces. The Persian Foreign Minister has admitted privately that many were honest and efficient and that most were probably idealists driven into communism by the rottenness of Persia. This is the general impression both inside and outside Persia, and *the executions have consequently aroused strong feelings, particularly since they have been conducted inefficiently.* In short the incident has been a particularly successful exercise in repression, but emphasises once again the vital importance of constructive action by the Persian regime to remedy a situation in which so many honest, efficient and idealistic young men can find no alternative to communism.[76]

This statement indicates that these actions were taken as 'anti-Communist measures', which were originally designed to prevent, or suppress, subversive activities. However, the Shah conducted them too brutally and they served only to cultivate anti-governmental sentiment amongst the population.

The eruption of deep discontent amongst the people against their own government can also be seen in the context of the Iraqi Revolution. As noted earlier, Iraq – Britain's most reliable ally in the region, especially under the premiership of Nuri al-Said – was considered to have the strongest anti-Communist government in the region, introducing repressive security regulations such as the Association Law. Under the law, Said Qazzaz – the Iraqi Minister of the Interior and Nuri al-Said's right-hand man for internal security – was exclusively empowered to conduct robust anti-Communist measures. It is perhaps unsurprising that after the Iraqi Revolution, Qazzaz and Bahjat Attiyah were the first civilians to be executed by the new revolutionary government on the grounds of 'multiple murders and physical torture of anti-government demonstrators and political detainees'.[77] Sir Sam Falle, Oriental Counsellor at the British Embassy in Baghdad (1957–61), who observed the developments in Iraq before and after the Revolution, recalls that Said Qazzaz's 'crime was that he was an effective anti-communist'.[78] Nuri al-Said, who escaped from his house on the morning of the Revolution, was discovered the next day disguised as an Arab woman. He was killed and his body was dragged through the streets by a mob.[79]

This raises the important question about whether Britain contributed to the excessive use and abuse of interrogation techniques, such as torture. As torture was illegal in British national law, the British Security Service abstained from its use. Eliza Manningham-Buller, former Director-General of MI5 (2002–7), proudly notes MI5's strict adherence to the rule of law during the Second World War.[80] Cases of abuse of power, such as the ill-treatment of prisoners, were indeed brought to a court martial, as can be seen from the case of Bad Nenndorf, a post-war interrogation centre in Germany. The Commandant, Colonel Robin 'Tin Eye' Stephens, faced a court martial for claims of ill-treatment and brutality by his subordinates, but was later acquitted and employed by MI5.[81] It is highly unlikely that Scotland Yard's training course on interrogation techniques given to Middle Eastern security services would have suggested torture or ill-treatment.[82]

This assumption is supported from the other side of the Atlantic. The CIA was also deeply involved in training SAVAK officers and even in interfering in their operational matters. However, Earnest Oney – a former CIA officer, whose mission was to train SAVAK officers in Iran in the late 1950s (1957–9) and early 1960s (1962 and 1964) – has refuted any allegation that the Americans were involved in training the officers in the Third Department of SAVAK, responsible for the internal security of Iran, and particularly denied training in the use of torture.[83] Documentary evidence now seems to support his claim. The declassified CIA interrogation manual, codenamed *KUBARK – CIA's Counter-Intelligence*

Interrogation Manual – drafted in July 1963, states that 'intense pain is quite likely to produce false confessions, concocted as a means of escaping from distress', and that interrogation must be 'conducted for the sake of information and not for police purposes'.[84] Moreover, according to a former SAVAK officer, who noted that the organisation was largely trained by the Americans, British and Israelis, SAVAK was 'trained by those countries *not* for torture', 'but to learn how to spy, to do research – that sort of thing'.[85]

As part of his training, the British had also told General Fardust that physical torture should not be employed as a technique of interrogation. Yet Fardust admitted that 'the brutal method of torture' was commonplace in SAVAK. According to him, SAVAK resorted to such interrogation techniques in sensitive political situations, when national security appeared threatened. Torture was necessary 'in order to get speedy results or to create terror and fear'. The aim therefore extended beyond acquiring information, to 'breaking the suspect and creating panic in society'.[86] Conditions in the Middle East, with constant rumours of plots and coups, helped facilitate excessive security measures. Earnest Oney also recalled that SAVAK received 'dozens of reports of plotting against the Shah' over the years, which was an 'endemic' condition in Iran.[87] Additionally, Sir Sam Falle notes that 'the Shah's tyranny came from fear'.[88] A similar case can be found in Iraq, where anti-governmental sentiments were commonplace. MI5 itself was also concerned that Nuri al-Said 'might at any moment be assassinated'.[89]

Britain's Reaction to the Abuse of Human Rights

Britain did not endorse human rights abuses during various training courses. Yet this raises a further question of whether British personnel became aware of such activity and, if so, whether they criticised it. Iraq forms an early example of this issue. In late 1948 and early 1949, the Iraqi CID raided houses of Iraqi Communists and arrested hundreds of revolutionaries, which also led to a retrial of the three foremost leaders of the ICP, who were later convicted of 'having led the party from the prison'.[90] In February 1949, the three leaders, plus another individual, were hanged in different squares in Baghdad, and their bodies were 'left hanging for several hours so that the common people going to their work would receive the warning'.[91] Sir Henry Mack, who had not been informed by the Iraqi government about these executions, reported to the Foreign Secretary, Ernest Bevin, that:

> Information received from secret sources indicates that the trial was not conducted in accordance with British ideas of judicial impartiality, but it must be admitted that the Iraqi Government needed to make an example and there is no doubt that these men were intent on undermining the Iraqi States. All of them had long records of subversive activity . . . [and evidence for their connection with the Soviet Union] shows that their aims were revolutionary and Government in Iraq is not so firmly established that it can afford to be lenient when such men fall into their hands.[92]

Once the news reached Britain that 160 other alleged Communists were still being held in custody and more executions were likely to be carried out, Bevin found himself under pressure to intervene. The Foreign Office then tried to stop further executions by the Iraqis on the grounds that they were 'violating fundamental human rights'.[93] British diplomats also feared that acting too ruthlessly against the Communists would only intensify Communist activities and would be exploited by propaganda accusing the Iraqi government of human rights abuses.[94]

Observing the executions of the Iraqi Communist leaders, Arkady Suvorov, the secretary of the Soviet Legation, queried:

> Does Nuri as-Said [al-Said] or the ruling class . . . think that the hanging of these men or of others will put an end to the Communist movement in Iraq? They are only being foolish . . . They may now shatter the party and incarcerate thousands of its members . . . but this will not avail them for long. The rotten state of things will of necessity rouse the people and not only the Communists to protests and eventually to revolution.[95]

Despite a strong anti-Communist stance by the authorities, Communist activities in Iraq actually intensified throughout the 1950s. The public executions in 1949 marked a turning point for the Communist struggle against the Iraqi government. Fahd, one of those killed, 'dead proved more potent than Fahd living', as 'Communism became now surrounded with the halo of martyrdom'.[96] Sir Henry Mack duly but gently reproved the Iraqi Prime Minister, Nuri al-Said, for the deaths, which had 'gone quite far enough'. Nuri al-Said, however, responded that this practice had been adopted since 1921 in accordance with the law, and told Mack that 'with a third world war possible it was essential to ensure that these anarchists would not be able to repeat what they had done in the past'.[97] Despite the British intervention, the Iraqi government carried out further executions, and another ICP leader was hanged in May 1949, though the dead body was not exposed in public this time.[98]

Another case occurred in Iran in the second half of the 1950s. British officials became aware of excessive anti-Communist measures, involving the torture of political prisoners. Britain contemplated an intervention, but in the end simply looked on at the unwelcome developments. As we have seen, Iranian authorities intensified measures against the Tudeh Party after the 1953 coup, including purging their members and sympathisers from the army and police. The person in charge of this operation was General Bakhtiar, then Military Governor of Tehran. Those interned have since accused Bakhtiar of flogging political prisoners with a whip at 'the renowned "bath-house" (hammam)', and being personally involved in the torture of prisoners.[99] The Iranian government kept the British Embassy in Tehran in ignorance of developments and the only explanation given by General Bakhtiar himself was that he had received an order from the Shah that he 'should use whatever methods he considered necessary to gain information'.[100]

As the Tudeh elements and International Communists gained ground by exploiting the situation with subversive propaganda, diplomats at the British Embassy in Tehran judged that the allegation of torture was accurate. They discussed whether they should intervene by suggesting the Shah dismiss General Bakhtiar from his post. The argument for intervention was that 'our reputation will suffer unless we do something about it'.[101] However, an MI6 officer, Edward de Haan, who headed the Tehran Station (1954–7), intervened and noted that:

> Whatever one may say against General Bakhtiar's methods, he is an extremely able individual who is likely to have many years of service under the Shah. He is, as you know, highly regarded by the Shah . . . [who] has no intention of keeping him in the post of Military Governor for very much longer . . . If General Bakhtiar believed that he had been dismissed from his post because of British objections to his methods of treatment of prisoners, we might alienate him forever. This would be a serious blow when he reaches higher posts, as he almost certainly will. The price would not be worth improving our stock in other quarters of Tehran.[102]

Indeed, General Bakhtiar relinquished his post as Military Governor of Tehran and assumed a new post, the first Head of SAVAK. Given his subsequent career as the Head of SAVAK (1957–61), which also entitled him to assume the post of Deputy Prime Minister, it was most likely that no intervention was made regarding his treatment of prisoners. Even if the intervention was made, there was no visible consequence.[103]

Britain's non-interventionist attitude was more apparent towards the treatment of the Kurds by Iran, Turkey and to a lesser extent Iraq, throughout the period between 1949 and 1963. As we have seen, British policy was to maintain good relationships with these governments and, as the regional governments were 'sensitive' to the Kurdish question, the Foreign Office refused to raise concerns about their treatment of the Kurds.[104] Despite British awareness of this politically sensitive issue since the end of the First World War, the treatment of the Kurds by the local governments had never caught much attention outside the region until the heroic return of Mulla Mustafa Barzani from his exile in the Soviet Union to Iraq in October 1958. As noted in Chapter 5, the Iranian and Turkish governments shared intelligence in order to keep a close eye on him and his activities in Iraq. Once Barzani announced his proposal for the unification of his Kurdistan

Democratic Party (KDP) in Iraq and the Kurdistan Democratic Party of Iran (KDPI) under a single secretary-general, SAVAK readily rounded up '250 suspected KDPI activists' without trial, and the KDPI 'almost ceased to exist'.[105]

The Turkish government also conducted precautionary security measures against the Kurds. Shortly after the civilian Menderes Government was overthrown by Turkish Army officers in May 1960, a group of Kurds began demanding Kurdish autonomy. The new military government moved fast and arrested 248 Kurds who were 'believed to have supported agitation for a free Kurdish State'.[106] Once news about the treatment of the Kurds by the Iranian and Turkish governments reached Britain, John Profumo, then Minister of State for Foreign Affairs, was asked by William Owen, a Labour MP, at the House of Commons in May 1960 about Britain's view on 'the recent disturbances in Turkey and Iran' and if these authorities consulted Britain as a CENTO member.[107] Profumo replied that Britain was not consulted by them and restated Britain's non-intervention policy towards the minority movements that 'the internal affairs of each country are a matter for that country alone'.[108]

Conclusion

The training of Middle Eastern security services in anti-Communist measures was a recurrent theme of Britain's policy in the region. Akin to the security training implemented throughout the colonies, policymakers in London – such as those of the AC (O) Committee – also hoped that, through British training, strong Middle Eastern security services would safeguard British interests in the region. Strengthening the political police certainly forestalled the Communist advance in these countries and sustained the existence of local governments, but once internal subversion by the Communists, the Soviet Union or Egypt intensified, the local authorities felt increasingly threatened. As their security services were the only means to keep these governments in power, Middle Eastern leaders often adopted more vigorous and ruthless counter-measures, including torture of prisoners.

Despite these efforts, internal subversion persisted, and the repression fostered anti-governmental feelings amongst the population. As a result, Middle Eastern governments faced internal subversion, not by the Communists, but by their own people. The inevitable consequence was that local security services became part of the problem rather than the solution. To maintain good relations with the local authorities, Britain looked the other way as the local authorities conducted excessive counter-subversion, and ultimately kept intervention at a minimum. Consequently, British influence over the policy of Middle Eastern governments was also limited.

Conclusion: The Twilight of the British Empire in the Middle East

Those who consider it [Britain's engagement in the post-war Middle East] to have been a period of failure are the sentimentalists who do not understand why things should not have gone on as they were before. A more correct judgement is that though we made mistakes like everyone else involved, we have so far come through an unusually difficult and complex period without more damage to our real interests in the Middle East.

Lord Trevelyan[1]

It is just possible, I suppose, that the West knows how a country like Persia *ought* to be governed in the best interests of the people, but that it knows how it *could* be so governed has always seemed to me very unlikely.

Lt.-Col. Geoffrey Wheeler[2]

The retention of the British Empire was, in the words of esteemed diplomat, Lord Franks, 'part of the habit and furniture of the minds'.[3] When it looked to be under threat, policymakers expected the intelligence services to intervene and protect Britain's interests. This worked effectively in many colonies where decolonisation involved a relatively smooth and successful transition to Commonwealth, thereby allowing law enforcement bodies to play an important role in safeguarding British influence. It was more difficult in the Middle East where policymakers also expected intelligence to maintain British interests in an altogether difference context, this time by working with local authorities to promote anti-Communist measures. MI5 and colonial police officers were deployed in the region and expected to perform the same tasks as they had in the colonies. Similarly, policymakers hoped that British training, again transposed from the imperial context, of strong Middle Eastern security services would also safeguard their regional interests.

It was often Middle Eastern governments that took the initiative in requesting British advice on anti-Communist measures, but Britain gladly agreed and provided assistance as a means of influencing policy. At the time, Middle Eastern governments saw Britain as their most reliable ally in fighting subversive elements at home. This was mostly due to its reputation for organisational reliability, as well as personal relationships developed through Britain's involvement in the region over many years.

Despite Britain's dominant influence in the region in the early post-war period, several crises in the 1950s meant that British influence gradually faded away. The year 1958, in which the Iraqi Revolution occurred, has received particular scholarly attention as a turning point for British Middle Eastern policy.[4] It was certainly a setback for British intelligence and security liaison. Duncan MacIntosh's career as Security/Police Adviser in Baghdad came to an abrupt end. A total of 108 pro-British influential Iraqis – including key liaison contacts, such as Said Qazzaz, Bahjat Attiyah and General Ghazi Dashistani – were arrested and accused of being 'criminal traitors' by the revolutionary government.[5] In addition, the Lebanese Crisis in the same year led to the resignation of Emir Farid Chehab from his post as the Head of the Sûreté Générale.[6] Colonel Sir Patrick Coghill, meanwhile, noted in his diaries that 1958 marked the end of informal regional intelligence/security cooperation between Jordan, Lebanon, Iraq, Iran and Turkey on subversive activities in the region.[7]

Yet, a degree of continuity in intelligence liaison remained after 1958 and was even sustained beyond the period of this study. A notable example is the Liaison and Counter-Subversion Committees under CENTO, which continued until the dissolution of CENTO in 1979.[8] Duncan MacIntosh moved to Jordan as Police Adviser in 1958, and served there until 1962. Until 1979, the Shah of Iran maintained a close connection with MI6 officers, including Sir Maurice Oldfield, as well as MI6 agents, Sir Shapoor Reporter and General Hussein Fardust. There is also evidence to suggest that MI6 benefited from ongoing relationships with contacts in the Iraqi Police and armed forces and among businessmen after the 1958 Revolution. A retired member of the British intelligence community recalls that even the Egyptians in the 1970s and 1980s, who had been uncooperative during the period of Nasser's rule from 1952 to 1970, were 'good allies' with British intelligence, especially against Libya.[9] Such continuation of British intelligence liaison with its Middle Eastern counterparts could not, however, match the relationships of the 'informal' Empire of the 1950s. British influence in the region declined once it lost its strategic allies.

The role of intelligence is to guide the policymaking process. It should therefore be asked whether intelligence and security officers were able to discern the socio-political challenges correctly at the time, which, in turn, would then have informed policy. An enquiry into state secrets inevitably faces methodological hurdles, yet there is no evidence to suggest that intelligence forewarned about the loss of British influence. There was no advance warning provided of either the Egyptian Revolution in 1952 or the Iraqi Revolution in 1958. This was largely because British intelligence depended on local authorities in every respect. They relied on these local authorities staying in power and relied on their sources for information. But whilst these partners proved useful in providing anti-Communist intelligence, they were less successful at heading off other threats. Intelligence provided to the British invariably came from a narrow anti-Communist perspective. In addition, liaison made it more difficult for Britain to conduct espionage operations on its friends even though this would have provided a more accurate picture. Whitehall's anti-Communist approach therefore had an unintended consequence: it hampered Britain's own independent espionage operations through fear of eroding goodwill. To make matters worse, MI6 officers also conducted their own covert anti-Communist actions, which threatened, if uncovered, to erode trust. These were not intelligence failures, rather inevitable consequences of an initial policy failure.

There is also no evidence to suggest that MI6 or MI5 officers in the region warned policymakers in London that the Communist threat was not prominent. There were certainly some sceptics, such as Guy Liddell and David Stewart, who saw training of local services in anti-Communist measures as failing to serve British interests. However, their views formed a minority and were over-ridden by Britain's strategic, anti-Communist and oil interests in supporting the friendly foreign regimes. As a result, instead of preventing army disaffection, understanding rapid demographic growth, urbanisation and social protest, and assessing the abiding strength of political Islam, policymakers in London prioritised anti-Communist measures. British intelligence and security officers, as well as IRD officials, were not necessarily blind or seeing these challenges through a Cold War lens, but their activi-ties and priorities were all directed by government policy. And British governments were preoccupied with the spread of the 'Communist menace'.

The quotation of Lord Trevelyan above suggests that, despite some mistakes in the short run, Britain's engagement in the region was successful in the long run. Yet, an examination of the years between 1948 and 1963 suggests otherwise. Despite the shared anti-Communist attitudes, Britain conducted counter-subversion in the post-war Middle East in a similar manner as it had done in the British Empire. But there was a key difference which under-mined the approach. Unlike in colonial territories, measures con-ducted in the post-war Middle East were inevitably in the hands of foreign authorities. Back in London, policymakers ignored the fact that many of these regimes had already banned Communism and ignored the side-effects of anti-Communist measures.

Throughout the period, the British government attempted to rectify the repressive characteristics of Middle Eastern govern-ments. Towards the late 1950s and early 1960s, General Hussein Fardust, the closest aide of the Shah, for instance, was chosen to influence domestic policy of the Iranian government. Nevertheless, as the above quotation from Geoffrey Wheeler reveals, the British proved unable to influence the policy of the Shah. Such limited influence also indicates that the 'informal' Empire was based on narrow grounds of anti-Communism and faded away throughout the period.

Above all, Britain's policy served to prop up increasingly unpop-ular authoritarian regimes against a rising tide of anti-British sentiment. In this regard, it was inherently flawed from the start. We will never know if the Iraqi Revolution would still have happened if British anti-Communist measures had not been implemented, or if Middle Eastern governments would have been less oppressive. It is probable, though, that fewer anti-Communist measures would have been conducted by local authorities and that pro-British Middle Eastern regimes might have survived longer. Lord Trevelyan's argument that Britain escaped with little damage to its interests therefore holds little water since the British strategic vision of maintaining influence was short-sighted and ended in failure.

Britain was not the only country guilty of this and other instances can be found elsewhere in the Cold War. Using similar methods to sustain its own short-term interests, the United States, Britain's closest ally against the Soviet Union, also failed in the long term, for instance, in Guatemala and Vietnam.[10] From a rather different perspective, similar arguments have been made about the Soviet Union with regard to Eastern Europe.[11] More noteworthy is what Britain's engagement with the post-war Middle East reveals about intelligence liaison, a ubiquitous and fundamental part of the secret world.[12] Liaising with local authorities was advantageous for Britain insofar as they formed unique local assets. Firstly, Britain was able to access intelligence on Communist activities in the region, including police records, which would otherwise have been inaccessible. Secondly, as a strong security service was regarded as essential to forestall Communist subversion, training such organisations was deemed the best way to influence the conduct of anti-Communist measures by Middle Eastern states.

Yet training foreign security forces is a double-edged sword as it is difficult to control how the imparted knowledge will be applied. Although British intelligence liaison with its Middle Eastern counterparts had a shared interest in countering Communism, local authorities used their newfound techniques and methods to serve their own purposes; and this proved damaging if the foreign government was a non-democratic regime. In the end, the implementation of security measures was in the hands of foreign governments.

Clear differences between the UK and the Middle East hampered intelligence liaison. Firstly, despite a close connection with the local authorities, there was no common intelligence culture. Middle Eastern security services dominated both internal security and propaganda in their home countries, and, despite frequent interactions with their British counterparts, these services frequently held views that contrasted sharply with the policing and information-oriented approach of the British. This rift was most noticeable and destructive in the Counter-Subversion Committee and in the use of excessive security measures, including torture of political prisoners. The intelligence and security culture of these Middle Eastern services was derived, to a considerable extent, from the political culture of the regimes they served. In some cases, such as Iran, there was strong adherence to the military culture from which the intelligence personnel sprang. From their point of view, MI5's constitutional principle, stipulated by the Maxwell-Fyfe Directive in 1952 as being apolitical in the defence of the realm, was totally incomprehensible.

Secondly, British and Middle Eastern governments interpreted the subversive threats differently. Britain saw them more narrowly and focused on Communist Party members or those who had close connections with the Soviets. By contrast, Middle Eastern governments saw any subversive activities, including those of Communists or minorities, which challenged the status quo as the threats. This led to the politicisation of intelligence and political considerations defining subversive threats.

Counter-subversion itself was subjective and the demarcation line between Communist and non-Communist subversive activities was often blurred. This was particularly the case in the Middle East, where Communist activities were illegal and often worked in tandem with other underground groups. For the Middle Eastern authorities, without differentiating Communist from non-Communist threats, these activities were illegal and threatened the very survival of the regime. It is also worth pointing out that both threats identified by the British and Middle Eastern governments served the interests of the Soviet Union but their standpoints differed significantly. As a result, despite the desire of the British imperial architects to foster anti-Communist measures in the region, local authorities acted against subversive elements rigorously, as demonstrated in the attempts to counter the Kurds.

Developing local security forces in the Middle East had unintended consequences for Britain. London did not realise that most regional governments were already anti-Communist and that they maintained strong security services which had the reputation of being secret police, infringing on human rights. Indeed, the formation of Communist Parties had already been banned across the region. British anti-Communist policy and training in counter-subversion could therefore be considered as contributing simply to the oppressive nature of local security services. The post-war Middle East predominantly consisted of foreign countries. The local authorities were not puppets or clients of the British Empire. The balance of intelligence liaison, as well as their relationship in general, was that local authorities were often stronger than their patrons. Middle Eastern governments listened to and sought advice from the British, but only on the narrow issue of anti-Communist measures, which they understood by their own interpretations. In addition, Middle Eastern security authorities were right to be labelled secret police. They were highly politicised and merely served as an instrument of the local authorities. The inevitable consequence of this was that Middle Eastern security services became part of the problem rather than the solution. Certain Middle Eastern governments actually undermined their own security as the repressive nature of their regimes alienated and bred resentment among their own populations.

Recent works emphasise the role of intelligence in successfully assisting Britain's decolonisation policy.[13] Asserting that intelligence was vital for perpetuating Britain's influence overseas, Calder Walton argues that intelligence 'allowed London to punch far above its weight in the years after 1957, for the rest of the Cold War'.[14] In the case of the Middle East, however, there is no evidence to suggest that intelligence delayed the twilight of the 'informal' Empire or rectified the policymakers' narrow views towards the region. Despite the desire of policymakers in London, British intelligence and security services, as well as the IRD, struggled to maintain British influence in a similar manner as they had achieved in the Empire. Intelligence unintentionally fostered and accelerated the decline of the British 'informal' Empire in the Middle East.

Notes

Introduction

1 On the Suez Crisis, cf. Keith Kyle, *Suez: Britain's End of Empire in the Middle East* (London: St Martin's Press, 1991); W. Scott Lucas, *Divided We Stand: Britain, the US and the Suez Crisis* (London: Hodder & Stoughton, 1991); Saul Kelly and Anthony Gorst (eds), *Whitehall and the Suez Crisis* (London: Frank Cass, 2000); Wm. Roger Louis and Roger Owen (eds), *Suez 1956: The Crisis and Its Consequences* (Oxford: Oxford University Press, 1989).

2 The term is generally used by imperial historians and has long been at the centre of debates about its meaning since the 1950s. Cf. John Gallagher and Ronald Robinson, 'The Imperialism of Free Trade', *The Economic History Review*, vol. 6, no. 1 (1953), pp. 1–15; Wm. Roger Louis (ed.), *Imperialism* (London: New Viewpoints, 1976). For the 'informal' empire, cf. Yoav Alon, 'Historiography of Empire: The Literature on Britain in the Middle East', in Zach Levey and Elie Podeh (eds), *Britain and the Middle East: From Imperial Power to Junior Partner* (Brighton: Sussex Academic Press, 2008), pp. 34–5; Glen Balfour-Paul, 'Britain's Informal Empire in the Middle East', in Judith M. Brown and Wm. Roger Louis (eds), *The Oxford History of the British Empire: vol. IV, The Twentieth Century* (Oxford: Oxford University Press, 1999); John Darwin, 'An Undeclared Empire: The British in the Middle East, 1918–39', *Journal of Imperial and Commonwealth History*, vol. 27, no. 2 (1999), pp. 159–76; Peter Sluglett, 'Formal and Informal Empire in the Middle East', in Robin W. Winks (ed.), *The Oxford History of the British Empire: vol. V, Historiography* (Oxford: Oxford University Press, 1999), pp. 416–36.

3 Anthony Parsons, *They Say the Lion: Britain's Legacy to the Arabs: A Personal Memory* (London: Jonathan Cape, 1986), p. xiv; see

also D. K. Fieldhouse, *Western Imperialism in the Middle East, 1914–1958* (Oxford: Oxford University Press, 2006), chs 7, 8.

4 Among some exceptional studies, see Wm. Roger Louis, *The British Empire in the Middle East, 1945–1951* (Oxford: Clarendon Press, 1984); Levey and Podeh, *Britain and the Middle East*. For a 'classical' or 'traditional' account, see Elizabeth Monroe, *Britain's Moment in the Middle East, 1914–1971* (London: Chatto & Windus, 1981). A 'revisionist' account is provided by Nigel J. Ashton, *Eisenhower, Macmillan and the Problem of Nasser* (London: Macmillan, 1996); Robert McNamara, *Britain, Nasser and the Balance of Power in the Middle East 1952–1967* (London: Frank Cass, 2003). On its colonial, foreign and defence policies in South Arabia, cf. Peter Hinchcliffe, John T. Ducker and Maria Holt, *Without Glory in Arabia* (London: I. B. Tauris, 2006); Spencer Mawby, 'The "Big Lie" and the "Great Betrayal": Explaining the British Collapse in Aden', in Nigel J. Ashton (ed.), *The Cold War in the Middle East: Regional Conflict and the Superpowers, 1967–73* (London: Routledge, 2007), pp. 167–87; Simon Smith, *Britain's Revival and Fall in the Gulf* (London: Routledge, 2004).

5 Cf. John Kent, *British Imperial Strategy and the Origins of the Cold War 1944–49* (Leicester: Leicester University Press, 1993); Michael J. Cohen, 'The Strategic Role of the Middle East after the War', in Michael J. Cohen and Martin Kolinsky (eds), *Demise of the British Empire in the Middle East* (London: Frank Cass, 1998), pp. 23–37; Anthony Gorst, '"We must cut our coat according to our cloth": The Making of British Defence Policy, 1945–8', in Richard J. Aldrich (ed.), *British Intelligence, Strategy and the Cold War, 1945–51* (London: Routledge, 1992), pp. 143–63. On the importance of the Egyptian base, see John Kent, 'The Egyptian Base and the Defence of the Middle East, 1945–54', *Journal of Imperial and Commonwealth History*, vol. 21, no. 3 (1993), pp. 45–65. On the convergence of the Anglo-American strategic (offensive) interests, and subsequent formation of the Baghdad Pact, see Michael J. Cohen, *Fighting World War Three from the Middle East* (London: Frank Cass, 1997); Michael J. Cohen, 'From "Cold" to "Hot" War: Allied Strategic and Military Interests in the Middle East after the Second World War', *Middle Eastern Studies*, vol. 43, no. 5 (2007), pp. 725–48.

6 Oliver Franks, 'Britain and the Tide of World Affairs', *Listener*, 52/1314 (11 November 1954), p. 788, quoted in Philip Darby,

British Defence Policy East of Suez, 1947–1968 (London: Oxford University Press, 1973), p. 22; Note that Prime Minister Clement Attlee, a 'committed internationalist, [who] actively opposed a military strategy based on the traditional imperial pattern', also acknowledged that foreign affairs including Commonwealth or colonial affairs, economic policy and defence were Bevin's sphere and it would be 'a mistake to intervene personally'. Raymond Smith and John Zametica, 'The Cold Warrior: Clement Attlee Reconsidered, 1945–7', *International Affairs*, vol. 61, no. 2 (1985), pp. 237, 251. See also Clement Attlee, *As It Happened* (London: William Heinemann, 1954), p. 169; Alan Bullock, *Ernest Bevin: Foreign Secretary, 1945–1951* (London: W. W. Norton, 1983), pp. 215, 399.

7 Of course, there is a vast literature on the role of intelligence in counter-insurgencies in the region. On the counter-insurgency campaign in Palestine, pre-eminent works include David Charters, *The British Army and Jewish Insurgency in Palestine, 1945–47* (London: Macmillan, 1989); David Charters, 'British Intelligence in the Palestine Campaign, 1945–47', *Intelligence and National Security* (hereafter *INS*), vol. 6, no. 1 (1991), pp. 115–40; Steven Wagner 'British Intelligence and the Jewish Resistance Movement in the Palestine Mandate, 1945–46', *INS*, vol. 23, no. 5 (2008), pp. 629–57; Steven Wagner, 'British Intelligence and the "Fifth" Occupying Power: The Secret Struggle to Prevent Jewish Illegal Immigration to Palestine', *INS*, vol. 29, no. 5 (2014), pp. 698–726; Calder Walton, 'British Intelligence and the Mandate of Palestine: Threats to British National Security Immediately after the Second World War', *INS*, vol. 23, no. 4 (2008), pp. 435–62. On counter-insurgency campaigns in Cyprus, see Panagiotis Dimitrakis, 'British Intelligence and the Cyprus Insurgency, 1955–1959', *International Journal of Intelligence and Counterintelligence* (hereafter *IJIC*), vol. 21, no. 2 (2008), pp. 375–94. For discussions on the role of intelligence in counter-insurgencies, see Richard Popplewell, '"Lacking Intelligence": Some Reflections on Recent Approaches to British Counter-Insurgency, 1900–1960', *INS*, vol. 10, no. 2 (1995), pp. 336–52; Calder Walton, *Empire of Secrets* (London: HarperCollins, 2013), pp. xi–xxxii. On the role of intelligence in the British Empire in general, see Walton, *Empire of Secrets*; David Anderson and David Killingray (eds), *Policing and Decolonisation: Politics, Nationalism, and the Police, 1917–65* (Manchester: Manchester University Press, 1992); Richard J. Popplewell, *Intelligence and Imperial Defence* (London: Frank Cass, 1995); Martin Thomas,

Empires of Intelligence: Security Service and Colonial Disorder after 1914 (London and Los Angeles: University of California Press, 2008). For the IRD in general, see Andrew Defty, *Britain, America and Anti-Communist Propaganda, 1945–1958: The Information Research Department* (London: Routledge, 2003); Paul Lashmar and James Oliver, *Britain's Secret Propaganda War 1948–1977* (London: Sutton, 1999); Hugh Wilford, 'The Information Research Department: Britain's Secret Cold War Weapon Revealed', *Review of International Studies*, vol. 24, no. 3 (1998), pp. 353–69; Scott Lucas and C. J. Morris, 'A Very British Crusade: The Information Research Department and the Beginning of the Cold War', in Aldrich (ed.), *British Intelligence, Strategy and the Cold War, 1945–51*, pp. 85–110; Lyn Smith, 'Covert British Propaganda: The Information Research Department: 1947–77', *Millennium: Journal of International Studies*, vol. 9, no. 1 (1980), pp. 67–83; Wesley Wark, 'Coming in from the Cold: British Propaganda and Red Army Defectors, 1945–1952', *The International History Review*, vol. 9, no. 1 (1987), pp. 48–72; Philip Deery, 'Confronting the Cominform: George Orwell and the Cold War Offensive of the Information Research Department, 1948–50', *Labour History*, vol. 73 (1997), pp. 219–25. On the colonial territories, see Susan L. Carruthers, *Winning Hearts and Minds: British Governments, the Media and Colonial Counter-Insurgency, 1944–60* (Leicester: Leicester University Press, 1995). For the Middle Eastern context, see James Vaughan, *The Failure of American and British Propaganda in the Arab Middle East, 1945–1957: Unconquerable Minds* (Basingstoke: Palgrave, 2005); James Vaughan, 'Propaganda by Proxy?: Britain, America, and Arab Radio Broadcasting, 1953–1957', *Historical Journal of Film, Radio, and Television*, vol. 22, no. 2 (2002), pp. 157–72; James Vaughan, '"A Certain Idea of Britain": British Cultural Diplomacy in the Middle East, 1945–57', *Contemporary British History*, vol. 19, no. 2 (2005), pp. 151–68; James Vaughan, '"Cloak without Dagger": How the Information Research Department Fought Britain's Cold War in the Middle East, 1948–56', *Cold War History*, vol. 4, no. 3 (2004), pp. 56–84; Johan Franzen, 'Losing Hearts and Minds in Iraq: Britain, Cold War Propaganda and the Challenge of Communism, 1945–58', *Historical Research*, vol. 83, no. 222 (2010), pp. 747–62.

8 See Christopher Andrew, *The Defence of the Realm: The Authorized History of MI5* (London: Allen Lane, 2009), pp. 442–82.

9 While there is some literature which indicates that MI5 operated in the post-war Middle East, there is no serious academic study on this aspect. Cf. Nigel West, *The Friends: Britain's Post War Secret Intelligence Operations* (London: Weidenfeld & Nicolson, 1988), p. 17; Anthony Cavendish, *Inside Intelligence: The Revelations of an MI6 Officer* (London: HarperCollins, 1990), chs 4–5; Richard Deacon, *'C': A Biography of Sir Maurice Oldfield* (London: Futura, 1984), ch. 4; Alistair Horne, *But What Do You Actually Do?* (London: Weidenfeld & Nicolson, 2011), chs 3–4; Ian Black and Benny Morris, *Israel's Secret Wars: A History of Israel's Intelligence Services* (New York: Grove Weidenfeld, 1991), pp. 74–5.

10 Richard J. Aldrich, *GCHQ* (London: Harper, 2011), pp. 155–64. See also David Easter, 'Spying on Nasser: British Signals Intelligence in Middle East Crises and Conflicts, 1956–67', *INS*, vol. 28, no. 6 (2013), pp. 824–44.

11 Important memoirs and works include: memoirs of the British account of Operation Boot, C. M. Woodhouse, *Something Ventured* (London: Granada, 1982), chs 8–9; of the American account of Operation TPAJAX, Kermit Roosevelt, *Countercoup: The Struggle for the Control of Iran* (New York: McGraw-Hill, 1979); Donald Wilber, 'Clandestine Service History: Overthrow of Premier Mossadeq of Iran, November 1952–August 1953', *Foreign Policy Bulletin*, vol. 11, no. 3 (2000), pp. 90–104. For academic works on the subject, cf. Brian Lapping, *End of Empire* (London: Guild, 1985), ch. 4; Mark J. Gasiorowski and Malcolm Byrne (eds), *Mohammad Mosaddeq and the 1953 Coup in Iran* (New York: Syracuse University Press, 2004). For the intelligence dimension, see Stephen Dorril, *MI6: Inside the Covert World of Her Majesty's Secret Intelligence Service* (London: Free Press, 2000), ch. 28; John Prados, *Safe for Democracy: The Secret War of the CIA* (Chicago: Ivan R. Dee, 2006), ch. 6.

12 On MI6's activities during the Cold War in general, see Dorril, *MI6*; Richard J. Aldrich, *The Hidden Hand* (Woodstock: Overlook, 2001). On the 'special operations' in the region, see Clive Jones, *Britain and the Yemen Civil War 1962–65: Foreign Policy and the Limits of Covert Action* (Brighton: Sussex Academic Press, 2004); Spencer Mawby, 'The Clandestine Defence of Empire: British Special Operations in Yemen 1951–64', *INS*, vol. 17, no. 3 (2002), pp. 105–30; Lucas, *Divided We Stand*, pp. 193–5. See also note 14 below.

13 The subject of liaison in the region is dominated by the

Anglo-American 'special intelligence' relationship. Cf. Richard J. Aldrich, 'Intelligence, Anglo-American Relations and the Suez Crisis, 1956', *INS*, vol. 9, no. 3 (1994), pp. 544–54; Anthony Gorst and W. Scott Lucas, 'The Other Collusion: Operation Straggle and Anglo-American Intervention in Syria, 1955–56', *INS*, vol. 4, no. 3 (1989), pp. 576–95; Matthew Jones, 'The "Preferred Plan": The Anglo-American Working Group Report on Covert Action in Syria, 1957', *INS*, vol. 19, no. 3 (2004), pp. 401–15; Scott Lucas and Alistair Morey, 'Hidden "Alliance": The CIA and MI6 before and after Suez', *INS*, vol. 15, no. 2 (2000), pp. 95–120; Len Scott and Peter Jackson once remarked in 2004 that it is 'a final "missing dimension"' in the field. Len Scott and Peter Jackson, 'Journeys in Shadows', in Len Scott and Peter Jackson (eds), *Understanding Intelligence in the Twenty-First Century* (London: Routledge, 2004), pp. 20–1. This remains the same. A recent survey of the academic research published in the past four decades in *INS* and *IJIC* has shown that liaison comes at the bottom of rankings as the least-studied subject in the field. See Damien Van Puyvelde and Sean Curtis, '"Standing on the Shoulders of Giants": Diversity and Scholarship in Intelligence Studies', *INS*, vol. 31, no. 7 (2016), pp. 1040–54.

14 The field of Intelligence Studies has been dominated by Western perspectives, but non-Western perspectives have been emerging recently. See Philip H. J. Davies and Kristian Gustafson (eds), *Intelligence Elsewhere* (Washington DC: Georgetown University Press, 2013); Rob Dover, Michael Goodman and Claudia Hillebrand (eds), *Routledge Companion to Intelligence Studies* (London: Routledge, 2014), part IV. More than two decades ago, however, there was also a comparative study done on intelligence organisations, including Japanese and Chinese ones; see Jeffrey Richelson, *Foreign Intelligence Organizations* (Cambridge, MA: Ballinger, 1988).

15 Documentary evidence of such dealings has been found in Tripoli as a result of the turmoil in Libya. Cf. Richard Norton-Taylor, 'Sir Mark Allen: The Secret Link between MI6, the CIA and Gaddafi', *The Guardian*, 4 September 2011; Nick Hopkins, 'The Libya Papers: A Glimpse into the World of 21st-Century Espionage', *The Guardian*, 9 September 2011.

16 Stephen Lander, 'International Intelligence Cooperation: An Inside Perspective', *Cambridge Review of International Affairs*, vol. 17, no. 3 (2004), pp. 483–4, 489.

17 Yaacov Caroz, *The Arab Secret Services* (London: Corgi, 1978), p. 13.

18 Bernard Porter, *Plots and Paranoia* (London: Unwin Hyman, 1989), p. vii. He referred to counter-subversive activities as 'domestic espionage', but what he meant was counter-subversion.

19 Cf. Walter Laqueur, *Communism and Nationalism in the Middle East* (London: Routledge and Kegan Paul, 1956); Tareq Ismael, *The Communist Movement in the Arab World* (London: Routledge, 2005); Cf. Caroz, *Arab Secret Services*, pp. 1–19.

20 On the formation of the Baghdad Pact, see Ayesha Jalal, 'Towards the Baghdad Pact: South Asia and Middle East Defence in the Cold War, 1947–1955', *The International History Review*, vol. 11, no. 3 (1989), pp. 409–33; Nigel J. Ashton, 'The Hijacking of a Pact: The Formation of the Baghdad Pact and Anglo-American Tensions in the Middle East, 1955–1958', *Review of International Studies*, vol. 19, no. 2 (1993), pp. 123–37; Brian Holden Reid, 'The "Northern Tier" and the Baghdad Pact', in John W. Young (ed.), *The Foreign Policy of Churchill's Peacetime Administration 1951–1955* (Leicester: Leicester University Press, 1988), pp. 159–79; Elie Podeh, 'The Perils of Ambiguity: The United States and the Baghdad Pact', in David W. Lesch (ed.), *The Middle East and the United States* (Boulder, CO: Westview Press, 2003), pp. 100–19. On CENTO as a defence alliance, see David R. Devereux, *The Formulation of British Defence Policy towards the Middle East, 1948–56* (London: Macmillan, 1990); Panagiotis Dimitrakis, *Failed Alliances of the Cold War* (London: I. B. Tauris, 2012). On the interpretation of the Baghdad Pact, see Richard Jasse, 'The Baghdad Pact: Cold War or Colonialism?', *Middle Eastern Studies*, vol. 27, no. 1 (1991), pp. 140–56. See also a classic and basic text, Royal Institute of International Affairs, *The Baghdad Pact: Origins and Political Setting* (London: Information Department of the Royal Institute of International Affairs, 1956).

21 Neville Stack, 'CENTO – The Unknown Alliance', *RUSI Journal*, vol. 117, no. 3 (1972), p. 51. He compares it with the other Cold War treaty organisations, such as NATO and SEATO.

22 Ibid. p. 51. Note that the Military Committee was aimed at military coordination against the aggression of the Communist bloc; the Economic Committee was for economic and societal developments of the signatories including developing atomic energy, proposed either by the United Kingdom or United States through their financial support.

23 Dimitrakis, *Failed Alliances*, p. 4.

24 Daniel Pipes, 'Dealing with Middle Eastern Conspiracy Theories', *Orbis*, vol. 36, no. 1 (1992), p. 43.

25 See Rory Cormac, *Confronting the Colonies: British Intelligence and Counterinsurgency* (London: Hurst, 2013); Benjamin Grob-Fitzgibbon, *Imperial Endgame* (London: Palgrave Macmillan, 2011); and Wm. Roger Louis and Ronald Robinson, 'The Imperialism of Decolonization', *The Journal of Imperial and Commonwealth History*, vol. 22, no. 3 (1994), pp. 462–511.

26 There are some exceptional studies. On the Communist movements in the region, see Laqueur, *Communism and Nationalism in the Middle East*; Ismael, *Communist Movement in the Arab World*. See also Sepehr Zabih, *The Communist Movement in Iran* (Los Angeles: University of California Press, 1966); George Harris, *The Origins of Communism in Turkey* (Stanford: Stanford University Press, 1967); Hanna Batatu, *The Old Social Classes and the Revolutionary Movements of Iraq* (Princeton: Princeton University Press, 1978).

27 See Hanna Batatu's classic work on the Iraqi context, *The Old Social Classes and the Revolutionary Movements of Iraq*. On Middle Eastern security services in general, see Caroz, *Arab Secret Services*, ch. 1.

28 Cf. Mark Townsend, 'Ex-MI6 Officer Joins Guantanamo Inmate in Hunger Strike', *The Observer*, 10 August 2013; Ian Cobain, Mustafa Khalili and Mona Mahmood, 'How MI6 Deal Sent Family to Gaddafi's Jail', *The Guardian*, 9 September 2011.

29 One of the authoritative revisionist perspectives on British counter-insurgency is David French; see David French, *The British Way in Counter-Insurgency, 1945–1967* (Oxford: Oxford University Press, 2011). For a general revisionist account of the British decolonisation, see Grob-Fitzgibbon, *Imperial Endgame*. On the Palestine Mandate, see David Cesarani, *Major Farran's Hat: Murder, Scandal, and Britain's Secret War against Jewish Terrorism, 1945–1948* (London: William Heinemann, 2009). For discussions on the orthodoxy and revisionist schools, cf. Huw Bennett, *Fighting the Mau Mau: The British Army and Counter-Insurgency in the Kenya Emergency* (Cambridge: Cambridge University Press, 2013), pp. 1–7; David M. Anderson, 'Mau Mau in the High Court and the "Lost" British Empire Archives: Colonial Conspiracy or Bureaucratic Bungle?', *The Journal of Imperial and Commonwealth History*, vol. 39, no. 5 (2011), pp. 699–716.

30 Philip Murphy, 'Creating a Commonwealth Intelligence Culture: The View from Central Africa, 1945–1965', *INS*, vol. 17, no. 3 (2002), pp. 131–62; Andrew, *Defence of the Realm*, p. 334.

31 Walton, *Empire of Secrets*, pp. 26–9.

32 Cf. Bruce Quarrie, *The World's Secret Police* (London: Octopus, 1986), pp. 108–29.

33 Cf. Ian F. W. Beckett, *Modern Insurgencies and Counter-Insurgencies* (London: Routledge, 2001).

34 Frank Kitson, *Low Intensity Operations: Subversion, Insurgency and Peacekeeping* (London: Faber and Faber, 1971), p. 3.

35 Ibid.

36 See Christopher Mayhew, *A War of Words: A Cold War Witness* (London: I. B. Tauris, 1998), pp. 14–47. Sir Roger Stevens, the British Ambassador in Tehran (1954–8), who saw 'Communist propaganda' undermining the 'morale and confidence' of the Baghdad Pact countries by twisting 'the truth', once noted in 1956 that the 'truth must be told and people should have a correct view of events and policies'. The National Archives, London (hereafter TNA): Public Record Office (hereafter PRO) FO371/121283: V10710/8: telegram by Sir Roger Stevens, Tehran, to FO, 5 April 1956.

37 TNA: PRO FO371/121283: V10710/28: letter by P. G. D. Adams, Beirut, to FO, 10 May 1956.

38 TNA: PRO KV4/238: Pol.F.1001/1/H.S.: report, 'SIME Record Note', by W. M. T. Magan to R. W. G. Stephens, 28 April 1951.

39 See Andrew, *Defence of the Realm*, pp. 442–82.

40 Cf. TNA: PRO FO371/75022: E7391/G: letter by B. A. B. Burrows to Sir Rupert Hay, Political Resident, 17 June 1949; PRO FO371/82127: EA15313/1: letter by Pelly, Bahrain, to G. W. Furlonge of FO, 10 July 1950.

41 Cf. TNA: PRO FO371/104426: EA1646/5: letter by B. A. B. Burrows to D. A. Greenhill, 20 August 1953.

42 A notable example for the personal connection is Sir Maurice Oldfield, who was in charge of counter-intelligence in the region until 1947 and who maintained some connections with Israelis even after 1948. See Deacon, 'C', chs 3–4.

43 Tom Bower, *The Perfect English Spy* (London: Heinemann, 1995), p. 239. According to Bower, it was in 1960 that MI6 officially contacted Mossad and posted a liaison officer in Israel. Ibid. pp. 240–1.

Chapter I

1 The term 'Communist menace' can often be found in official records, but was first referred to by Foreign Secretary Ernest Bevin in his memorandum to Prime Minister Clement Attlee in the context of the establishment of the Official Committee on Communism (Overseas). See TNA: PRO PREM8/1365: PM/49/115: memorandum by Bevin to Attlee, Top Secret, 17 August 1949.

2 TNA: PRO PREM11/1582: memorandum by Anthony Eden, 10 December 1955.

3 TNA: PRO FO371/121261: V1073/294G: COS (56) 270: report by Chiefs of Staff Committee, 'United Kingdom Commitments under the Baghdad Pact', 13 July 1956.

4 TNA: PRO CAB158/33: JIC (58) 72 (Final): report by the Joint Intelligence Committee, 'Intelligence Targets', 21 November 1958.

5 Cf. Julian Lewis, *Changing Direction*, 2nd edn (London: Frank Cass, 2002); Percy Cradock, *Know Your Enemy* (London: John Murray, 2002), pp. 25–49; Aldrich, *Hidden Hand*, pp. 43–63.

6 Cf. Ray Merrick, 'The Russia Committee of the British Foreign Office and the Cold War, 1946–47', *Journal of Contemporary History*, vol. 20, no. 3 (1985), pp. 453–68.

7 Wilford, 'The Information Research Department'.

8 Cf. Ritchie Ovendale, 'William Strang and the Permanent Under-Secretary's Committee', in John Zametica (ed.), *British Officials and British Foreign Policy, 1945–50* (Leicester: Leicester University Press, 1990), pp. 212–27.

9 TNA: PRO CAB134/2: AC (M) (51) 3: note by the Secretary of the Cabinet, 19 May 1951. On the AC (O) Committee, see also Chikara Hashimoto, 'British Security Liaison in the Middle East: The Introduction of Police/Security Advisers and the Lebanon–Iraq–Jordan "Anti-Communist Triangle" from 1949 to 1958', *INS*, vol. 27, no. 6 (2012), pp. 850–4; Rory Cormac, 'The Pinprick Approach: Whitehall's Top-Secret Anti-Communist Committee and the Evolution of British Covert Action Strategy', *Journal of Cold War Studies*, vol. 16, no, 3 (2014), pp. 5–28.

10 See TNA: PRO CAB134/53: Committee on Communism, from May until December 1949.

11 TNA: PRO PREM8/1365: Annual Report on Strategic Policy by the Commandant of the Imperial Defence College, Air Chief Marshal Sir John Slessor, 20 July 1948.

12 TNA: PRO PREM8/1365: PM/49/69: minute by Ernest Bevin to PM, 19 April 1949.

13 The committee was also referred to by the names of the chairs, such as the 'Jebb Committee', the 'Dixon Committee' or even the 'Cold War Committee'. Cf. TNA: PRO KV4/472: the Liddell Diaries, 25 May, 13 June, 22 June, 14 November, 1 December 1950; PRO KV4/473: the Liddell Diaries, 6 February 1951. Note that, although the Russia Committee, which he also chaired, is mentioned, not surprisingly, Sir Gladwyn Jebb mentions nothing at all about the AC (O) Committee in his memoirs. See Lord Gladwyn, *The Memoirs of Lord Gladwyn* (London: Weidenfeld & Nicolson, 1972), pp. 226–7.

14 Cf. TNA: PRO PREM8/1365: note by Sir Norman Brook to Mr Helsby, 13 February 1950; PRO CAB134/3: AC (O) (49) 1: note by the Secretary of the Cabinet, 'Composition and Terms of Reference', 31 December 1949. TNA: PRO CAB21/2992: letter by John Shaw of MI5 to P. Mason of FO, 19 February 1953; letter by J. A. Harrison of MI5 to C. A. L. Cliffe of Cabinet Office, 15 December 1953.

15 TNA: PRO PREM8/1365: minute by Ernest Bevin to Clement Attlee, 19 April 1949; PRO CAB134/4: AC (O) (50) 1st meeting: minute, 'Terms of Reference and Procedure of the Committee', 25 January 1950.

16 Other members included Lord President, Foreign Secretary, Chancellor of the Exchequer and Minister of Defence. See TNA: PRO CAB134/2: AC (M) (49) 1: note by the Secretary of the Cabinet, 31 December 1949.

17 TNA: PRO PREM8/1365: note, 'The Cold War', by the Commandant of the Imperial Defence College, annex A to Annual Report on Strategic Policy, Top Secret, 20 July 1948. On Slessor, see Aldrich, *Hidden Hand*, pp. 145–9.

18 TNA: PRO CAB21/5003: agenda for 'meeting of Ministerial Committee on Communism' by Sir Norman Brook to PM, 20 December 1950. The AC (M) Committee indeed approved MI6's 'full cooperation with the Americans' on anti-Communist activities behind the Iron Curtain. See TNA: PRO CAB21/5003: letter by PM Office to C. A. L. Cliffe of Cabinet Office, 21 December 1950.

19 Richard J. Aldrich (ed.), *Espionage, Security and Intelligence in Britain, 1945–1970* (Manchester: Manchester University Press, 1998), pp. 191–2; Aldrich, *Hidden Hand*, pp 161–6; Philip H. J.

Davies, *MI6 and the Machinery of Spying* (Frank Cass: London, 2004), pp. 199–211, 217–19.

20 NSC Directive 10/2 (1948), quoted in William Leary (ed.), *The Central Intelligence Agency: History and Documents* (Tuscaloosa: University of Alabama Press, 1984), pp. 131–3. On the Doolittle Report, see *Report on Covert Activities of the Central Intelligence Agency*, available at <http://cryptome.org/cia-doolittle.pdf> (last accessed 29 August 2016).

21 On 'collegiality', see Michael Herman, *Intelligence Power in Peace and War* (Cambridge: RIIA, 1996), pp. 259, 269–70; Michael Goodman, 'The British Way in Intelligence', in Matthew Grant (ed.), *The British Way in Cold Warfare: Intelligence, Diplomacy and the Bomb, 1945–1975* (London: Continuum, 2009), pp. 136–7.

22 Aldrich, *Hidden Hand*, pp. 13–15, 43–63.

23 Ibid. pp. 179, 315–19, 324–41. For instance, Aldrich asserts that 'by 1951 the desire of the British military to do something about winning the Cold War was being effectively contained'. Ibid. p. 319.

24 TNA: PRO CO1035/116: COS (55)262: memorandum by the Chiefs of Staff, 'Cold War – Countering Covert Aggression', 12 October 1955; also in PRO DEFE13/331, which contains an extra page.

25 Ibid.

26 TNA: PRO PREM11/1582: PM/55/142: minute by Macmillan to PM, Top Secret, 19 October 1955.

27 Dorril, *MI6*, pp. 481–517.

28 TNA: PRO PREM11/1582: PM55/142: minute by Harold Macmillan to PM, 19 October 1955.

29 TNA: PRO PREM11/1582: minute by Norman Brook to PM, 21 October 1955.

30 Ibid. MI6's special political actions being conducted against the Soviet Bloc at the time of 1955 were unclear from this report, but existing literature indicates some activities against them. On Operation Lyautey, see Aldrich, *Hidden Hand*, pp. 178–9; Bower, *Perfect English Spy*, pp. 261–2; Paul Maddrell, 'British Intelligence through the Eyes of the Stasi: What the Stasi's Records Show about the Operations of British Intelligence in Cold War Germany', *INS*, vol. 27, no. 1 (2012), pp. 54–5; Paul Maddrell, 'What We Have Discovered about the Cold War Is What We Already Knew: Julius Mader and the Western Secret Services during the Cold War', *Cold War History*, vol. 5, no. 2 (2005), pp. 250–1. See also Dorril, *MI6*,

pp. 483–517; Paul Maddrell, *Spying on Science* (Oxford: Oxford University Press, 2006), pp. 176–204.

31 TNA: PRO PREM11/1582: minute by Norman Brook to PM, 21 October 1955.

32 Ibid. It also recorded that 'One of the disadvantages of the term "cold war" is that it has tempted the Chiefs of Staff to think that it is their business. This Committee [the AC (O) Committee] was originally appointed at a time when the Chiefs of Staff were restive about the conduct of foreign policy and thought that the Foreign Office were not doing enough to counter Communist encroachments abroad ... Now that the risk of "hot war" has become more remote, the Chiefs of Staff have again become restive about the conduct of the "cold war".'

33 TNA: PRO CO1035/116: minute by D. Watson to Sir T. Lloyd, 21 February 1956.

34 Referring to this incident, Duncan Watson, head of the newly established ISD of the Colonial Office, recorded in his minute to Sir Thomas Lloyds, the Permanent Under-Secretary of State for the Colonies, that 'you may wish to let the Secretary of State know how Sir N. Brook reacted'. TNA: PRO CO1035/116: minute by D. Watson to Sir T. Lloyd, 21 February 1956.

35 TNA: PRO PREM11/1582: minute by Brook to PM, 28 November 1955. There was also a similar episode in 1949. See Aldrich, *Hidden Hand*, p. 316.

36 TNA: PRO CAB21/5003: memorandum by G. P. Young to Norman Brook, 'AC (O) and AC (M)', 31 January 1955.

37 Minute by Patrick Dean to Sir I. Kirkpatrick, 31 December 1955. OPS/1/55, obtained under the FOIA at my request (REF: 1258-12), 8 March 2013.

38 Minute by Sir I. Kirkpatrick to the Foreign Secretary, 13 February 1956. OPS/1/56, obtained under the FOIA at my request (REF: 1258-12), 8 March 2013, which states: 'For example, they constantly allege that the Foreign Office block *all* proposals for action against the Communists. This they are told by some of their low-level representatives.' Original emphasis.

39 TNA: PRO PREM11/1582: minute by Norman Brook to PM, 28 November 1955.

40 Note of a Cabinet meeting 'Counter-Subversion', OPS/1/56, S.50/94/4/1st meeting, 24 February 1956. Obtained under the FOIA at my request (REF: 1258-12), 8 March 2013.

41 TNA: PRO CAB130/114: GEN 520/1st meeting, 'Committee on

Counter-Subversion in Colonial Territories', 16 March 1956. It was composed of the representatives of the Foreign, Colonial and Commonwealth Offices, Ministry of Defence, MI6 and MI5, excluding the Chiefs of Staff. After the Colonial Policy Committee ceased to exist in late 1963 as a consequence of the reorganisation of Cabinet committees and government departments, the Committee on Counter-Subversion was renamed the 'Counter-Subversive Committee' and placed under the new Official Committee on Defence and Overseas Policy. See also TNA: PRO CAB21/5379, the file entitled, 'Counter-Subversion'.

42 Minute by the Foreign Office 'The Russia Committee and the Overseas Planning Committee', 18 July 1957. O/1/57. Obtained under the FOIA at my request (REF: 1258-12), 8 March 2013.

43 Minute by Patrick Dean to Sir I. Kirkpatrick, 31 December 1955. OPS/1/55; note of a Cabinet meeting 'Counter-Subversion', OPS/1/56, S.50/94/4/1st meeting, 24 February 1956. Obtained under the FOIA at my request (REF: 1258-12), 8 March 2013. This was at the suggestion of Selwyn Lloyd 'in order to keep the Chiefs of Staff informed' of counter-subversive activities in foreign countries. TNA: PREM11/1582: minute by Brook to PM, 23 February 1956.

44 Minute by Patrick Dean to Sir I. Kirkpatrick, 31 December 1955. OPS/1/55, obtained under the FOIA at my request (REF: 1258-12), 8 March 2013.

45 Ibid.

46 Note of a Cabinet meeting 'Counter-Subversion', OPS/1/56, S.50/94/4/1st meeting, 24 February 1956. Obtained under the FOIA at my request (REF: 1258-12), 8 March 2013.

47 TNA: PRO PREM11/1582: memorandum by Anthony Eden, 10 December 1955.

48 Ibid.

49 On the development of the JIC in 1957, cf. Rory Cormac, 'A Whitehall "Showdown"?: Colonial Office–Joint Intelligence Committee Relations in the Mid-1950s', *The Journal of Imperial and Commonwealth History*, vol. 39, no. 2 (2011), pp. 249–67; Michael Herman, *Intelligence Services in the Information Age* (London: Frank Cass, 2001), ch. 5.

50 Minute by Patrick Dean to M. S. Williams, 'Organisation of Intelligence in the Foreign Office', 22 December 1955. Obtained under the FOIA at my request (REF: 1258-12), 8 March 2013.

51 Ibid.

52 Dean emphasised that the expressions 'Communists' or 'Sino/ Soviet' being used in his minute were not to 'denote purely Communist or Russian/Chinese plans: they would include also extreme nationalist plans etc., which are likely to receive support and comfort from the Sino-Soviet bloc and local Communist movements'. Ibid.

53 TNA: PRO PREM11/1582: memorandum by Anthony Eden, 10 December 1955.

54 Letter by Sir Ivone Kirkpatrick to Ambassador/Minister overseas, 17 May 1956. OPS/1/56, obtained under the FOIA at my request (REF: 1258-12), 8 March 2013.

55 Ibid.

56 TNA: PRO PREM11/1582: PM/55/142: minute by Macmillan to PM, Top Secret, 19 October 1955.

57 Ibid.

58 Quoted in F. S. Northedge, 'Britain and the Middle East', in Ritchie Ovendale (ed.), *The Foreign Policy of the British Labour Governments, 1945–1951* (Leicester: Leicester University Press, 1984), p. 149. See also Peter Hennessy, *Never Again: Britain 1945–1951* (London: Vintage, 1992), pp. 239–40.

59 Louis, *British Empire in the Middle East*, p. 10.

60 Scott Lucas, 'The Path to Suez: Britain and the Struggle for the Middle East, 1953–56', in Ann Deighton (ed.), *Britain and the First Cold War* (London: Macmillan, 1990), pp. 253–72; Ritchie Ovendale, 'Egypt and the Suez Base Agreement', in John W. Young (ed.), *The Foreign Policy of Churchill's Peacetime Administration 1951–1955* (Leicester: Leicester University Press, 1988), pp. 135–58.

61 The foundation of the Pact was cooperation between the so-called Northern Tier countries, Iraq and Turkey, in February 1955. Reid, 'The "Northern Tier" and the "Baghdad Pact"'.

62 TNA: PRO FO371/121261: V1073/294G: COS (56) 270: report by Chiefs of Staff Committee, 'United Kingdom Commitments under the Baghdad Pact', 13 July 1956.

63 Among sources and scholarly works on post-war imperial defence strategy, cf. Gorst, '"We must cut our coat according to our cloth"'; Bullock, *Ernest Bevin*, p. 215; Ovendale, 'William Strang', p. 217. See also Michael Goodman, *The Official History of the Joint Intelligence Committee, vol. 1* (London: Routledge, 2014), pp. 348–9.

64 For discussions about war planning including the DTC and the Government War Book, see Peter Hennessy, *The Secret State:*

Preparing for the Worst, 1945–2010, 2nd edn (London: Penguin, 2010).

65 The backbone of it remained the same but was constantly reviewed and revised by relevant departments throughout the Cold War. Cf. TNA: PRO CAB21/3420: file entitled 'Departmental War Books: Reports of Progress on Preparation', from November 1952 to August 1953, which includes MI5.

66 TNA: PRO CAB175/1: Government War Book, 'Chapter III: Internal Security Measures', November 1948. See also PRO KV4/470: the Liddell Diaries, 27 July, 31 December 1948; PRO KV4/471: the Liddell Diaries, 1 January, 21 April 1949. The authorised history of MI5 testifies that they kept a close eye on the Communist Party of Great Britain (CPGB) lest they had to act against them in the event of war. See Andrew, *Defence of the Realm*.

67 TNA: PRO CAB21/3419: DTC (52)1, Defence (Transition) Committee, 'Preparation of Departmental War Books', 19 December 1950; letters by Guy Liddell, DDG of MI5, to Brigadier A. T. Cornwall-Jones, Secretary of War Book Sub-Committee of the DTC, Cabinet Office, 28 November 1950, 12 December 1951.

68 Note that the 1951 Government War Book was more relevant to SIME, which included 'limited war', TNA: PRO CAB21/3393.

69 Note that TNA: PRO CAB158 and PRO CAB159 series contain the JIC estimates which regularly assessed the Soviet military threat to the Middle East area.

70 For the case of the colonies, see TNA: PRO CO537/5082: Defence Transition Committee: Government War Book Sub-Committee: 'Evacuation of Civilian Population from Certain Colonies in the Event of War' (1949).

71 The exception was Israel.

72 TNA: PRO CAB158/9: JIC (50) 20: memorandum, 'Communist Influence in the Middle East', 21 April 1950.

73 TNA: PRO CAB81/133: JIC (46) 70 (0) (FINAL), 'The Spread of Communism throughout the World and the Extent of Its Direction from Moscow', 23 September 1946; PRO CAB159/5: JIC (49) 28th meeting, 'Scale and Nature of Attack on the Colonies', 16 March 1949; also annex to JIC (48) 128 (Final) Revise, 'Fifth Column Activities', 11 January 1949.

74 TNA: PRO CAB134/4: AC (O) (50) 18th meeting of Cabinet Official Committee on Communism (Overseas): minute, 'Communist Influence in the Middle East', 2 June 1950.

75 Ibid.

76 Minute by Patrick Dean to the Foreign Secretary, 19 March 1956. Obtained under the FOIA at my request (REF: 1258-12), 8 March 2013. Emphasis added. As noted earlier, the JIB was also a member of the Overseas Planning Committee, but the link with the JIB before the reorganisation in 1955/6 is unclear. On the JIB, see Huw Dylan, 'The Joint Intelligence Bureau: (Not So) Secret Intelligence for the Post-War World', *INS*, vol. 27, no. 1 (2012), pp. 27–45. See also Huw Dylan, *Defence Intelligence and the Cold War* (Oxford: Oxford University Press, 2014).

77 Goodman, *Official History*, pp. 215–18; Richard J. Aldrich, 'Secret Intelligence for a Post-War World: Reshaping the British Intelligence Community, 1944–51', in Aldrich (ed.), *British Intelligence, Strategy and the Cold War, 1945–51*, pp. 16–19; Cf. Michael Goodman, 'Learning to Walk: The Origins of the UK's Joint Intelligence Committee', *IJIC*, vol. 21, no. 1 (2008), pp. 40–58; Herman, *Intelligence Services*, pp. 112–29.

78 Andrew, *Defence of the Realm*.

79 Ibid. p. 443; Bower, *Perfect English Spy*, pp. 219–20; Dorril, *MI6*, p. 31; Walton, *Empire of Secrets*, pp. 23–4.

80 SIME Charter, para. 3. See Appendix.

81 Keith Jeffery, *MI6: The History of the Secret Intelligence Service, 1909–1949* (London: Bloomsbury, 2010), pp. 620–1.

82 Davies, *MI6*, pp. 175–92; Philip H. J. Davies, 'Organizational Politics and the Development of Britain's Intelligence Producer/Consumer Interface', *INS*, vol. 10, no. 4 (1995), pp. 113–32, pp. 113–32; Aldrich, *Espionage, Security and Intelligence*, pp. 27–9. Private information obtained through an interview.

83 Aldrich, *Espionage, Security and Intelligence*, pp. 191–2; Aldrich, *Hidden Hand*, pp 161–6; Davies, *MI6*, pp. 199–211, 217–19.

84 Christopher Andrew once noted that 'unlike any previous prime minister, Churchill was sometimes in danger of showing too much enthusiasm for secret intelligence and too much hastiness in using it'. Christopher Andrew, 'Churchill and Intelligence', *INS*, vol. 3, no. 3 (1988), p. 192.

85 On his use of MI6, a notable example is in Iran in 1953. Churchill famously said to Kim Roosevelt, who briefed Churchill on Operation Ajax/Boot, '"Young man," ... "if I had been but a few years younger, I would have loved nothing better than to have served under your command in this great venture!"' Quoted in Roosevelt, *Countercoup*, p. 207. See also Andrew, 'Churchill and Intelligence', p. 182.

86 On MI6's plot against Nasser, see Douglas Dodds-Parker, *Political Eunuch* (Ascot: Springwood, 1986), pp. 102–4; Lucas, *Divided We Stand*, pp. 193–5. See also obituary of John McGlashan of MI6, *The Telegraph*, 10 September 2010.

87 Nigel J. Ashton, 'Macmillan and the Middle East', in Richard Aldous and Sabine Lee (eds), *Harold Macmillan and Britain's World Role* (Basingstoke: Macmillan, 1996), p. 37.

88 TNA: PRO PREM11/1582: PM/55/142: minute by Macmillan to PM, Top Secret, 19 October 1955.

89 Cf. Dorril, *MI6*, pp. 529–677; Jones, 'The "Preferred Plan"'; Lucas and Morey, 'Hidden "Alliance"'; Jones, *Britain and the Yemen Civil War 1962–65*; Mawby, 'The Clandestine Defence of Empire'; Bower, *Perfect English Spy*, pp. 185–201.

90 Woodhouse, *Something Ventured*, pp. 132–3.

91 The King's College London Liddell Hart Military Archives (KCLHMA): GB0099 the Private Papers of Col. Hon. Christopher Montague Woodhouse (hereafter Woodhouse Papers) 8/1: letter by Woodhouse (recipient unknown), classified confidential, 10 December 1954. His response was, 'I said jokingly: "You tell that to the Colonial Office!"' The recipient of the letter was perhaps 'C'.

92 TNA: PRO PREM11/1582: PM/55/142: minute by Macmillan to PM, Top Secret, 19 October 1955. Emphasis added.

93 TNA: PRO FO371/121283: V10710/2: letter by A. A. Dudley, Singapore, to W. D. Allen, FO, 24 January 1956.

94 Minute by Patrick Dean to the Foreign Secretary, 19 March 1956. Obtained under the FOIA at my request (REF: 1258-12), 8 March 2013.

95 Minute by Patrick Dean to the Foreign Secretary, 16 December 1955. Obtained under the FOIA at my request (REF: 1258-12), 8 March 2013.

96 TNA: PRO PREM11/1582: minute by Norman Brook to PM, 21 October 1955. Emphasis added.

97 Goodman, *Official History*, p. 363.

98 It has been the subject of numerous studies, including Lucas, *Divided We Stand*; Ashton, *Eisenhower, Macmillan and the Problem of Nasser*; Ritchie Ovendale, *Britain, the United States and the Transfer of Power in the Middle East, 1945–1962* (London: Leicester University Press, 1996); Stephen J. Blackwell, 'A Transfer of Power? Britain, the Anglo-American Relationship and the Cold War in the Middle East, 1957–1962', in Michael F. Hopkins,

M. Kandiah and G. Staerck (eds), *Cold War Britain, 1945–1964: New Perspectives* (Basingstoke: Palgrave, 2003), pp. 168–79; Tore T. Petersen, *The Middle East between the Great Powers* (London: Macmillan, 2000).

99 Cf. Nicholas Thatcher, 'Reflections on US Foreign Policy towards Iraq in the 1950s', in Robert Fernea and Wm. Roger Louis (eds), *The Iraqi Revolution of 1958* (London: I. B. Tauris, 1991), pp. 62–76; Frederick Axelgard, 'US Support for the British Position in Pre-Revolutionary Iraq', in Fernea and Louis (eds), *The Iraqi Revolution of 1958*, pp. 77–94. See also Wilbur Crane Eveland, *Ropes of Sand: America's Failure in the Middle East* (London: W. W. Norton, 1980), pp. 46–7, 49; Waldemar Gallman, *Iraq under General Nuri: My Recollections of Nuri al-Said, 1954–58* (Baltimore: Johns Hopkins University Press, 1964), pp. 182–99.

100 Ovendale, *Britain, the United States and the Transfer of Power*, pp. 1–23, 242–7.

101 Louis and Robinson, 'The Imperialism of Decolonization', p. 462.

102 See Nigel J. Ashton, 'Harold Macmillan and the "Golden Days" of Anglo-American Relations Revisited, 1957–63', *Diplomatic History*, vol. 29, no. 4 (2005), pp. 691–723; Nigel J. Ashton, *Kennedy, Macmillan and the Cold War: The Irony of Interdependence* (New York: Palgrave Macmillan, 2002).

103 Dwight D. Eisenhower Presidential Library: Box 48, file folder 'Syria (3)': memorandum of conference, Dwight D. Eisenhower, Secretary Dulles, Mr. Loy Henderson, Secretary Rountree, Secretary Quarles, General Twining, General Whisenand, General Cabell, Mr. Wisner, General Cutler, General Goodpaster, 7 September 1957.

104 Cf. Scott Lucas and Ray Kakeyh, 'Alliance and Balance: The Anglo-American Relationship and Egyptian Nationalism, 1950–57', *Diplomacy and Statecraft*, vol. 7, no. 3 (1996), pp. 631–51; Lucas, *Divided We Stand*; Aldrich, *Hidden Hand*.

105 Cf. Bradley Smith, *The Ultra-Magic Deals: And the Most Secret Special Relationship, 1940–1946* (Novato, CA: Presidio, 1993); Jeffrey Richelson and Desmond Ball, *The Ties That Bind* (Boston: Allen & Unwin, 1985).

106 Cf. Cohen, 'The Strategic Role of the Middle East after the War; Cohen, *Fighting World War Three*; Cohen, 'From "Cold" to "Hot" War .

107 United States National Archives & Records Administration

(hereafter NARA): RG226: Entry 120: Box 19: Folder 81: SIME security summaries, 1945. This has also been noted by Richard Aldrich, 'Never-Never Land and Wonderland? British and American Policy on Intelligence Archives', *Contemporary Record*, vol. 8, no. 1 (1994), p. 150, n.23.

108 Essential memoirs include Woodhouse, *Something Ventured*, chs 8–9; Roosevelt, *Countercoup*; Wilber, 'Clandestine Service History'.

109 Eden noted: 'it was impossible without the Americans'. Woodhouse, *Something Ventured*, p. 133. See also ibid. chs 8–9; KCLHMA: GB0099 Woodhouse Papers 8/1: draft of his autobiography, *Something Ventured*, 16 August 1976. See also Hugh Wilford, *America's Great Game: The CIA's Secret Arabists and the Shaping of the Modern Middle East* (New York: Basic Books, 2013), pp. 160–74.

110 Letter by Sir Ivone Kirkpatrick to Ambassador/Minister overseas, 17 May 1956. OPS/1/56, obtained under the FOIA at my request (REF: 1258-12), 8 March 2013.

111 Minute by Patrick Dean to the Foreign Secretary, 19 March 1956. Obtained under the FOIA at my request (REF: 1258-12), 8 March 2013.

112 TNA: PRO FO371/134072: letter by Sir Charles Johnston, Amman, to E. M. Rose of FO, 6 May 1958. The file has been declassified under the FOIA at my request (REF: 0894-11), 27 October 2011.

113 Charles Johnston, *The Brink of Jordan* (London: Hamish Hamilton, 1972), p. 44.

114 TNA: PRO FO371/134072: letter by Sir Charles Johnston, Amman, to E. M. Rose of FO, 6 May 1958. The file has been declassified under the FOIA at my request (REF: 0894-11), 27 October 2011. 'I doubt whether the American Military Attaché makes any attempt to influence Jordanian staff officers against the British Embassy. He has frequently expressed the opinion that the Jordan Arab Army has been built up on British lines and that it should continue so . . . As for the Jordanians the tendency is to believe that they can get more for the Army from the Americans than they can from us. I should add that there is no sign of a widespread anti-British trend within the Army.'

115 Jack O'Connell, *King's Counsel: A Memoir of War, Espionage, and Diplomacy in the Middle East* (New York: W.W. Norton, 2011), pp. 1–14.

116 Eveland, *Ropes of Sand*, pp. 125, 155–8, 299. See also Wilford, *America's Great Game*, pp. 175–88.
117 Podeh, 'The Perils of Ambiguity'.
118 Ibid. p. 113.
119 TNA: PRO PREM11/2754: MO1/P(58)303: report by the Chief of the Imperial General Staff 'A Policy for the Middle East', 9 August 1958. The file has been declassified under the FOIA at my request (REF: F0029264), 17 March 2012.
120 Report of Central Intelligence Bulletin, 22 September 1959, pp. 3, 5. CIA-RDP79T00975A004700190001-9, available at <http://www.foia.cia.gov/sites/default/files/document_conversions/5829/CIA-RDP79T00975A004700190001-9.pdf > (last accessed 29 August 2016).
121 Minute by Patrick Dean to the Foreign Secretary, 19 March 1956. Obtained under the FOIA at my request (REF: 1258-12), 8 March 2013.
122 TNA: PRO PREM11/2754: ME (M) (59) 6: memorandum 'Middle East Policy' by FO to PM, 10 March 1959. The file has been released under the FOIA at my request (REF: F0029264), 17 March 2012.
123 TNA: PRO PREM11/2754: memorandum 'Short-Term Policy in the Middle East', 23 July 1958; COS (58) 183: memorandum by the Chiefs of Staff 'Position in the Middle East', 28 July 1958. See also PRO PREM11/2754: M87/59: minute by PM to Foreign Secretary, 11 March 1959. The file has been released under the FOIA at my request (REF: F0029264), 17 March 2012. According to *The Macmillan Diaries*, the inclusion of the United States in the Baghdad Pact as a full member had already been in Macmillan's mind in November 1955. See Peter Catterall (ed.), *The Macmillan Diaries: The Cabinet Years 1950–195* (London: Pan Books, 2004), p. 511.

Chapter 2

1 Mohamed Heikal, *Nasser: The Cairo Documents: The Private Papers of Nasser* (London: New English Library, 1972), pp. 24–5. Mohamed Heikal was a close confidant to the Egyptian presidents, such as Col. Gamal Abdul Nasser and Anwar El Sadat.
2 Anwar El Sadat, *Revolt on the Nile* (London: Allan Wingate, 1957), p. 79.

3 John Curry, *The Security Service 1908–1945: The Official History* (Kew: PRO, 1999), pp. 396–9.

4 Christopher Andrew, *Secret Service: The Making of the British Intelligence Community* (Sevenoaks: Sceptre, 1986), p. 684.

5 Ibid.

6 Walton, *Empire of Secrets*, p. 125. See also A. W. Cockerill, *Sir Percy Sillitoe* (London: W. H. Allen, 1975), pp. 178–91; Percy Sillitoe, *Cloak without Dagger* (London: Cassell, 1955), pp. 190–5.

7 Walton, *Empire of Secrets*, pp. 143–5.

8 Andrew, *Defence of the Realm*, p. 332.

9 Walton, *Empire of Secrets*, pp. 145–7. See also Rory Cormac, 'Organizing Intelligence: An Introduction to the 1955 Report on Colonial Security', *INS*, vol. 25, no. 6 (2010), p. 805; Cormac, 'A Whitehall "Showdown"?'; TNA: PRO CAB158/30: annex to JIC (57) 115, 8 November 1957.

10 TNA: PRO CAB158/30: annex to JIC (57) 115, 'Review by the Security Intelligence Adviser of the Development of Intelligence Organisation in Colonial Territories, 1954–1957', 8 November 1957.

11 Andrew, *Defence of the Realm*, p. 462.

12 Walton, *Empire of Secrets*, p. 146.

13 TNA: PRO CAB21/2925: Report on Colonial Security by General Sir Gerald Templer, 23 April 1955, p. 25.

14 TNA: PRO CO1035/55: attachment to ISD 69/70/01, 'Senior Colonial Police Course', 10 May 1956; circular 1280/55, ref: ISD 69/70/01, despatch, 'Special Branch Training', by Alan Lennox-Boyd, Secretary of State for the Colonies, 20 December 1955.

15 TNA: PRO CO885/119: record of the Conference of Colonial Commissioners of Police at the Police College, Ryton-on-Dunsmore, April 1951.

16 See Peter Wright, *Spycatcher* (Richmond, VIC: William Heinemann, 1987), pp. 34–5.

17 TNA: PRO KV4/473: the Liddell Diaries, 8 May 1951.

18 TNA: PRO CAB21/2925: Report on Colonial Security by General Sir Gerald Templer, 23 April 1955, pp. 13, 25.

19 TNA: PRO CAB158/30: annex to JIC (57) 115, 8 November 1957.

20 TNA: PRO CAB134/3: AC (O) (50) 34: circular despatch, 'internal security: lessons of the emergency in Malaya', 11 July 1950;

FO371/80199: J1641/1G: minute by Gladwyn Jebb, 24 February 1950.

21 TNA: PRO CAB134/3: AC (O) (50) 43: memorandum 'Training of Foreign Police Officers', 23 August 1950.

22 Ismael, *Communist Movement in the Arab World*, pp. 1–16.

23 TNA: PRO FO371/82410: E41019/1G: letter by Sir Henry Mack, Baghdad, to Ernest Bevin, 7 November 1950.

24 Cf. TNA: PRO FO371/80354: JE10111/10G: report by SIME to G. N. Jackson, 'Communism in Egypt, June 1949–June 1950', 15 July 1950; PRO FO371/82704: ET1015/4G: report by HQ Arab Legion, Amman, 'Communism on the West Bank', 8 August 1950; PRO FO371/95274: RK1018/6: report by Scott Fox, Ankara, to Anthony Eden, 'Communism in Turkey', 10 December 1951.

25 Laqueur, *Communism and Nationalism in the Middle East*, p. 174.

26 On Attiyah, see Batatu, *Old Social Classes*, pp. 465, 479, 486, 488, 553, 606.

27 Private Papers of Emir Farid Chehab in possession of the family of Emir Farid Chehab (hereafter Chehab Papers 'F'): report by Keith Wheeler [sic], Middle East correspondence of TIME, 'Subject Communism in the Middle East', 13 November 1954, designated '4Q', p. 2.

28 TNA: PRO KV4/473: the Liddell Diaries, 25 June 1951.

29 TNA: PRO FO371/81904: E1018/5: report by Glubb Pasha 'Communism in Syria, Lebanon and Jordan', 20 April 1950.

30 Cf. Caroz, *Arab Secret Services*, p. 7; Said Aburish, *Beirut Spy* (London: Bloomsbury, 1990), *passim*. See also Andrew Rathmell, *Secret War in the Middle East: The Covert Struggle for Syria, 1949–61* (London: I. B. Tauris, 1995).

31 TNA: PRO FO371/81904: E1018/5: report by Glubb Pasha 'Communism in Syria, Lebanon and Jordan', 20 April 1950.

32 TNA: PRO FO371/73476: J1781/G: minute by R. W. Bailey, 1 March 1949.

33 TNA: PRO CAB134/3: AC (O) (50) 28: draft memorandum by the Joint Secretaries, 'Constitutional and Administrative Measures to Combat Communism, particularly in the Middle East', 15 June 1950; AC (O) (50) 44: draft despatch to His Majesty's Representatives: Baghdad, Damascus, Beirut, Amman and Tehran, September 1950.

34 TNA: PRO FO371/91177: E1017/2G: letter by Sir Ralph Stevenson, British Ambassador to Cairo to Patrick Reilly, 28 February 1951;

E1017/3G: memorandum by H. A. Dudgeon, 'Anti-Communist Measures in Middle Eastern Countries', 1 March 1951.

35 TNA: PRO CAB134/3: AC (O) (50) 28: draft memorandum by the Joint Secretaries, 'Constitutional and Administrative Measures to Combat Communism, particularly in the Middle East', 15 June 1950; AC (O) (50) 44: draft despatch to His Majesty's Representatives: Baghdad, Damascus, Beirut, Amman and Tehran, September 1950.

36 TNA: PRO FO371/82391: EP1641/2G: minute by [name removed, presumably by MI5] to G. N. Jackson of PUSD, 3 August 1950; PRO FO371/82314: EP1017/17G: letter by Haldane-Porter of MI5 to G. N. Jackson, 26 October 1950.

37 TNA: PRO KV4/472: the Liddell Diaries, 30 October 1950.

38 TNA: PRO FO371/82391: EP1641/1G: letter by Francis Shepherd, Ambassador to Persia, to Michael Wright, 26 June 1950; PRO FO371/82391: EP1641/3G: minute by Nigel Bicknell, 18 September 1950.

39 Ibid. 6 November 1950. Guy Liddell gave a lecture about 'a rough idea' of the roles and responsibilities of MI5; Roger Hollis, Director of C Division (Security), talked about protective security; and Malcolm Cumming gave a lecture on 'technical aids' with 'the crudest form of microphone'.

40 TNA: PRO FO371/82314: EP1017/17G: letter by Haldane-Porter of MI5 to G. N. Jackson, 26 October 1950.

41 TNA: PRO KV4/472: the Liddell Diaries, 6 November 1950. This was the case not only with the Iranians, but also with the Jordanians. 'Only one of them [Jordanians] could speak much English, but they seemed to think that they had learned something.' Quoted in TNA: PRO KV4/473: the Liddell Diaries, 8 October 1951.

42 Hashimoto, 'British Security Liaison in the Middle East', pp. 857–8, 863.

43 TNA: PRO KV4/473: the Liddell Diaries, 8 October 1951; PRO FO371/81989: E1642/7: letter by Chancery at British Legation, Beirut, to FO, 8 July 1950.

44 TNA: PRO FO371/115796: VQ1643/2: letter by A. R. H. Kellas, Baghdad, to Levant Department, 14 November 1955.

45 TNA: PRO KV4/473: the Liddell Diaries, 7 February 1951.

46 TNA: PRO FO371/80199: J1641/1G: minute by Patrick Reilly, 26 April 1950. Note that while the name of MI6 has been redacted in the 'weeding' process, it is logically, and also easily,

assumed that the redacted word was MI6 by cross-referencing the materials.

47 TNA: PRO FO371/91178: E1018/1G: memorandum by C. E. King, head of the Overseas Planning Section, 7 May 1951.

48 TNA: PRO CAB134/2: AC (M) (51) 4: memorandum, 'The Work of the Official Committee on Communism (Overseas)', 23 June 1951. Archival research does not shed much further light on the meaning of the sentence, 'take steps to segregate and re-educate politically persons . . .'.

49 Minute by Patrick Dean to the Foreign Secretary, 19 March 1956. Obtained under the FOIA at my request (REF: 1258-12), 8 March 2013. Sir Patrick Dean noted in his minute to Sir Ivone Kirkpatrick: 'We have Ministerial approval for expending an extra £25,000 a year on this and we must make sure that full use is made of this.'

50 Martin Thomas, *The French Empire at War, 1940–45* (Manchester: Manchester University Press, 1998); Martin Thomas, *The French Empire between the Wars: Imperialism, Politics and Society* (Manchester: Manchester University Press, 2005).

51 TNA: PRO CAB134/3: AC (O) (50) 18: JIC report (annex), 'Communist Influence in the Middle East', 21 April 1950.

52 Ibid.

53 Ibid.

54 TNA: PRO CAB134/4: AC (O) (50) 18th meeting: minute, 'Communist Influence in the Middle East', 2 June 1950.

55 TNA: PRO FO371/75319: E3456/G: telegram by Houstoun-Boswall to FO, no. 142 of 15 March 1949, which notes: 'the spread of Communism was a great source of anxiety to the Lebanese Government and it was felt that new methods must be devised to meet the menace . . . I think it is important from every point of view to meet this request. What they want advice about is *how* to organise an effective counter espionage against the Communists.'

56 Nicholas Nassif, *Ser Aldawlah: fousol fe tarekh ala'men ala'am 1945–1977* [*State Secret: Chapters in the History of the Sûreté Générale in Lebanon, 1945–1977*] (Lebanon: General Security, 2013), pp. 21–4.

57 See Meir Zamir, 'The "Missing Dimension": Britain's Secret War against France in Syria and Lebanon, 1942–45 – Part II', *Middle Eastern Studies*, vol. 46, no. 6 (2010), pp. 791–899. On the Anglo-French tensions in the region, see also Elie Kedourie, *The Chatham House Version and other Middle-Eastern Studies* (London: Weidenfeld & Nicolson, 1970), ch. 8; A. B. Gaunson,

The Anglo-French Clash in Lebanon and Syria, 1940–45 (London: Macmillan, 1987).

58 TNA: PRO FO371/75319: E3456/G: minute by L. Thirkell, 17 March 1949.

59 Ibid. Note that Mitchell was then in B (Counter-Espionage) Division, later Deputy Director-General of MI5 under Sir Roger Hollis.

60 TNA: PRO FO371/75319: E7476/G: report (Flag C) by Mitchell, 'Lebanon: Defence against Communism', 17 June 1949 (hereafter Mitchell Report), p. 1.

61 Cf. Stephen Longrigg, *Syria and Lebanon under French Mandate* (Oxford: Oxford University Press, 1958), p. 138.

62 Chikara Hashimoto, 'Emir Farid Chehab: Chief of Lebanese Secret Police', in Paul Maddrell, Christopher Moran, Ioanna Iordanou and Mark Stout (eds), *Spy Chiefs: Volume II. Intelligence Leaders in Europe, the Middle East, and Asia* (Washington DC: Georgetown University Press, 2018).

63 TNA: PRO FO371/75319: E8783/G: report by D. Beaumont-Nesbitt to Head Office [MI5] (B1) and SIME (B), 27 June 1949 (hereafter Beaumont-Nesbitt Report).

64 Ibid. The name of David Beaumont-Nesbitt also appears in William Magan, *Middle Eastern Approaches* (Norwich: Michael Russell, 2001), p. 149.

65 Ibid.

66 Ibid.

67 Youmna Asseily and Ahmad Asfahani (eds), *A Face in the Crowd* (London: Stacey International, 2007), p. xi.

68 Hashimoto, 'Emir Farid Chehab'.

69 Chehab Papers 'F': report by Keith Wheeler [sic], Middle East correspondent of *TIME*, 'Subject Communism in the Middle East', 13 November 1954, designated '4Q', p. 14.

70 Asseily and Asfahani, *Face in the Crowd*, p. 191.

71 Ibid. pp. 9, 193–4, 202.

72 TNA: PRO FO371/75319: E7476/G: report (Flag D) by Mitchell, 'Suggested Recommendation to Be Tendered to Prime Minister at Second Interview', 17 June 1949.

73 Hashimoto, 'Emir Farid Chehab'.

74 Mitchell Report, p. 3.

75 Beaumont-Nesbitt Report.

76 TNA: PRO FO371/75319: telegram from Beirut to FO, 18 July 1949.

77 TNA: PRO FO371/75319: E10297/G: letter by R. C. Mayall, Sudan Gov. Agency, to Thirkell, 23 August 1949; PRO FO371/82267: EL1015/13G: letter by Ronald Beiley to G. W. Furlonge, 14 March 1950.

78 TNA: PRO CAB134/4: AC (O) (50) 18th meeting: minute, 'Communist Influence in the Middle East', 2 June 1950.

79 Asseily and Asfahani, *Face in the Crowd*, p. 10.

80 TNA: PRO FO371/91177: E1017/6G: letter by Ronald W. Bailey, acting Chargé d'Affaires in Beirut, to Herbert Morrison, Foreign Secretary then, 1 June 1951; PRO KV4/473: the Liddell Diaries, 25 June 1951.

81 TNA: PRO FO371/82267: EL1015/16G: letter by Houstoun-Boswell to Bevin, 28 November 1950.

82 TNA: PRO FO371/91178: E1018/1G: minute by H. A. Dudgeon, 18 May 1951.

83 TNA: PRO KV4/473: the Liddell Diaries, 25 June 1951.

84 Ibid.

85 TNA: PRO CAB134/3: AC (O) (50) 18: JIC report (annex), 'Communist Influence in the Middle East', 21 April 1950.

86 TNA: PRO FO371/82314: EP1017/3G: letter by Colonel D. K. Betts to Brigadier V. Boucher of DDMI, 'Defection of Soviet Subject', 27 January 1950.

87 TNA: PRO FO371/82314: EP1017/1G: minute by H. A. A. Hankey, 2 February 1950.

88 TNA: PRO FO371/82314: EP1017/1G: minute by A. Leavett, 26 January 1950.

89 TNA: PRO FO371/82314: EP1017/3G: letter by Colonel D. K. Betts to Brigadier V. Boucher of DDMI, 'Defection of Soviet Subject', WO, no. 307 of 27 January 1950, which states that 'Vassilev was, I understand, deputy manager of the Soviet controlled transport company named "Iransovtrans" which operates in Persia. The C. G. S. [General Razmara] said that Vassilev brought with him a number of letters which showed that certain Soviet controlled commercial concerns in this country were falsifying the figures submitted to the Persian Minister of Finance, in order to turn over undeclared profits to the financing of Soviet propaganda and espionage in this country.'

90 TNA: PRO FO371/82314: EP1017/3G: letter by Colonel D. K. Betts to Brigadier V. Boucher of DDMI, WO, no. 518 of 28 January 1950.

91 TNA: PRO FO371/82314: EP1017/11G: report by Haldane-Porter

of MI5, 'Report on Visit to Tehran', 14 April 1950 (hereafter Haldane-Porter Report).

92 Note that Magan's wartime experience in Iran as a liaison officer of the Intelligence Bureau in India with the Persian government can be found in Magan, *Middle Eastern Approaches*. See also Middle East Centre Archive (hereafter MECA), St Antony's College, Oxford: Private Papers of W. M. T. Magan and Alan Roger (MAGAN/ROGER), Collection GB165-0199: letter by Magan to Denis Wright, 3 February 1981.

93 TNA: PRO FO371/82314: EP1017/1G: minute by H. A. A. Hankey, 2 February 1950; EP1017/4G: minute by H. A. A. Hankey, 8 February 1950. His brief visit was proposed to be kept secret and thus he would have to be sent 'in the guise of an officer from G. H. Q. [General Headquarters in Cairo]'.

94 TNA: PRO FO371/82314: EP1017/4G: minute by Sir William Strang, 9 February 1950.

95 TNA: PRO FO371/82314: EP1017/4G: minute by H. A. A. Hankey, 21 February 1950; EP1017/1G: telegram by FO to Tehran, 24 February 1950; EP1017/6G: telegram by FO to Tehran, no. 109 of 9 March 1950; EP1017/8G: letter by Haldane-Porter of MI5 to H. A. A. Hankey, 9 March 1950.

96 TNA: PRO FO371/82314: EP1017/1G: telegram by FO to Tehran, 24 February 1950.

97 Haldane-Porter Report, p. 4.

98 Ibid.

99 Ibid.

100 Ibid.

101 Ibid.

102 Cf. TNA: PRO FO371/82314: EP1017/3G: letter by Colonel D. K. Betts to Brigadier V. Boucher of DDMI, 28 January 1950. Indeed, MI6 was given responsibility for intelligence collection in Iran after the end of the Second World War. See the India Office Library Records (IOLR), the British Library: L/WS/1/1570: cipher telegram from the War Office to C-in-C Middle East, C-in-C India, GOC-in-Persia and Iraq, desp. 092320 of August 1945.

103 Haldane-Porter Report, p. 4.

104 Forter was present in Tehran during the period just before the 1953 coup and was also recruited by MI6 and later the Head of Station in Baghdad. Cf. Bower, *Perfect English Spy*, p. 236; Dorril, *MI6*, p. 570; West, *Friends*, p. 122. Forter was also a junior officer of SIME, seconded from the RAF, for a short period in 1947. Cf.

TNA: PRO KV4/438: report by J. C. Robertson, 'Report on Visit to Middle East', 14 April–14 June 1947, p. 8. Forter died in Paris in 1983, when he was the Head of Station there. See Horne, *But What Do You Actually Do?*, p. 55.

105 Haldane-Porter Report.

106 Ibid.

107 Dorril, *MI6*, p. 559.

108 TNA: PRO CAB134/4: AC (O) (50) 18th meeting of the AC (O) Committee: minute, 'Communist Influence in the Middle East', 2 June 1950.

109 TNA: PRO FO371/82314: EP1017/13G: minute by K. G. Younger to PM, 21 June 1950. Note that instead of becoming the Security Adviser in Tehran, Sir 'George' Jenkin took up the post of the Adviser to the Special Branch/Criminal Investigation Department, and was later designated Director of Intelligence in Malaya. He resigned in 1952 due to his differences with the local government over the reorganisation of the Malayan Police. See Leon Comber, *Malaya's Secret Police 1945–60: The Role of the Special Branch in the Malayan Emergency* (Clayton, VIC: Monash University Press, 2008), p. 131.

110 TNA: PRO FO371/82314: EP1017/13G: minute by K. G. Younger, Minister of State at FO, to PM, 'Assistance to the Persian Army in Countering Subversive Activities', 21 June 1950.

111 TNA: PRO FO371/82314: EP1017/18G: minute by PM, C. R. A. 'Assistance to the Persian Army in Countering Subversive Activities', 21 June 1950.

112 The Deputy Director of Intelligence Bureau in India was also the Director of Intelligence in the Bureau. See also Walton, *Empire of Secrets*, pp. 152–3, 173–4, which misspelled Jenkin's name as 'Jenkins'.

113 Haldane-Porter Report.

114 John Briance was then recruited by MI6, and later became a personal assistant to 'C', Sir Dick White. See Bower, *Perfect English Spy*, pp. 172, 209. See also Dorril, *MI6*, p. 570. Note that this assumption is made on the timing of his appointment to the British Embassy in Tehran, and given that MI5 and MI6 were discussing the post at the same time. See TNA: PRO FO371/82314: EP1017/11G: letter by J. V. W. Shaw of MI5 to H. A. A. Hakey, 20 April 1950, which states 'We [MI5] are discussing [redacted, presumably with the name of an MI6 officer] various details in connection with the appointment of a resident British adviser and

have in fact someone in mind for this post.' See also Guy Liddell's entry in his diaries, TNA: PRO KV4/474: the Liddell Diaries, 16 September 1952.

115 TNA: PRO KV4/474: the Liddell Diaries, 16 September 1952.
116 Woodhouse, *Something Ventured*, pp. 110–11.
117 TNA: PRO FO371/82314: EP1017/18G: letter by Sir Francis Shepherd to Bevin, no. 324 of 3 November 1950.
118 TNA: PRO FO371/82314: EP1017/17G: letter by Haldane-Porter to G. N. Jackson, 26 October 1950; PRO FO371/82391: EP1641/1G: letter by Sir Francis Shepherd, Ambassador to Persia, to Michael Wright, 26 June 1950.
119 TNA: PRO FO371/82391: EP1641/1G: letter by Sir Francis Shepherd, Ambassador to Persia, to Michael Wright, 26 June 1950.
120 TNA: PRO FO371/82314: EP1017/18G: letter by Sir Francis Shepherd to Bevin, no. 324 of 3 November 1950.
121 TNA: PRO KV4/474: the Liddell Diaries, 16 September 1952; PRO KV4/475: the Liddell Diaries, 21 April 1953.
122 TNA: PRO FO248/1514: G10101: letter from British Embassy, Tehran, to Sir James Bowker of FO, 12 March 1951.
123 TNA: PRO FO248/1514: G10101: *Pravda* article by Ya. Viktorov, 'Mysterious Doings in Iran', translated by Joint Press Reading Service, 18 March 1951.
124 TNA: PRO FO371/98637: EP1193/1G: letter by Sir George Clutton, Tehran, to Sir James Bowker of FO, 3 June 1952.
125 There was evidence of the presence of MI6 officers in Tehran before and after the Iranian coup in August 1953. Cf. Woodhouse, *Something Ventured*; Cavendish, *Inside Intelligence*, pp. 140–2.
126 On the shifting of British strategy from Egypt to Iraq, see Lucas, 'The Path to Suez'.
127 TNA: PRO CAB134/3: AC (O) (50) 18: JIC report (annex), 'Communist Influence in the Middle East', 21 April 1950.
128 Ibid. For detailed reports on the raid by the Iraqi CID on the ICP in 1949, see TNA: PRO FO371/75130; 75131. See also Batatu, *Old Social Classes*.
129 TNA: PRO FO371/91177: E1017/9G: letter by Sir John Troutbeck to Herbert Morrison, 27 June 1951.
130 TNA: PRO FO371/82410: EQ1019/1G: Letter by Sir Henry Mack to Ernest Bevin, 7 November 1950.
131 On the Point Four Program, see Vaughan, *Failure of American and British Propaganda*, p. 111. See also TNA: PRO FO371/98276: E11345/7: minute, 25 January 1952, enclosing 'United States

Economic and Social Interest in the Middle East', undated; NARA: RG59: 511.80/4/1653, Clark to Sanger, 16 April 1953, enclosing 'Information Policy for the Point IV Program', 3 March 1953.

132 TNA: PRO FO371/104719: EQ1641/9G: letter by Troutbeck to Falla, 13 October 1953.

133 Dorril, *MI6*, pp. 541–2.

134 Although no reference was made to his career in MI5, his service as Head of the Special Branch in India a few years earlier is revealed in his autobiography. Roger Lees, *In the Shade of the Peepul Tree* (private publication, 1998), p. 89.

135 TNA: PRO FO371/104719: EQ1641/9G: minute by Patricia M. Hutchinson, 19 October 1953.

136 TNA: PRO FO371/111043: VQ1641/5: letter by H. S. Stephenson of BMEO to R. Allen, 24 January 1954.

137 TNA: PRO FO371/104719: EQ1641/13G: letter by Troutbeck to Falla, 24 November 1953.

138 TNA: PRO FO371/104719: EQ1641/16G: memorandum by P. Mallet, 'Iraqi Request for Assistance in Re-organising Police', 18 December 1953, which noted that placing a British security/police officer in Iraq would be 'more valuable to nip Communism in the bud than to fight against well-established Communist organisations'.

139 Eveland, *Ropes of Sand*, p. 67.

140 TNA: PRO FO371/104719: EQ1641/16G: memorandum by P. S. Falla, 'Police Expert for Iraq', 23 December 1953; letter by R. Allen of FO to A. E. Drake of Treasury, 30 December 1953.

141 Note that queries by the Foreign Office to the Home Office were readily turned down on the grounds that there were 'no specialists in riot control and no funds with which to second an expert or send a police mission to Iraq'. Cf. TNA: PRO FO371/104719: EQ1641/11G: letter by R. Lloyd-Thomas of Police Division, HO to R. L. Joseph of FO, 10 November 1953; EQ1641/16G: memorandum by P. S. Falla, 'Police Expert for Iraq', 23 December 1953; letter by R. Allen of FO to A. E. Drake of Treasury, 30 December 1953.

142 For instance, while the search for a suitable candidate for the Security Adviser position at the Lebanese Sûreté was being conducted by the Foreign Office, Sir William Houstoun-Boswall complained that MI5 was 'largely responsible' for the failure to find one. MI5 was not responsible for interviewing candidates. See

TNA: PRO FO371/75319: E10297/G: minute by L. G. Thirkell of FO, 14 September 1949.

143 TNA: PRO FO371/104719: EQ1641/9G: letter by Sir John Troutbeck to Falla, 13 October 1953.

144 TNA: PRO FO371/104719: EQ1641/9G: minute by P. L. V. Mallet, 26 October 1953. Although MI5 could not find 'anyone else with the dual qualifications', they instead suggested Sir John Troutbeck assure the Iraqi Interior Minister that he was capable of giving 'considerable under-cover assistance', alongside police advisers who would also be able to advise on CID reorganisation. See TNA: PRO FO371/104719: EQ1641/10G: telegram by FO to Baghdad, 31 October 1953.

145 See TNA: PRO FO371/115796: VQ1643/3: letter by R. W. J. Hooper, Baghdad, to R. M. Hadow, of FO, 2 December 1955. Magan, *Middle Eastern Approaches*, pp. 150–4.

146 TNA: PRO FO371/104719: EQ1641/13G: letter by Troutbeck to Falla, 24 November 1953.

147 TNA: PRO FO371/104719: EQ1641/14G: telegram by Sir J. Troutbeck to FO, 14 December 1953; PRO FO371/111043: VQ1641/1G: letter by H. P. Goodwyn of MI5 to Miss P. M. Hutchinson of FO, 1 January 1953 [sic. 1954]. A passage referring to MI6 has been recovered under the FOIA at my request (REF: 1344-11), 25 January 2012, which clearly states that Jenkin was 'recommended by our friends'. See TNA: PRO FO371/111043: VQ1641/10G: report 'Police and CID Advisers to the Iraq Government', undated (c. March 1954).

148 TNA: PRO FO371/111043: VQ1641/2: letter by M. B. Ramage of CO to Falla, 15 January 1954.

149 TNA: PRO FO371/111043: VQ1641/14G: telegram by FO to Baghdad, no. 334 of 31 March 1954. Lloyd Thomas observed the nature of police and CID work as inseparable, with the latter 'to some extent subordinate' to the former. The Foreign Office commented: 'we cannot guarantee that J [Jenkin] would work happily "with but after" M [MacIntosh]'. A passage recovered under the FOIA at my request (REF: 1344-11, 25 January 2012) states that MacIntosh was 'recommended by our friends [MI6] as an all-rounder'. See TNA: PRO FO371/111043: VQ1641/10G: report 'Police and CID Advisers to the Iraq Government', undated (c. March 1954).

150 TNA: PRO FO371/111043: VQ1641/27: telegram by Sir John Troutbeck to FO, 23 September 1954. On the formation of the

new government, see Lord Birdwood, *Nuri As-Said: A Study in Arab Leadership* (London: Cassell, 1959), p. 227.

151 TNA: PRO FO371/115796: VQ1643/3: letter by R. W. J. Hooper, Baghdad, to R. M. Hadow, of FO, 2 December 1955.

152 TNA: PRO CAB134/2: AC (M) (51) 4: memorandum, 'The Work of the Official Committee on Communism (Overseas)', 23 June 1951. Archival research does not shed much further light on the meaning of the sentence, 'take steps to segregate and re-educate politically persons . . .'.

153 TNA: PRO FO371/119367: JF1022/1G: letter by Sir Michael Wright, Baghdad, to T. E. Bromley, African Department of FO, 17 January 1956; PRO FO371/132519: E1641/1: letter by Sir Michael Wright, Baghdad, to E. M. Rose of FO, 12 May 1958.

154 Ronen Yitzhak, 'The Beginnings of Transjordanian Military Intelligence: A Neglected Aspect of the 1948 War', *Middle East Journal*, vol. 57, no. 3 (2003), pp. 449–68.

155 TNA: PRO CAB134/3: AC (O) (50) 18: JIC report (annex), 'Communist Influence in the Middle East', 21 April 1950.

156 TNA: PRO FO371/81904: E1018/7G: diplomatic despatch by Sir A. Kirkbride, Amman, to Ernest Bevin, 20 October 1950; PRO FO371/81989: E1642/7: letter by Chancery at British Legation, Beirut, to FO, 8 July 1950; PRO FO371/91790: ET1016/4G: minute by J. M. Hunter of FO, 28 September 1951; PRO KV4/473: the Liddell Diaries, 8 October 1951.

157 TNA: PRO FO371/91790: ET1016/4G: letter by Furlonge of FO to Amri Abdul Majid Haidar, Envoy Extraordinary and Minister Plenipotentiary, the Jordan Legation, 29 October 1951.

158 A former commander of the Arab Legion, Peter Young, gives Colonel Coghill's title as the 'Director of CID [Criminal Investigation Department]'. Peter Young, *Bedouin Command with the Arab Legion 1953–1956* (London: William Kimber, 1956), p. 174.

159 James Lunt, *The Arab Legion, 1923–1957* (London: Constable, 1999), pp. 140–1.

160 Cf. TNA: PRO WO216/890: letter by Colonel Sir Patrick Coghill to Major General W. P. Oliver of WO, 27 November 1955.

161 Ibid.

162 Ibid.

163 The Imperial War Museum, London (hereafter IWM): Private Papers of Lieutenant-Colonel Sir Patrick Coghill: memoir/diary, entitled 'Before I Forget . . .', vol. 2, p. 108–9.

164 Ibid. p. 122.

165 Ibid. p. 123.

166 Ibid. p. 123.

167 Ibid. pp. 120–2.

168 Ibid. p. 118.

169 Ibid.

170 IWM: Private Papers of Patrick Coghill, 'Before I Forget . . .', vol. 1, p. 44. Haj Amin al-Hussini had also been closely watched by SIME. Cf. TNA: PRO KV2/2085–2092, all of which are Personal Files of MI5 on him. See also TNA: PRO FO371/111094: telegram by Sir Chapman Andrews, Beirut, to FO, 16 December 1954.

171 TNA: PRO FO371/111043: VQ1641/27: telegram by Sir J. Troutbeck to FO, 18 September 1954.

172 TNA: PRO WO216/890: letter by Colonel Sir Patrick Coghill to Major General W. P. Oliver of WO, 27 November 1955.

173 Asseily and Asfahani, *Face in the Crowd*, p. 68.

174 TNA: PRO FO371/115467: V1016/4: letter from Information Division, Beirut, IRD of FO, 15 June 1955.

175 TNA: PRO FO371/91177: E1017/3G: letter by Furlonge of FO, 4 May 1951. See also PRO CAB134/2: AC (M) (51) 4: memorandum by Pierson Dixon, successor to Sir Gladwyn Jebb, 'The Work of the Official Committee on Communism (Overseas)', 23 June 1951.

176 TNA: PRO FO371/91177: E1017/10G: letter of FO to Sir John Troutbeck, Baghdad, 4 October 1951.

177 TNA: PRO FO371/91177: E1017/10G: minute by H. A. Dudgeon, 5 September 1951.

178 Cf. TNA: PRO WO216/890: report by Colonel Sir Patrick Coghill, 'Jordan and the Baghdad Pact', 26 November 1955; PRO FO371/121423: V1691/1: letter from Ankara to E. M. Rose of FO, 9 January 1956.

179 Cf. TNA: PRO FO371/104890: ET1017/16E: letter from British Embassy, Amman, to Eastern Dept. of FO, 19 March 1953; PRO FO371/110875: VJ1015/2: letter from British Embassy, Amman, to Levant Dept. of FO, 31 March 1954.

180 TNA: PRO FO371/115706: VJ1641/2G: letter by C. B. Duke to C. A. E. Shuckburgh, 3 June 1955. Uriel Dann notes that King Hussein had also been 'toying for over a year with the idea of "demilitarizing" the security services'. See Uriel Dann, *King Hussein and the Challenge of Arab Radicalism: Jordan, 1955– 1967* (Oxford: Oxford University Press, 1989), p. 35. Of course,

in an international context, King Hussein was forced to distance Jordan from the British connection in response to the Egyptian challenge. See Nigel J. Ashton, *King Hussein of Jordan: A Political Life* (London: Yale University Press, 2008), ch. 2.

181 According to Nigel Ashton, he has not found the name of MacIntosh during his archival research at the Hashemite Archives, under the authorisation of King Abdullah. Email exchange, 11 September 2011.

182 The information is derived from the official website of the General Intelligence Department of Jordan, available at <http://www.gid.gov.jo/en/home.html> (last accessed 29 August 2016). The Jordanian Police was reorganised during MacIntosh's four-year tenure in Amman, which laid the foundations for the Jordanian Police and the Security Service today. Evidence of continuity from the reorganisation by MacIntosh was that it was first headed by Colonel Muhammand Rasul Al Kailani, who had been the Deputy Director of the CID, and who had been separated from the Public Security by MacIntosh. See TNA: FO371/170335: EJ1641/2: letter by Sir Roderick Parkes, Ambassador to Jordan, to L. C. W. Figg of Eastern Department, 28 December 1962.

183 TNA: FO371/170335: EJ1641/2: letter by Sir Roderick Parkes, Ambassador to Jordan, to L. C. W. Figg of Eastern Department, 28 December 1962.

184 TNA: FO371/170335: EJ1641/3: letter by Alexander Stirling, First Secretary and Consul in Amman, to P. J. Cairns of FO, 14 February 1963.

185 See Chapter 1. See also O'Connell, *King's Counsel*.

186 TNA: CAB134/4: AC (O) (50) 18th meeting: minute of the AC (O) Committee meeting, 2 June 1950; PRO FO371/82851: letter by C. E. King to Captain Liddell, 6 February 1951.

187 TNA: PRO FO371/91178: E1018/1G: Minute by H. A. Dudgeon, 18 May 1951.

Chapter 3

1 An earlier version of this chapter was published as Chikara Hashimoto, 'Fighting the Cold War or Post-Colonialism?: Britain in the Middle East from 1945 to 1958: Looking through the Records of the British Security Service', *The International History Review*, vol. 36, no. 1 (2014), pp. 19–44.

2 El Sadat, *Revolt on the Nile*, p. 50. Anwar El Sadat was the Egyptian president (1970–81).

3 For brief discussions, see F. H. Hinsley and C. A. G. Simkins, *British Intelligence in the Second World War, vol. 4: Security and Counter-Intelligence* (London: Her Majesty's Stationery Office, 1990), pp. 162–7; Michael Howard, *British Intelligence in the Second World War, vol. 5: Strategic Deception* (London: Her Majesty's Stationery Office, 1990), pp. 31–52, 110. All of the articles on the wartime SIME are by H. O. Dovey. See H. O. Dovey, 'Maunsell and Mure', *INS*, vol. 8, no. 1 (1993), pp. 60–77; 'Security in Syria, 1941–45', *INS*, vol. 6, no. 2 (1991), pp. 418–46; 'The Middle East Intelligence Centre', *INS*, vol. 4, no. 4 (1989), pp. 800–12; 'Operation Condor', *INS*, vol. 4, no. 2 (1989), pp. 357–73; 'The False Going Map at Alam Haifa', *INS*, vol. 4, no. 1 (1989), pp. 165–8; 'The Unknown War: Security in Italy, 1943–45', *INS*, vol. 3, no. 2 (1988), pp. 285–311. For discussion of MI6's role, see West, *Friends*, p. 17; Cavendish, *Inside Intelligence*, chs 4–5; Deacon, *'C'*, ch. 4; Horne, *But What Do You Actually Do?*, chs 3–4. In connection with the Israelis, see Black and Morris, *Israel's Secret Wars*, pp. 74–5. Academic works that refer to SIME in the post-war era include Roger Arditti, 'Security Intelligence in the Middle East (SIME): Joint Security Intelligence Operations in the Middle East, c. 1939–58', *INS*, vol. 31, no. 3 (2016), pp. 369–96; Aldrich, *Hidden Hand*, pp. 99–101, 260; Richard J. Aldrich, 'Soviet Intelligence, British Security and the End of the Red Orchestra: The Fate of Alexander Rado', *INS*, vol. 6, no. 1 (1991), pp. 196–217; Philip H. J. Davies, 'The SIS Singapore Station and the Role of the Far East Controller: Secret Intelligence Structure and Process in Post-War Colonial Administration', *INS*, vol. 14, no. 4 (1999), pp. 105–29; Dorril, *MI6*, p. 555; Walton, *Empire of Secrets*, pp. 77, 87, 89, 96, 144, 172, 301.

4 Quoted in David Mure, *Practise to Deceive* (London: William Kimber, 1977), p. 262.

5 TNA: PRO KV4/383: 'Security Intelligence, Middle East Charter', undated. See also Andrew, *Defence of the Realm*, p. 138. Note that at the outbreak of war in 1939, MI5 officers were located in the 'permanent establishment of the Security Service overseas', such as Gibraltar, Malta, Cairo, Aden, Singapore and Hong Kong. The officers were also provided with 'a small staff of military personnel'. Curry, *Security Service*, pp. 396–7.

6 Hinsley and Simkins, *British Intelligence*, pp. 150–3; Howard, *British Intelligence*, p. 32.

7 Hinsley and Simkins, *British Intelligence*, p. 152.

8 Curry, *Security Service*, pp. 273–4. Cf. TNA: PRO KV4/238: Pol.F.1001/1/H.S.: report, 'SIME Record Note', by W. M. T. Magan to R. W. G. Stephens, 28 April 1951, p. 6. The security matters in Iran and Iraq were administered by the RAF and came under the auspices of the Combined Intelligence Centre Iraq/Iran (CICI), responsible to Persia and Iraq Command, known as PAIFORCE.

9 Dovey, 'Operation Condor'.

10 Cf. Mohammad A. Tarbush, *The Role of the Military in Politics: A Case Study of Iraq to 1941* (London: KPI, 1985).

11 TNA: PRO KV4/197: Part II: 3: 'Instructions (Provisional) for the Interrogation and Disposal of Suspects', by Colonel R. J. Maunsell, Head of SIME, SIME/500/15/9, 19 March 1943; KV4/240: appendix XV, 'Special Interrogation of Travellers & Interrogation of Captured Agents in the Middle East', 18 February 1943.

12 By comparison, 1,003 security suspects were interned by the security authority in India.

13 TNA: PRO KV4/383: Paper no. 19: SIME by Head of SIME, undated, c. 1945–6.

14 An exception was in the late 1940s, when Anthony Cavendish operated as a German prisoner of war in Cairo. Cavendish, *Inside Intelligence*, pp. 25–41.

15 Hinsley and Simkins, *British Intelligence*, p. 164

16 Howard, *British Intelligence*, p. 32; cf. also Hinsley and Simkins, *British Intelligence*, pp. 152–3.

17 Hinsley and Simkins, *British Intelligence*, p. 44.

18 Cf. ibid. *passim*.

19 IWM: Private Papers of R. J. Maunsell: 4829 80/30/1, pp. 2, 5. The relationship between Maunsell and Jenkins is also noted in Hinsley and Simkins, *British Intelligence*, p. 150.

20 Indeed, SIME was just one of a number of wartime intelligence organisations operating in the Middle East. In addition to SIME, there were the Combined Intelligence Centre Iraq/Iran (CICI), a security organisation administered by the RAF; the Inter-Services Liaison Department (ISLD), a regional headquarters of MI6; the Middle East Intelligence Centre (MEIC), a political intelligence assessment centre; the Political Warfare Executive (PWE), responsible for British propaganda; the Special Operations Executive

(SOE); and the Combined Bureau Middle East (CBME), a regional section of the Government Code & Cipher School (GC&CS). See Adam Shelley, 'British Intelligence in the Middle East, 1939–46' (PhD thesis, University of Cambridge, 2008).

21 IOLR: L/WS/1/1570: cipher telegram from the War Office to C-in-C Middle East, C-in-C India, GOC-in-Persia and Iraq, desp. 092320 of August 1945.

22 TNA: PRO KV4/234: 56b: SIME Charter, attachment to note, 'Future Organisation of SIME' by Percy Sillitoe to Secretary of JIC, 17 August 1946; 82A: attachment to note, 'Statement to CIGS' by Douglas Roberts to Percy Sillitoe, 25 November 1946.

23 TNA: PRO KV4/384: report of visit by Mr A. J. Kellar to the Middle East, 'III: Organisational Problems of SIME and CICI', p.15, February Feb 1945, p. 15.

24 Cf. TNA: PRO KV4/238: Pol.F.1001/1/H.S.: report, 'SIME Record Note', by W. M. T. Magan to R. W. G. Stephens, 28 April 1951 (hereafter Magan Report), p. 12.

25 TNA: PRO KV4/383: minute by D. G. White, 'Report on Future of SIME', 22 January 1946.

26 Ibid.

27 Ibid. See also TNA: PRO KV4/383: JIC (46) 3rd meeting: minute of JIC (MEF) meeting, 17 January 1946.

28 Ibid. See also TNA: PRO KV4/383: appendix 'A' to JIC/49/ME, 'Recommendations for the future organisation of SIME by the Joint Intelligence Committee Middle East', 18 January 1946; letter by N. Bates, JIC ME, to Secretary, JIC, 'Future Organisation of SIME', 18 January 1946; PRO KV4/234: SF.205/ME/5/D, 'Security Intelligence Middle East Charter', 17 August 1946.

29 Magan, *Middle Eastern Approaches*, p. 98.

30 Ibid. pp. 98–9.

31 MI5 was administratively responsible to the Home Secretary under the 1952 Maxwell Fyfe Directive. See Andrew, *Defence of the Realm*, 324–5.

32 TNA: PRO KV4/472: the Liddell Diaries, 6 July 1950.

33 TNA: PRO KV4/442: SF51/30/85: letter by MI5 to DDMI, War Office, 24 May 1945.

34 Aden Colony was added to the list of its outstations from 1953. See TNA: PRO KV4/475: the Liddell Diaries, 12 February, 9 April 1953.

35 TNA: PRO KV4/467: the Liddell Diaries, 13 May 1946; PRO KV4/469: the Liddell Diaries, 5 December 1947.

36 TNA: PRO KV4/470: the Liddell Diaries, 22 January 1948.

37 TNA: PRO KV4/438: report on visit to Middle East by Mr J. C. Robertson, 14 April–14 June 1947, pp. 34–6. See also TNA: PRO KV4/468: the Liddell Diaries, 4 December 1946; PRO KV4/469: the Liddell Diaries, 2 October, 3 November 1947.

38 TNA: PRO KV4/438: report on visit to Middle East by Mr J. C. Robertson, 14 April–14 June 1947, p. 35.

39 TNA: PRO KV4/438: report on visit to Middle East by Mr J. C. Robertson, 14 April–14 June 1947, pp. 34–6.

40 TNA: PRO KV4/384: report of visit by Mr A. J. Kellar to the Middle East, July 1946, p. 14; PRO KV4/470: the Liddell Diaries, 27 February 1948.

41 Ibid. p. 37. See also TNA: PRO KV4/469: the Liddell Diaries, 21 November 1947. As a consequence, Morton was placed under 'a virtual ban on his participation in any diplomatic social engagements' for a while.

42 TNA: PRO KV4/384: report of visit by Mr A. J. Kellar to the Middle East, July 1946, pp. 12–13.

43 TNA: PRO KV4/236: 173b: minute by J. C. Robertson, B3a, to DB, White, and DDG, Liddell, 14 May 1948.

44 TNA: PRO CAB301/29: note of a meeting held in Sir Edward Bridges' Room, 12 August 1947.

45 Andrew, *Defence of the Realm*, p. 129.

46 Ibid. p. 443; Bower, *Perfect English Spy*, pp. 219–20; Dorril, *MI6*, p. 31; Walton, *Empire of Secrets*, pp. 23–4.

47 SIME Charter, para. 3. See Appendix.

48 Jeffery, *MI6*, pp. 634–9. See also Arditti, 'Security Intelligence in the Middle East (SIME)'.

49 TNA: PRO KV4/472: the Liddell Diaries, 9 January 1950.

50 TNA: PRO CAB301/30: memorandum by Sir William Strang to 'C', 17 April 1950; memorandum by Sir Edward Bridges to Sir Percy Sillitoe, 17 April 1950.

51 TNA: PRO KV4/425: p. 2/SIFE/HSIFE: minute, 23 June 1953. Note that the post of the Joint Intelligence Division of SIFE was headed by MI6 officers such as Maurice Oldfield and Fergie Dempster. See further TNA: PRO FO1093/393, file entitled 'Relations between the Security Service (MI5) and the Secret Intelligence Service (SIS): Memorandum of Agreement', March–December 1949.

52 TNA: PRO FO371/75319: minute by Bernard Burrows to William Hayter, 21 October 1949; minute by [name illegible], 31 October 1949.

53 An exception was Norman Himsworth of MI5, who was posted as the Security Liaison Officer (SLO) in Iraq (1953–6). See TNA: PRO FO371/115796: VQ1643/3: letter by R. W. J. Hooper, Baghdad, to R. M. Hadow, of FO, 2 December 1955.

54 Bower, *Perfect English Spy*, p. 232; Horne, *But What Do You Actually Do?*, p. 58. Cf. Aldrich, 'Secret Intelligence for a Post-War World'; Davies, *MI6*, pp. 128–30, 192.

55 TNA: PRO KV4/438: report on visit to Middle East by Mr J. C. Robertson, 14 April–14 June 1947.

56 Ibid. See also TNA: PRO KV4/470: the Liddell Diaries, 2 March 1948.

57 TNA: PRO KV4/473: the Liddell Diaries, 1 August 1951.

58 Davies, 'The SIS Singapore Station', p. 117.

59 Kim Philby, *My Silent War* (St Albans: Panther, 1969), p. 125.

60 Cf. TNA: PRO KV4/234: 50z: circulating letter by SIME to DSOs in the area, 27 December 1944.

61 TNA: PRO KV4/236: 171: minute by J. C. Robertson, B3a, to DB, White, 23 April 1948.

62 TNA: PRO KV4/438: report on visit to Middle East by Mr J. C. Robertson, 14 April–14 June 1947. See also TNA: PRO FO1093/391: letter by M. C. S. Philips of MI5 to M. G. L. Joy of PUSD, FO, 29 August 1949.

63 The authorised history of MI5 records that as of 1968, ten countries played host to both representatives of MI5 and MI6. Andrew, *Defence of the Realm*, p. 481.

64 TNA: PRO KV4/471: the Liddell Diaries, 12 October 1949. Sir Alistair Horne notes that SIME was also receiving SIGINT. See Horne, *But What Do You Actually Do?*, pp. 56–7.

65 TNA: PRO FO141/1455: 1016/3/52G: letter by H. S. Stephenson, Chairman of JIC/ME to Creswell of FO, 15 April 1952. The whole file has been declassified under the FOIA at my request (REF: 0903-12), 9 October 2012.

66 TNA: PRO KV4/471: the Liddell Diaries, 12 October 1949. Cf. also PRO KV4/471: the Liddell Diaries, 20 October 1949.

67 Cavendish, *Inside Intelligence*, pp. 50–1.

68 Philby, *My Silent War*, ch. 9.

69 Andrew, *Defence of the Realm*, pp. 344–5; Deacon, '*C*', p. 78; Philby, *My Silent War*, pp. 116–20; Christopher Andrew and Vasili Mitrokhin, *The Mitrokhin Archive II* (London: Allen Lane, Penguin, 2005), pp. 182–3.

70 A. W. Sansom, *I Spied Spies* (London: George G. Harrap, 1965),

p. 234. See also Christopher Andrew and Vasili Mitrokhin, *The Mitrokhin Archive* (London: Allen Lane, 1999), pp. 202–3.

71 TNA: PRO KV4/438: report on visit to Middle East by Mr J. C. Robertson, 14 April–14 June 1947, p. 30.

72 TNA: PRO KV4/384: report of visit by Mr A. J. Kellar to the Middle East, July 1946, pp. 10–11.

73 Ibid.

74 Horne, *But What Do You Actually Do?*, p. 56.

75 TNA: PRO KV4/438: report on visit to Middle East by Mr J. C. Robertson, 14 April–14 June 1947.

76 TNA: PRO FO141/1455: 1016/3/52G: letter by H. S. Stephenson, Chairman of JIC/ME to Creswell of FO, 15 April 1952. The whole file has been declassified under the FOIA at my request (REF: 0903-12), 9 October 2012.

77 In his memoir, Magan states: 'I felt particularly nervous of the Iraqi Army which might try to seize power and which I felt that the Iraqi intelligence authorities had not got sufficiently covered.' Magan, *Middle Eastern Approaches*, pp. 146–7. Cf. TNA: PRO CAB159/16: JIC (54) 67th meeting, 'Liaison with Iraq', 29 July 1954.

78 TNA: PRO CAB158/34: JIC (58) 102: JIC report, 'Reasons for the Failure of the Iraqi Intelligence Services to Give Warning of the Revolution of July 14', 8 October 1958. See also Allen Dulles, *The Craft of Intelligence* (New York: Signet, 1965), p. 144.

79 TNA: PRO CAB159/11: JIC (52) 2nd meeting, minute, 'Coordination of Intelligence in the Middle East', 3 January 1952.

80 He was better known as the Commandant of Camp 020, the wartime 'spy prison', and its counterpart in post-war Germany, Bad Nenndorf. On Robin Stephen in Camp 020 and Bad Nenndorf, see Oliver Hoare (ed.) *Camp 020: MI5 and the Nazi Spies* (Richmond: PRO, 2000), pp. 1–30. He was the SLO in the Gold Coast after Germany. See Andrew, *Defence of the Realm*, p. 451. He was seconded from the Army.

81 Magan Report, p. 24.

82 TNA: PRO KV4/238: 290a: letter by R. W. G. Stephens, Head of SIME, to Head Office, 14 July 1951.

83 TNA: PRO KV4/238: 297a: letter by J. V. W. Shaw, DOS, to R. W. G. Stephens, HS, 16 August 1951.

84 Magan, *Middle Eastern Approaches*, p. 166. Before then, Magan was seconded from the Army to MI5 as the DSO in Palestine (1946); acting Head of SIME (1947); and Head of SIME (1947–51).

During the Second World War, he was in Persia for intelligence/ security purposes: creating a stay-behind network, and controlling double-agents in Persia against the Axis Powers. See ibid. ch. 5.

85 Bower, *Perfect English Spy*, p. 144. In addition to his longest tenure as Director of E Branch, Magan remained a Director, for example, of C Branch (Protective Security) and F Branch (Counter-Subversion at home). Magan, *Middle Eastern Approaches*, p. 166. Nigel West, for instance, notes that 'No history of the postwar Security Service would be complete without a reference to Brigadier William M. T. Magan, one of the most remarkable intelligence officers of his generation.' Nigel West, *Historical Dictionary of British Intelligence* (Lanham, MD: Scarecrow, 2005), p. 321.

86 TNA: PRO KV4/238: 294a: minute by W. M. T. Magan, B1g, to Alex Kellar, OS, 8 August 1951.

87 Ibid.

88 On MI5 and Zionist extremists, cf. Andrew, *Defence of the Realm*, pp. 352–66; Walton, 'British Intelligence and the Mandate of Palestine'; Walton, *Empire of Secrets*, ch. 3; Wagner, 'British Intelligence and the Jewish Resistance Movement'; Wagner, 'British Intelligence and the "Fifth" Occupying Power.

89 TNA: PRO KV4/438: report by J. C. Robertson to DG, 'IV: DSO Palestine', 14 April–14 June 1947, pp. 18, 21.

90 Sir Alistair Horne notes the Soviet section of SIME was 'a long way behind' the Jewish, which was 'by far the biggest' section, and the Arab section, which came second. See Horne, *But What Do You Actually Do?*, p. 54. I am grateful to Sir Alistair Horne for pointing this out.

91 TNA: PRO KV4/234: SIME/008/232/T: report by Brigadier Douglas Roberts, Head of SIME, to Field Marshal Sir Bernard ('Monty') Montgomery, the Chief of the Imperial General Staff, 'Investigation of Left-Wing Activity', 8 April 1946; SIME/700/ XI/1: statement by H/SIME to CIGS, 'Russian Intelligence and Subversion', 25 November 1946.

92 Andrew and Mitrokhin, *Mitrokhin Archive II*, p. 223.

93 A senior officer at MI5 Registry noted that the record-keeping at SIME Registry through 'the card-index system' was an 'instrument of primary importance to the whole organisation'. TNA: PRO KV4/436: extract of telegram, 'Office Instruction no. 97', by Mr Power, 27 March 1946. See also Horne, *But What Do You Actually Do?*, pp. 57–8.

94 TNA: PRO KV4/436: SIME Instruction: 7/53, by W. H. Oughton

(for Head of SIME), 'SIME Headquarters: Carding Principles and Procedure', 31 March 1953.

95 TNA: PRO KV4/436: letter by C. J. H. Foulkes, DSO Cairo, to SIME, 6 June 1953.

96 TNA: PRO KV4/436: letter by R. E. R. Lees, DSO Baghdad, to SIME, 9 June 1953.

97 TNA: PRO KV4/436: letter by JEF, DSO Canal, to SIME, 1 May 1953.

98 TNA: PRO KV4/436: letter by A. N. Druce, DSO Cyprus, to SIME, 25 April 1953.

99 TNA: PRO KV5/65: report 'Jamiyat Al Abad Al Islamiya – The Moslem Ethical Society', p. 6, October 1948.

100 Ibid.

101 For discussions about war planning including the DTC and the Government War Book, see Hennessy, *Secret State*.

102 Note that PRO CAB158 and PRO CAB159 series contain the JIC estimates, which regularly assessed Soviet military threat to the Middle East area.

103 TNA: PRO KV4/436: SIME Instruction: 7/53 by W. H. Oughton (for Head of SIME), 'SIME Headquarters: Carding Principles and Procedure', 31 March 1953.

104 TNA: PRO KV4/436: draft Heads of Agreement reached at a meeting held between representatives of the Security Service and SIS to consider modifications in the integration of the two services in the Middle East, December 1953.

105 TNA: PRO KV4/436: SIME Instruction: 7/53 by W. H. Oughton (for Head of SIME), 'SIME Headquarters: Carding Principles and Procedure', 31 March 1953.

106 Even when good security liaison was maintained, the planning for security measures in the event of war was concealed from local authorities even in the case of Egypt in 1950. See TNA: PRO FO141/1402: MIL/1243/ME: Security Directive, Joint Standing Instruction No. 2 (Plan Celery), issued by the Commanders-in-Chief, Middle East, 29 September 1950.

107 On Iraq and the Communist Movement, see Batatu, *Old Social Classes*.

108 TNA: PRO FO371/75131: report by the representative of MI5 in Baghdad, Philip Bicknell Ray, 'The Iraqi Communist Party': 'XII. Russian Links with the Party', March 1949, pp. 55–8.

109 Ibid. See also PRO KV4/470: the Liddell Diaries, 29 December 1948.

110 TNA: PRO KV4/474: the Liddell Diaries, 9 June 1952.

111 TNA: PRO AIR23/8605: Joint Standing Instruction No. 3: Security Directive, issued by Commanders-in-Chief, Middle East, 24 November 1950.

112 TNA: PRO KV4/474: the Liddell Diaries, 9 June 1952. See also Hashimoto, 'British Security Liaison in the Middle East', p. 863.

113 TNA: PRO AIR23/8605: appendix 'C' to the Air Headquarters Iraq Security Plan, 'Security Measures in Iraq', attached to letter by R. Lloyd, Wing Commander, for Air Vice-Marshal, Air Officer Commanding, British Forces in Iraq, to Military Division, BMEO, 30 March 1951.

114 TNA: PRO AIR23/8605: report on 'Security Planning', produced by R. E. R. Lees, attached to minutes of a meeting by Wing Commander A. J. Douch, Senior Intelligence Officer, 10 June 1953, p. 2.

115 TNA: PRO AIR23/8605: letter by R. E. R. Lees, AHQ detachment, RAF, British Embassy Section, Baghdad, to P. S. Davies, Wing-Commander, SIO, Habbaniya, 'Security Measures in Iraq in the Event of War', 19 May 1952.

116 Ibid.

117 TNA: PRO AIR23/8605: report on 'Security Planning', attached to a letter by Group Captain H. M. White, Headquarters, Middle East Air Force, to Air Vice-Marshal J. G. Hawtrey, Air Officer Commanding, British Forces in Iraq, 'Security Planning in Iraq', 23 July 1953.

118 TNA: PRO KV4/474: the Liddell Diaries, 9 June 1952.

119 TNA: PRO AIR23/8605: letter by R. E. R. Lees [DSO], AHQ detachment, RAF, British Embassy Section, Baghdad, to P. S. Davies, Wing-Commander, SIO, Habbaniya, 'Security Measures in Iraq in the Event of War', 19 May 1952.

120 TNA: PRO AIR23/8605: report on 'Security Planning', attached to a letter by Group Captain H. M. White, Headquarters, Middle East Air Force, to Air Vice-Marshal J. G. Hawtrey, Air Officer Commanding, British Forces in Iraq, 'Security Planning in Iraq', 23 July 1953.

121 Ibid.

122 TNA: PRO AIR23/8605: minute of a meeting, the Local Security Board, held in the Military Attaché's office on 9 June 1953, by A. J. Douch, Wing Commander, Senior Intelligence Officer, 10 July 1953; letter by [name redacted], AHQ detachment, RAF, British Embassy Section, Baghdad, to Wing Commander A. J.

Douch, Senior Intelligence Officer, Air Headquarters, Habbaniya, report on 'Security Planning', 16 June 1953.

123 TNA: PRO AIR23/8605: report on 'Security Planning', attached to a letter by Group Captain H. M. White, Headquarters, Middle East Air Force, to Air Vice-Marshal J. G. Hawtrey, Air Officer Commanding, British Forces in Iraq, 'Security Planning – Air Headquarters Iraq', 2 July 1953.

124 TNA: PRO AIR23/8605: letter by Group Captain H. M. White, Headquarters, Middle East Air Force, to Air Vice-Marshal J. G. Hawtrey, Air Officer Commanding, British Forces in Iraq, 'Security Planning in Iraq', 23 July 1953.

125 TNA: PRO AIR23/8605: letter by K. Dear, Squadron Leader, to Headquarters, (Main) Middle East Air Force, 'Security Measures in Iraq in the Event of War', 28 April 1955.

126 Richard J. Aldrich, 'Legacies of Secret Service: Renegade SOE and the Karen Struggle in Burma, 1948–50', *INS*, vol. 14, no. 4 (1999), pp. 130–48; Richard J. Aldrich, 'Unquiet in Death: The Post-War Survival of the "Special Operations Executive", 1945–51', in Anthony Gorst, Lewis Johnman and Scott Lucas (eds), *Contemporary British History, 1931–1961* (London: Pinter, 1991), pp. 193–217; Dorril, *MI6*, ch. 2; Jeffery, *MI6*, pp. 718–19.

127 Philip H. J. Davies, 'From Special Operations to Special Political Action: The "Rump SOE" and SIS Post-War Covert Action Capability 1945–1977', *INS*, vol. 15, no. 3 (2000), pp. 55–76; Davies, *MI6*, pp. 203–7. A glimpse of MI6's war planning can be found in Cavendish, *Inside Intelligence*, pp. 59–60, 65–7; David Smiley, *Irregular Regular* (Norwich: Michael Russell, 1994).

128 TNA: PRO FO1093/386: PR769/73/G: memorandum 'Intelligence for a Political Warfare Executive in the Event of Mobilisation', 1 April 1949; PRO FO1093/370: confidential annex to COS (48) 155th meeting, 'Intelligence Requirements for "Cold War" Planning', 3 November 1948. See also TNA: PRO FO1093/373: letter by 'C' to William Hayter, 2 November 1948, which mentions some planning in Turkey; TNA: PRO CAB301/16: memorandum 'C's Preparations for War', 16 December 1950, which contains a reference to the Middle East.

129 TNA: PRO CAB159/12: JIC (52) 75th meeting, 'Liaison between JIC (ME) and Commander-in-Chief, Southern Flank', 9 July 1952; JIC (53) 21st meeting, 'Evasion, Escape and Rescue Planning in the Middle East and Far Eastern Theatres', 25 January 1953.

130 TNA: PRO FO141/1465: JIC (ME) (52) – 44, minute of the JIC

(ME), 'The Co-operation to Be Expected from the Egyptians in the Event of a Major War', 18 September 1952. The file has been declassified under the FOIA at my request (REF: 0894-11), 27 October 2011. The minutes were circulated to relevant authorities, including Robin 'Tin Eye' Stephens, Head of SIME, and George K. Young, the Middle East Controller of MI6.

131 Nigel West suggests that 'Swinburn was the head of SIS's stay-behind network'. West, *Friends*, p. 141.

132 Mohamed H. Heikal, *Cutting the Lion's Tail: Suez: Through Egyptian Eyes* (London: Andre Deutsch, 1986), p. 154. See also Caroz, *Arab Secret Services*, p. 25. According to Jonathan Bloch and Patrick Fitzgerald, the Egyptian security service was tipped off by the Soviets, who 'in turn had obtained it from the MI6 double-agent George Blake'. See Jonathan Bloch and Patrick Fitzgerald, *British Intelligence and Covert Action* (London: Junction Books, 1983), p. 122. Obituary of John McGlashan, *The Telegraph*, 10 September 2010.

133 Andrew, *Defence of the Realm*, p. 464.

134 See Ritchie Ovendale (ed.), *British Defence Policy since 1945* (Manchester: Manchester University Press, 1994), pp. 106–8.

135 See ibid. pp. 111–15. See also the 1957 White Paper, *Defence: Outline of Future Policy*, Cmnd.124, presented by the Minister of Defence to Parliament, April 1957 (London: Her Majesty's Stationery Office, reprinted 1964). On 'East of Suez', see Darby, *British Defence Policy*; Saki Dockrill, *Britain's Retreat from East of Suez* (Basingstoke: Palgrave Macmillan, 2002).

136 Cormac, 'Organizing Intelligence', p. 805.

137 These included SIFE and one in Germany. For internal developments within the Ministry of Defence, see Dylan, *Defence Intelligence*.

138 Cf. Cormac, 'A Whitehall "Showdown"?'; Herman, *Intelligence Services*, ch. 5.

139 TNA: PRO KV4/426: note of a meeting held in DG's room on 5 January 1954, 6 January 1954. A similar development was also taking place in the Far East, where SIFE was reorganised accordingly. TNA: PRO KV4/427: letter by DG to R. Thistlethwaite, H/SIFE, 31 August 1955.

140 TNA: PRO CAB176/52: JIC Working Party report 'Review of Intelligence Tasks in the Middle East', 4 April 1955.

141 TNA: PRO KV4/426: letter by R. H. Hollis to SIME, 'Meeting between DG & Mr Fulton', 25 October 1955.

142 TNA: PRO CAB176/52: JIC Working Party report 'Review of Intelligence Tasks in the Middle East', 4 April 1955.

143 TNA: PRO KV4/427: draft latter by DG to H/SIFE, 30 November 1955.

144 TNA: PRO KV4/427: minute by W. T. Magan, 15 December 1955.

145 Ibid.

146 TNA: PRO CAB176/52: JIC/671/55: JIC report 'Existing Intelligence Staffs at HQ ME Command' by EEGL Searight, 8 March 1955. The differences between MI6's 'officers' and 'operators' are unclear from the records.

147 TNA: PRO PREM11/1582: minute by Sir Norman Brook to PM, 28 November 1955.

148 TNA: PRO KV4/426: note of discussion between DG and Sir Ivone Kirkpatrick on 13.1.55, 17 January 1955.

149 TNA: PRO KV4/426: letter by DG to R. Thistlethwaite, H/SIME, 31 August 1955.

150 TNA: PRO CAB159/18: JIC (55) 22nd meeting: JIC minute, 10 March 1955.

151 Ibid.

152 Bower, *Perfect English Spy*, p. 185. 'Robber barons' is a reference to the medieval knights who defied their sovereign and acted independently of any central authority; I am grateful to Nigel West for this.

153 Andrew, *Secret Service*, p. 689.

154 Bower, *Perfect English Spy*, p. 185.

155 On MI6's plot to kill Nasser, see obituary of John McGlashan, *The Telegraph*, 10 September 2010; Wilford, *America's Great Game*, pp. 221–2; Caroz, *Arab Secret Services*, pp. 21–7.

156 See Heikal, *Cutting the Lion's Tail*, pp. 103–4.

157 Wright, *Spy Catcher*, pp. 160–1.

158 Anthony Nutting recorded his conversation with Eden, who angrily said: 'I want him [Nasser] destroyed, can't you understand? I want him removed, and if you and the Foreign Office don't agree, then you'd better come to the Cabinet and explain why.' See Anthony Nutting, *No End of a Lesson: The Story of Suez* (London: Constable, 1967), pp. 34–5. See also Evelyn Shuckburgh, *Descent to Suez: Diaries 1951–56* (London: Weidenfeld & Nicolson, 1986), pp. 341, 346, 360.

159 Dodds-Parker, *Political Eunuch*, pp. 102–4. On Sir Charles Hambro, see M. R. D. Foot, *SOE: An Outline History of the*

Special Operations Executive 1940–1946 (London: Pimlico, 1999); William Mackenzie, *The Secret History of SOE: The Special Operations Executive, 1940–1945* (London: St Ermin's Press, 2000).

160 Magdalene College, Oxford: Private Papers of Douglas Dodds-Parker: MC: P2/5/2C/8: minute by Dodds-Parker to Lord Reading, classified as Top Secret, 'Future Aims in the Middle East', 14 August 1956. Also ibid: note by C. R. A. Rae to Dodds-Parker, 14 August 1956, which pondered, 'If we clobber Nasser quickly and then pull out, what guarantees are there that there will be no repeat performance by a successor Government?'

161 Cf. Sue Onslow, 'Unreconstructed Nationalists and a Minor Gunboat Operation: Julian Amery, Neil McLean and the Suez Crisis', *Contemporary British History*, vol. 20, no. 1 (2006), pp. 73–99.

162 Miles Copeland, *The Game Player* (London: Aurum Press, 1989), p. 201.

163 See Jones, 'The "Preferred Plan"'.

Chapter 4

1 TNA: PRO FO371/157497: EB1693/5G: minute on CENTO Counter-Subversion and Liaison Committee's report by C. F. R. Barclay, 2 February 1961. The whole file has been declassified under the FOIA at my request (REF: 0894-11), 27 October 2011.

2 Quoted in TNA: PRO CAB176/61: SF303/1/1/C: report annexed to 'Security Training of Iranians', by E. M. Furnival Jones of MI5, 24 April 1957. Roger Lees was the DSO in Baghdad (1951–3) and later advised the Shah of Iran on the establishment of the Iranian National Intelligence and Security Organisation, known as SAVAK.

3 Howard, *British Intelligence*, p. 31.

4 For a discussion of this, see Pipes, 'Dealing with Middle Eastern Conspiracy Theories'. See also Rathmell, *Secret War in the Middle East*.

5 For an analysis of Iraq's role in the formulation of the Baghdad Pact, see Elie Podeh, *The Quest for Hegemony in the Arab World: The Struggle over the Baghdad Pact* (Leiden: E. J. Brill, 1995). For an emphasis on the Turkish role, see Ara Sanjian, 'The

Formulation of the Baghdad Pact', *Middle Eastern Studies*, vol. 33, no. 2 (1997), pp. 226–66.

6 The foundation of this cooperation was personal connections between Colonel Sir Patrick Coghill, Director-General of Intelligence of the Arab Legion (1952–6); Emir Farid Chehab, Head of the Sûreté Générale (1948–58); and Bahjat Beg el-Attiyah, Director of the Iraqi CID, later promoted to the newly created post of Director-General of Security (1947–58).

7 See Chapter 2.

8 IWM: Private Papers of Patrick Coghill, 'Before I Forget . . .', vol. 2, p. 118.

9 Ibid. See also Owen Sirrs, *A History of the Egyptian Intelligence Service: A History of the Mukhabarat, 1910–2009* (London: Routledge, 2010), p. 36.

10 IWM: Private Papers of Patrick Coghill, 'Before I Forget . . .', vol. 2, p. 119.

11 Ibid. Coghill also noted in his diaries that he, Chehab and Attiyah 'had in fact ganged up to wreck the plan' to disrupt the creation of the Egyptians' Anti-Communist Bureau, but before the attempt was made, the Anti-Communist Bureau fell apart. Thus the objective was luckily achieved without 'provoking the suspicion' of their collusion.

12 Cf. TNA: PRO WO216/890: report by Colonel Sir Patrick Coghill, 'Jordan and the Baghdad Pact', 26 November 1955; PRO FO371/121423: V1691/1: letter from Ankara to E. M. Rose of FO, 9 January 1956.

13 TNA: PRO FO371/121423: V1691/1: letter from Ankara to E. M. Rose of FO, 9 January 1956.

14 IWM: Private Papers of Patrick Coghill, 'Before I Forget . . .', vol. 2, p. 119. The fact of this highly secret meeting is also confirmed by a record of the Turkish counterpart. Cf. Başbakanlık Devlet Arşivleri Genel Müdürlüğü [The State Archives in Ankara]: 30/0/18/12: 141/133/20, 9 January 1956.

15 Sir Michael Wright, the British Ambassador in Baghdad, noted in early 1956 that the Americans were in agreement on Iraq's claim that the Soviet Union was 'launching a major Communist offensive' in the region. See TNA: PRO PREM11/1938: telegram by Sir Michael Wright, Baghdad, to FO, 18 January 1956.

16 TNA: PRO PREM11/1938: V1073/1361: report by Sir Michael Wright, Baghdad, to Harold Macmillan, 'First Meeting of the Council of the Baghdad Pact', 22 November 1955.

17 TNA: PRO FO371/121283: V10710/2: letter by A. A. Dudley, Singapore, to W. D. Allen, FO, 24 January 1956. In the Far East, the Committee to Combat Communist Subversion, also known as the Committee of Security Experts (CSE), had been formed a few months earlier, and the British delegation was headed by Dick Thistlethwaite of MI5, Head of Security Intelligence Far East (1956–9). See also David McKnight, 'Western Intelligence and SEATO's War on Subversion, 1956–63', *INS*, vol. 20, no. 2 (2005), pp. 288–303.

18 Zabih, *Communist Movement in Iran*, pp. 208–45.

19 TNA: PRO FO371/121283: V10710/1: telegram by M. Wright to FO, 27 January 1956.

20 TNA: PRO FO371/121269: V1074/7: a summary of the meeting held in Baghdad by MI5, January 1956.

21 TNA: PRO FO371/121283: V10710/8: telegram by Sir R. Stevens, Tehran, to FO, 5 April 1956. See also Aldrich, *Espionage, Security and Intelligence*, pp. 223–5.

22 TNA: PRO FO371/121283: V10710/6: telegram by Sir Michael Wright, Baghdad, to FO, 15 December 1955; PRO FO371/121283: V10710/1: telegram by M. Wright to FO, 27 January 1956.

23 TNA: PRO FO371/121283: V10710/11: telegram by Shattock, POMEF, to FO, 7 April 1956.

24 'Security Organisation' as the name of the Security Committee also appears in Gallman, *Iraq under General Nuri*, p. 71.

25 TNA: PRO CAB176/58: JIC/2276/56: report 'Structure of the Baghdad Pact Committee and Secretariat Organisation', 12 September 1956.

26 TNA: PRO PREM11/1938: V1073/1361: report by Sir Michael Wright, Baghdad, to Harold Macmillan, 'First Meeting of the Council of the Baghdad Pact', 22 November 1955. The main idea was to protect the classified documents, chiefly handled by the Military Committee of the Baghdad Pact, and to enhance the security of the Pact.

27 Cf. TNA: PRO CAB176/61: JIC/1022/57, JIC report 'Inspection Report of the UK Baghdad Pact Registries', 6 May 1957.

28 TNA: PRO FO371/121269: V1074/7: letter by MI5 to P. L. Carter of FO, 26 January 1956.

29 TNA: PRO FO371/121269: V1074/3: record of the meeting of 'Security Organisation Committee' of Council of the Baghdad Pact, held at the Qasr al Zehoor, 19 December 1955.

30 TNA: PRO FO371/121269: V1074/5: telegram by GHQ MELF, to Ministry of Defence, London, 10 January 1956.

31 TNA: PRO FO371/121269: V1074/1G: minute by R. J. Bray of FO, 2 January 1956.

32 Ibid.

33 TNA: PRO CAB179/59: JIC/2854/56: report by Sir Michael Wright 'State of Security in Baghdad Pact Organisation', 21 November 1956.

34 TNA: PRO CAB21/4747: 2331/31/57: letter by R. S. Crawford, Baghdad, to A. C. I. Samuel of FO, 18 October 1957.

35 TNA: PRO FO371/157497: EB1693/6G: attachment to letter by C. A. G. Simkins of MI5 to R. Pleydell-Bouverie of FO, 'Suggested Re-draft of Bottom of p. 1 to Beginning of (4) on p. 3 of FO Draft', 9 October 1961. The whole file has been declassified under the FOIA at my request (REF: 0894-11), 27 October 2011.

36 TNA: PRO CAB159/34: JIC (60) 57th meeting: minutes of the JIC meeting, 17 November 1960; PRO FO371/157497: EB1693/4G: minute by P. G. D. Adams, Security Department of FO, 'CENTO Security', 7 September 1961. The file has been released under the FOIA at my request (REF: 0894-11), 27 October 2011. See also PRO FO371/170252: EB1692/6: report 'SENTO Security Organisation', 6 February 1963.

37 TNA: PRO CAB159/34: JIC (60) 40th meeting: minutes of the JIC meeting, 28 July 1960.

38 TNA: PRO FO371/121269: V1074/7: a summary of the meeting held in Baghdad by MI5, January 1956.

39 TNA: PRO CAB176/60: JIC/528/57: annex A, 'State of Security in Baghdad Pact Organisation', by A. C. I. Samuel of FO to Sir Michael Wright, Baghdad, 14 December 1956.

40 TNA: PRO CAB176/60: JIC/528/57: annex B, 'State of Security in Baghdad Pact Organisation', by R. S. Crawford, Baghdad, to A. C. I. Samuel of FO, 12 February 1957.

41 TNA: PRO FO371/157497: EB1693/4G: letter by C. A. G. Simkins of MI5 to P. G. D. Adams, Security Department of FO, 16 August 1961. The whole file has been declassified under the FOIA at my request (REF: 0894-11), 27 October 2011.

42 Magan, *Middle Eastern Approaches*, pp. 146–7.

43 TNA: PRO CAB21/4749: SF 295/C: report by James Robertson of MI5 to C. T. P. Potter of Cabinet Office, 'State of Security of Our NATO Allies', 1 December 1961.

44 Caroz, *Arab Secret Services*, pp. 27–8.

45 Ilya Dzhirkvelov, *Secret Servant: My Life with the KGB and the Soviet Elite* (London: Simon & Schuster, 1987), pp. 211–14, 223.

46 Ben Macintyre, *A Spy among Friends* (London: Bloomsbury, 2014), pp. 204–26.

47 Richard Beeston, *Looking for Trouble: The Life and Times of a Foreign Correspondent* (London: Tauris Parke, 2006), p. 34.

48 George Blake, *No Other Choice* (London: Jonathan Cape, 1990), pp. 166–82.

49 Andrew and Mitrokhin, *Mitrokhin Archive*, pp. 442–5.

50 For instance, Ephraim Kahana and Muhammad Suwaed (eds), *The A to Z of Middle Eastern Intelligence* (Lanham, MD: Scarecrow, 2009), pp. 122–3.

51 Cf. Woodhouse, *Something Ventured*, chs 8–9; Wilber, 'Clandestine Service History', the declassified American account of which clearly shows Britain's, i.e. MI6's, active involvement in the operation. See also Eveland, *Ropes of Sand*, pp. 108–9; Dorril, *MI6*, pp. 558–99; Wilford, *America's Great Game*, p. 163; Wm. Roger Louis, 'Britain and the Overthrow of the Mosaddeq Government', in Mark J. Gasiorowski and Malcolm Byrne (eds), *Mohammad Mosaddeq and the 1953 Coup in Iran* (New York: Syracuse University Press, 2004), pp. 126–77.

52 Mansur Rafizadeh, *Witness* (New York: William Morrow, 1987), p. 393, n.4. See also Ali Akbar Dareini (ed.), *The Rise and Fall of the Pahlavi Dynasty: Memoirs of Former General Hussein Fardust* (Delhi: Motilal Banarsidass, 1999), ch. 4, which also refers to a close connection between the Iranian and British intelligence services. On the other hand, a recent PhD on SAVAK, using mostly Iranian but secondary sources, only refers to the British involvement with a sentence. See K. Moravej, 'The SAVAK and the Cold War: Counter-Intelligence and Foreign Intelligence, 1957–1968' (PhD thesis, University of Manchester, 2011), p. 76.

53 TNA: PRO FO371/121269: V1074/5: telegram by GHQ MELF, to Ministry of Defence, London, 10 January 1956.

54 TNA: PRO FO371/121269: V1074/8: telegram by Hollis of MI5 to Clayton, sent through FO cable, 1 February 1956.

55 TNA: PRO CAB176/57: letter (annex A) by FO to Sir Roger Stevens, British Ambassador in Tehran, 17 February 1956. Clayton was also privately asked by General Hadjazi to provide security training to a few Iranians in Britain.

56 TNA: PRO FO371/121269: V1074/9: telegram by Sir Michael Wright, Baghdad, to FO, 4 February 1956.

57 TNA: PRO FO371/121269: V1074/12: telegram by Sir M. Wright, Baghdad, to FO, 15 February 1956.

58 TNA: PRO CAB176/58: report by Roger Lees of MI5 to JIC 'Security Training of Iranians', August 1956.

59 TNA: PRO CAB176/57: letter (annex A) by FO to Sir Roger Stevens, British Ambassador in Tehran, 17 February 1956.

60 TNA: PRO FO371/121269: V1074/19: telegram by Sir R. Stevens, Tehran, to FO, 16 March 1956.

61 TNA: PRO CAB176/57: letter (annex A) by FO to Sir Roger Stevens, British Ambassador in Tehran, 17 February 1956.

62 TNA: PRO CAB176/58: minute by Graham Mitchell of MI5 to the Secretary of JIC 'Provision of Security Training for Iran', 31 August 1956. See also his obituary, *The Telegraph*, 6 March 2009.

63 Although no reference was made to his career in MI5, his service as Head of the Special Branch in India a few years earlier is revealed in his autobiography. Lees, *In the Shade of the Peepul Tree*, p. 89.

64 TNA: PRO CAB176/61: SF303/1/1/C: report annexed to 'Security Training of Iranians', by E. M. Furnival Jones of MI5, 24 April 1957.

65 TNA: PRO CAB176/61: SF303/1/1/C: report annexed to 'Security Training of Iranians', by E. M. Furnival Jones of MI5, 24 April 1957. Note that The Iranian Cabinet approved a decree to establish SAVAK on 3 October 1956, which became effective in 1957. See Habib Ladjevardi (ed.), *Memoirs of Fatemeh Pakravan* (Cambridge, MA: Harvard University, Center for Middle Eastern Studies, 1998), p. 20, n.15.

66 TNA: PRO CAB176/58: report by Roger Lees of MI5 to JIC 'Security Training of Iranians', August 1956.

67 Ibid.

68 TNA: PRO CAB176/61: SF303/1/1/C: report annexed to 'Security Training of Iranians', by E. M. Furnival Jones of MI5, 24 April 1957.

69 Cf. TNA: PRO CAB176/60: JIC/528/57: annex B, 'State of Security in Baghdad Pact Organisation', by R. S. Crawford, Baghdad, to A. C. I. Samuel of FO, 12 February 1957.

70 Quoted in TNA: PRO CAB176/61: SF303/1/1/C: report annexed to 'Security Training of Iranians', by E. M. Furnival Jones of MI5, 24 April 1957.

71 Earnest Oney, interviewed by Seyyed Vali Reza Nasr, Maryland, 22 and 29 May 1991, the Oral History Office of Foundation for Iranian Studies (hereafter OHOFIS), transcript file no. 3, p. 54.

72 Rafizadeh, *Witness*, p. 393, n.4.

73 The recent (unpublished) PhD on SAVAK based mostly on secondary, but non-English, sources argues that it was Iran's concern about its enemies, the Soviet Union and Iraq, which contributed to the establishment of SAVAK. See Moravej, 'The SAVAK and the Cold War', pp. 65–76.

74 Dzhirkvelov, *Secret Servant*, p. 215.

75 Ibid. ch. 9, p. 211.

76 Yevgeni Primakov, *Russia and the Arabs* (New York: Basic Books, 2009), ch. 5; Jonathan Haslam, *Russia's Cold War* (London: Yale University Press, 2011), pp. 146, 154–6; Andrew and Mitrokhin, *Mitrokhin Archive II*, ch. 7.

77 Vartanian had attended the 'special NKVD espionage course' in Austria before joining the military service and being sentenced to imprisonment for life. TNA: PRO FO371/127861: VB1692/9: report by the Turkish Delegation on Communist Activities in Turkey, 23 May 1957.

78 TNA: PRO FO371/127861: VB1692/9: report by the Turkish Delegation on Communist Activities in Turkey, 23 May 1957. Herbrecht was sentenced to death, later commuted to imprisonment for life, due to his activities concerning his contact with the Kurdish independence movement, which was considered a direct threat to Turkish national security.

79 Concerning the discussion on the schedule of the communist-sponsored international events, the role of the security services was indeed to take necessary measures against them: for instance, making recommendations to their own authorities to refuse all applications of any individuals for exit visas in order to participate in the events. TNA: PRO FO371/127861: VB1692/9: report by the Turkish Delegation on Communist Activities in Turkey, 23 May 1957.

80 TNA: PRO FO371/149746: EB1691/2/G: draft report of the UK contribution to the CENTO Liaison Committee papers by MI5, 'Special Study 1: The Iraq Communist Party', 3 March 1960.

81 TNA: PRO FO1110/1353: PR146/20: monthly report on the CSO (January) by Peter Joy of FO, 5 February 1960.

82 TNA: PRO FO371/127861: VB1692/9: report by the Turkish Delegation on Communist Activities in Turkey, 23 May 1957. In addition, even those who had been released from prison after their initial imprisonment were placed under surveillance by the authorities.

83 From 1958 onwards the CIA became an official 'full' member of the Liaison Committee. Letter by Allen Dulles of CIA to Foster Dulles, the Secretary of State, Department of State, 9 January 1958: CIA-RDP80B01676R002600110028-4, approved for release, 29 January 2003, available at <http://www.foia.cia. gov/sites/default/files/document_conversions/5829/CIA-RD P80B01676R002600110028-4.pdf> (last accessed 29 August 2016).

84 TNA: PRO FO371/157497: EB1693/3G: report by A. J. Kellar of MI5 to P. G. D. Adams, Security Department of FO, 17 January 1961. The whole file has been declassified under the FOIA at my request (REF: 0894-11), 27 October 2011. Kellar was then Director of E Branch (responsible for security throughout the Empire, 1958–62).

85 The NATO Special Committee had very similar functions to the Liaison Committee of CENTO. Kellar was the chairman from 1960.

86 Ibid. Kellar's suggestions were also endorsed by MI6.

87 TNA: PRO FO371/164061: EB1692/1: letter by S. Ergin, Security Adviser, Ankara, to R. A. Hibbert, British Embassy in Ankara, 2 January 1961.

88 The Counter-Subversion Committee is discussed in Chapter 5.

89 TNA: PRO FO371/157497: EB1693/3G: report by A. J. Kellar of MI5 to P. G. D. Adams, Security Department of FO, 17 January 1961. The whole file has been declassified under the FOIA at my request (REF: 0894-11), 27 October 2011.

90 TNA: PRO FO371/157497: EB1693/5G: minute on CENTO Counter-Subversion and Liaison Committee's report by C. F. R. Barclay, 2 February 1961. The whole file has been declassified under the FOIA at my request (REF: 0894-11), 27 October 2011.

91 John Bruce Lockhart, 'The Relationship between Secret Services and Government in a Modern State', *RUSI Journal*, vol. 119, no. 2 (1974), p. 7.

92 TNA: PRO FO371/127861: VB1692/5: telegram by Karachi to FO, 28 May 1957.

93 TNA: PRO FO371/127861: VB1692/10G: letter by HPG/DNJ of MI5 to Miss P. Tower, PUSD, FO, 13 August 1957.

94 TNA: PRO FO371/127861: VB1692/10G: telegram by Sir H. Caccia, Washington, to FO, 26 September 1957; PRO FO371/127861: VB1692/12: letter by C. D. Wiggin, Baghdad, to D. J. Spears, FO, 5 November 1957.

95 TNA: PRO FO371/127860: VB1691/27: telegram by Karachi to FO, 29 May 1957.

96 TNA: PRO FO371/164061: EB1692/3: draft note, 'UK Delegation Brief for the Twelfth Session of the Counter-Subversion Committee of CENTO', undated, c. 1962.

97 TNA: PRO FO371/164060: EB1691/1: letter by B. A. B. Burrows, Ankara, to G. H. Hiller of FO, 15 February 1962.

98 TNA: PRO FO371/175633: EB1692/4G: report '12th Session of CENTO Liaison Committee', undated, c. 1964.

99 TNA: PRO FO371/127861: VB1692/10G: letter by HPG/DNJ of MI5 to Miss P. Tower, PUSD, FO, 13 August 1957.

100 Lockhart, 'The Relationship between Secret Services and Government', p. 7, referring to NATO.

101 TNA: PRO FO371/127861: VB1692/5G: telegram by Karachi to FO, 28 May 1957. The passages of the file have been declassified under the FOIA at my request (REF: 1145-11), 2 December 2011, which noted 'more bilateral exchange of intelligence information' was preferred to multilateral intelligence exchange at the Liaison Committee.

102 Apart from Britain and the United States.

103 TNA: PRO FO371/127860: VB1691/1: letter by A. R. H. Kellas, Baghdad, to FO, 5 January 1957.

104 TNA: PRO FO371/170252: EB1692/6: report, 'The United Kingdom Report of the Eleventh Session of the CENTO Liaison Committee (Washington, January 21–25)', prepared by the leader of the UK delegation, 6 February 1963.

105 OHOFIS: General Alavi-Kia, file no. 1, pp. 30–1, file no. 3, p. 10; OHOFIS: Yatsevitch, script no. 1, p. 37.

106 Aldrich, *GCHQ*, pp. 155–64.

107 Paul Lashmar, *Spy Flights of the Cold War* (Annapolis, MD: Naval Institute Press, 1996), pp. 121, 123. See also Robert Jackson, *High Cold War* (Sparkford: Patrick Stephens, 1998), chs 5, 7; Royal Air Force Historical Society, 'Seminar – Cold War Intelligence Gathering', *RAF Historical Society Journal*, vol. 23 (2010), p. 62; Royal Air Force Historical Society, 'Seminar – The RAF in the Mediterranean Region', *RAF Historical Society Journal*, vol. 38 (2007), p. 123.

108 Email exchange with Norman Denman, a former member of RAF 192 Squadron (stationed at Habbaniya), 4 June 2012.

109 TNA: PRO CAB176/52: JIC/949/55: JIC report 'Middle East Intelligence Organisation', 4 April 1955.

110 TNA: PRO KV4/240: minute by White to Liddell, 29 March 1943.

111 Horne, *But What Do You Actually Do?*, pp. 46–7.

112 Wright, *Spy Catcher*, pp. 82–4.

113 Ibid. p. 85.

114 'How valuable we have found this material and how much I appreciate the hard work and skill involved in its production', quoted in Aldrich, *Espionage, Security and Intelligence*, pp. 55–6.

115 Easter, 'Spying on Nasser'.

116 Matthew Aid, *The Secret Sentry* (New York: Bloomsbury, 2009), p. 134.

117 Cf. TNA: PRO HW12/298: 128879 of telegram from Foreign Ministry, Angora, to Turkish Chargé d'Affaires, London, 1 March 1944; 128898 of telegram from Ministry for Foreign Affairs, Tehran, to the Persian Legation, Washington, 2 March 1944; 128928 of telegram from Iraqi Minister, Cairo, to Minister for Foreign Affairs, Baghdad, 3 March 1944.

118 Bower, *Perfect English Spy*, p. 232; Eveland, *Ropes of Sand*, pp. 169–80. On MI6's plot to kill Nasser, see obituary of John McGlashan, *The Telegraph*, 10 September 2010. It is also noteworthy that a retired member of the British intelligence community noted that during the period up to the early 1960s, when the reform of MI6 by Sir Dick White began to take effect, the status of MI6 in Whitehall as an intelligence provider was 'not high': MI6 itself was 'tolerated rather than admired'. Email exchange, 18 September 2011.

119 Bower, *Perfect English Spy*, p. 236.

120 Cf. TNA: PRO FO371/140777: EB1691/7G: attached report of SF303/2/Supp/C/E2 by MI5 to S. J. Whitewell of FO, 23 July 1959; PRO FO371/149746: draft report by MI5 to FO 'Special Study II: Effects on the Security of the CENTO Area of the Relationship between International Communism and Radical Arab Nationalism', 3 March 1960. See also TNA: FO371/157497: EB1693/3G: report by A. J. Kellar of MI5 to P. G. D. Adams, Security Department of FO, 17 January 1961. The whole file has been declassified under the FOIA at my request (REF: 0894-11), 27 October 2011

121 John Earl Haynes and Harvey Klehr, *VENONA* (New Haven, CT: Yale University Press, 1999); Nigel West, '"Venona": The British Dimension', *INS*, vol. 17, no. 1 (2002), pp. 117–34. On the Australian dimension, see Andrew, *Defence of the Realm*, pp. 367–81.

122 All VENONA materials are accessible at TNA. According to the GCHQ historian, 'there is no secret store of VENONA material which has not been released'. Email exchange with the GCHQ historian, 19 September 2011.

123 See Chapter 2. According to the Liddell Diaries, the Russians used a small circle of minorities, such as the Armenians and the Kurds, to contact Communist members in the region. See TNA: PRO KV4/470: the Liddell Diaries, 29 December 1948. The use of the Armenians and the Kurds for contacting Communists by the Russians both in Lebanon and Syria was also noted in the private papers of the late Emir Farid Chehab. See Document of 16/9/34 in Asseily and Asfahani, *Face in the Crowd*, pp. 84–5.

124 TNA: PRO FO371/149746: EB1691/2/G: draft report of the UK contribution to the CENTO Liaison Committee papers by MI5, 'Special Study 1: The Iraq Communist Party', 3 March 1960.

125 Bower, *Perfect English Spy*, p. 236. See also Corinne Souza, *Baghdad's Spy: A Personal Memoir of Espionage and Intrigue from Baghdad to London* (London: Mainstream, 2003).

126 Jasse, 'The Baghdad Pact'.

Chapter 5

1 OHOFIS: Charles Naas, interviewed by William Burr, Maryland, 13 May 1988, script no. 1, p. 16.

2 L. C. W. Figg was the British representative at the Counter-Subversion Committee of the Baghdad Pact in 1956, who later became the British Ambassador to Ireland (1980–3). TNA: PRO FO371/121286: V10710/67(A): minute by L. C. W. Figg, 5 July 1956.

3 Pipes, 'Dealing with Middle Eastern Conspiracy Theories', p. 43.

4 An exception was Pakistan where a senior official of the Ministry of Interior was the Pakistani representative.

5 Baruch Hazan, *Soviet Propaganda: A Case Study of the Middle East Conflict* (Jerusalem: Israel University Press, 1976), pp. 144–8, 191–202, 212.

6 TNA: PRO FO371/128002: VL1017/1: letter by Sir George Middleton, the British Ambassador in Beirut, to Selwyn Lloyd, 18 March 1957.

7 TNA: PRO FO371/75131: report by the representative of MI5

in Baghdad, probably Philip Bicknell Ray, 'The Iraqi Communist Party': 'XII. Russian Links with the Party', pp. 55–8, March 1949.

8 TNA: PRO FO371/128002: VL1017/1: letter by Sir George Middleton, the British Ambassador in Beirut, to Selwyn Lloyd, 18 March 1957.

9 TNA: PRO WO216/890: letter by Colonel Sir Patrick Coghill to Major General W. P. Oliver of WO, 27 November 1955.

10 Hazan, *Soviet Propaganda*, p. 6.

11 TNA: PRO FO1110/1041: PR1093/5G: draft note for a talk for the Secretary of State with the Crown Prince of Iraq, 18 January 1957. It also included subversive propaganda by Saudi Arabia. See TNA: PRO FO371/136521: RK1821/3: letter by B. A. B. Burrows, Ankara, to F. D. W. Brown of FO, 17 December 1958.

12 Wilford, *America's Great Game*, pp. 151–9.

13 Gamal Abdel Nasser, *The Philosophy of the Revolution* (Buffalo, NY: Economica, 1959).

14 Caroz, *Arab Secret Services*, p. 84.

15 Heikal, *Nasser*, p. 159.

16 Anthony Eden, *Full Circle: The Memoirs of Sir Anthony Eden* (London: Cassell, 1960), p. 465.

17 Heikal, *Nasser*, p. 211. Indeed, Heikal's highly entertaining narrative of the events must be treated with caution as he was a prominent spokesman for Nasser's Egypt. Sir Colin T. Crowe notes in his unpublished memoir that 'Heikal is a curious character; he is not everybody's cup of tea. He is intense and nervous, brusque and can be very rude. But he is genuine, extremely intelligent and a first-class journalist.' MECA, St Antony's College, Oxford: Private Papers of CROWE: CROWE Collection GB165-0070: unpublished memoir, p. 102.

18 Heikal, *Nasser*, p. 159.

19 TNA: PRO FO1110/1251: PR146/65G: letter by F. J. Leishman, Tehran, to D. C. Hopson of FO, 1 October 1959.

20 Frantz Fanon, *A Dying Colonialism* (Harmondsworth: Penguin, 1965), pp. 53–80.

21 TNA: PRO FO371/127980: VJ1681/1: letter by R. H. Mason, Amman, to R. M. Hadow, FO, 17 July 1957.

22 Gallman, *Iraq under General Nuri*, pp. 39, 56–7.

23 Sam Falle, *My Lucky Life: In War, Revolution, Peace and Diplomacy* (Oxford: ISIS, 2004), p. 141.

24 Eveland, *Ropes of Sand*, p. 287, which also records the impact and

influence of Cairo Radio on politics in Lebanon. Ibid. pp. 205, 266, 291.

25 See ibid. p. 170. See also Miles Copeland, *The Game of Nations* (New York: Simon & Schuster, 1969), pp. 100, 127.

26 Keith Wheelock, *Nasser's New Egypt: A Critical Analysis* (London: Atlantic Books, 1960), pp. 251–2.

27 TNA: PRO FO371/133792: V10316/1: minute, 'Egyptian Subversive Activity in the Middle East', 19 July 1957. See also Caroz, *Arab Secret Services*, pp. 63–86; Wheelock, *Nasser's New Egypt*, pp. 251–2.

28 TNA: PRO CAB158/33: JIC (58) 83: JIC report, 'Lebanon and Jordan – Infiltration and Subversion by the United Arab Republic', 8 August 1958.

29 Nassif, *Ser Aldawlah*, p. 170.

30 Ibid. pp. 159–60, 165–9.

31 TNA: PRO CAB158/34: annex to JIC (58) 121: MI6 memorandum 'The Subversive Potential of Egyptian Teachers in the Middle East and Africa', undated (c. 1958).

32 Minute by Patrick Dean to the Foreign Secretary, 19 March 1956. Obtained under the FOIA at my request (REF: 1258-12), 8 March 2013. In addition to the Egyptian teachers, Britain also saw school teachers with 'communist leanings' elsewhere as a threat since they might inspire students to undertake possibly subversive activities. See TNA: PRO CO1035/59: file entitled 'Subversion Inspired by School Teachers with Communist Leanings: Background for Joint Intelligence Committee Paper', from January to December 1956.

33 Ibid.

34 TNA: PRO FO371/140777: EB1691/7G: report 'Assessment of the Threat of Communist Subversion in the Baghdad Pact Area', prepared by MI5, 23 July 1959.

35 TNA: PRO FO1110/1370: PR10116/4G: memorandum, 'Hostile Radio Propaganda from Cairo', 15 February 1961.

36 Wilford, 'The Information Research Department'.

37 Vaughan, *Failure of American and British Propaganda*, p. 103.

38 TNA: PRO FO1110/1074: PR146/12: telegram from FO to Baghdad, 14 January 1958.

39 TNA: PRO FO371/164061: EB1692/3: draft note, 'UK Delegation Brief for the Twelfth Session of the Counter-Subversion Committee of CENTO', 1 March 1962.

40 TNA: PRO FO371/127860: VB1691/5: letter by J. A. Speares, Baghdad, to P. G. D. Adams, Beirut, 9 January 1957.

41 Michael Thornhill, *Road to Suez: The Battle of the Canal Zone* (Phoenix Mill: Sutton, 2006), pp. 48, 58–63, 191–3; Gary Rawnsley, 'Overt and Covert: The Voice of Britain and Black Radio Broadcasting in the Suez Crisis, 1956', *INS*, vol. 11, no. 3 (1996), pp. 497–522.

42 Vaughan, '"Cloak without Dagger"'.

43 Vaughan, *Failure of American and British Propaganda*, p. 207.

44 TNA: PRO FO1110/1370: PR10116/4/G: memorandum 'Transmission X', 15 February 1961.

45 TNA: PRO FO1110/1220: PR10104/106G: letter by D. C. Hopson to C. F. R. Barclay, Regional Information Office in the Middle East, Beirut, 6 November 1959.

46 TNA: PRO FO1110/880: PR10131/10AG: EC (56) 62: memorandum by Foreign Secretary, Egypt Committee, 'Propaganda and Political Warfare in the Middle East', 24 October 1956.

47 TNA: PRO FO1110/1370: PR10116/4/G: memorandum 'Transmission X', 15 February 1961.

48 TNA: PRO PREM11/2754: ME (M) (59) 6: memorandum 'Middle East Policy' by FO to PM, 10 March 1959. The file has been released under the FOIA at my request (RFE: F0029264), 17 May 2012.

49 TNA: PRO PREM11/2754: memorandum 'Short-Term Policy in the Middle East', 23 July 1958; COS (58) 183: memorandum by the Chiefs of Staff 'Position in the Middle East', 28 July 1958. See also PRO PREM11/2754: M87/59: minute by PM to Foreign Secretary, 11 March 1959. The file has been released under the FOIA at my request (RFE: F0029264), 17 May 2012.

50 MECA, St Antony's College, Oxford: Private Papers of Sir Colin Tradescant Crowe (CROWE): CROWE Collection GB165-0070: unpublished memoir, p. 3.

51 Ibid. pp. 115–19.

52 TNA: PRO T219/1044: GS298/011: minute, 'Overseas Broadcasting OI (57)2', 23 January 1957. The file has been released under the FOIA at my request (REF: 10/915&10/920), 1 February 2011.

53 See also Vaughan, *Failure of American and British Propaganda*, p. 248.

54 Followed by Africa (9.9 per cent), Communist Europe (8.8 per cent), the Indian subcontinent (8.4 per cent) and the Far East (7.6 per cent).

55 TNA: PRO T219/1045: GS298/011: memorandum by the

Chancellor of the Exchequer, 'Overseas Information Meeting', 31 May 1957; PRO T219/671: GS6/65/014: M442/57: minute by Harold Macmillan, PM, to Chancellor of the Exchequer, 28 August 1957. These files have been released under the FOIA at my request (REF: 10/915&10/920), 1 February 2011.

56 According to James Vaughan, from the end of the Second World War until 1957 not only the IRD but also other bodies such as the British Council sought to bolster British prestige by a softer and more cultural approach to the region. Vaughan, '"A Certain Idea of Britain"'.

57 The members of the working party included representatives from the Cabinet Office, the Treasury, two from the FO, one from the CO, CRO, two from the Central Office of Information and one from the Post Office as secretary. TNA: PRO T219/670: GS6/65/014: minute of 1st meeting, 'Working Party on Broadcasting in the Middle East', 22 February 1957. The file has been released under the FOIA at my request (REF: 10/915&10/920), 1 February 2011.

58 Douglas Boyd, 'Sharq Al-Adna/The Voice of Britain: The UK's "Secret" Arabic Radio Station and Suez War Propaganda Disaster', *Gazette: The International Journal for Communication Studies*, vol. 65, no. 6 (2003), pp. 443–55. See also Beeston, *Looking for Trouble*, pp. 4–10.

59 TNA: PRO T219/671: GS6/65/014: M442/57: minute by Harold Macmillan, PM, to Chancellor of the Exchequer, 28 August 1957. The file has been released under the FOIA at my request (REF: 10/915&10/920), 1 February 2011.

60 Boyd, 'Sharq Al-Adna/The Voice of Britain', p. 452.

61 TNA: PRO FO371/121283: V10710/8: telegram by Sir R. Stevens, Tehran, to FO, 5 April 1956.

62 TNA: PRO FO371/164061: EB1692/3: draft note, 'UK Delegation Brief for the Twelfth Session of the Counter-Subversion Committee of CENTO', 1 March 1962.

63 TNA: PRO FO1110/1353: PR146/95: draft paper, 'Proposals for the Re-orientation of the Functions and Organisation of the Counter-Subversion Office', 12 July 1960.

64 TNA: PRO FO1110/934: IRD report 'Anti-Communist and other Material Supplied by the Information Department, Baghdad, and Reproduced by the Local Press during May 1956', 2 July 1956.

65 TNA: PRO FO1110/1193: IRD monthly report by J. A. Speares, Ankara, 16 April 1959.

66 TNA: PRO FO1110/1048: IRD monthly report by Regional Information Office, Beirut, 3 August 1957.

67 TNA: PRO FO1110/1814: PR10523/39G: training programme 'Information Research Department: CENTO Officers' Information Visit, June 29–July 7, 1964: Programme of Work', c. 1964. See also PRO FO1110/1450: PR109/2: training programme 'Information Training Courses for Foreign Service Officers – Seventh Course, 1961', November 1960.

68 OHOFIS: Charles Naas, interviewed by William Burr, Maryland, 13 May 1988, script no. 1, p. 15.

69 TNA: PRO FO1110/1251: PR146/65G: letter by D. C. Hopson of FO to F. J. Leishman, Tehran, 'Iranian Criticism of the CENTO Counter-Subversion Office', 19 October 1959.

70 TNA: PRO FO1110/1353: PR146/41G: minute by H. M. Carless of FO, 'Future of CSO', 26 February 1960.

71 TNA: PRO FO371/170252: minute, 'CENTO Liaison Committee (Washington, January 21–25)', by deGourcy Ireland, 14 January 1963.

72 TNA: PRO FO371/127861: VB1692/5: telegram by Karachi to FO, 28 May 1957.

73 Ibid.

74 TNA: PRO FO371/157497: EB1693/3G: report by A. J. Kellar of MI5 to P. G. D. Adams, Security Department of FO, 17 January 1961. The file has been declassified under the FOIA at my request (REF: 0894-11), 27 October 2011.

75 TNA: PRO FO371/170252: EB1692/6: report, 'The United Kingdom Report of the Eleventh Session of the CENTO Liaison Committee (Washington, January 21–25)', prepared by the leader of the UK delegation, 6 February 1963.

76 TNA: PRO FO1110/1251: PR146/65G: letter by F. J. Leishman, Tehran, to D. C. Hopson of FO, 1 October 1959; PRO FO371/170252: EB1692/9: attachment to letter by W. J. A. Wilberforce, Ankara, to Percy Cradock of FO, 16 December 1963.

77 SAVAK had two deputies: General Pakravan was responsible for external affairs, while General Hassan Alavi-Kia (1957–62) was responsible for internal affairs. General Pakravan later succeeded Bakhtiar as Head of SAVAK (1961–5).

78 TNA: PRO FO1110/1251: PR146/65G: letter by F. J. Leishman, Tehran, to D. C. Hopson of FO, 1 October 1959.

79 OHOFIS: Charles Naas, interviewed by William Burr, Maryland, 13 May 1988, script no. 1, p. 16.

80 A report 'US View on the Report of the Counter-Subversion Committee', 18 April 1960, pp. 16–17. CIA-RDP86 B00269R000400060004-7, available at <http://www.foia.cia.gov/sites/default/files/document_conversions/5829/CIA-RDP86 B00269R000400060004-7.pdf> (last accessed 29 August 2016).

81 A specific strategy was formed (Project OMEGA) to confront Nasser's increasing popularity throughout the region. See Salim Yaqub, *Containing Arab Nationalism: The Eisenhower Doctrine and the Middle East* (Chapel Hill, NC: University of North Carolina Press, 2004), p. 265.

82 Cf. Eveland, *Ropes of Sand*, *passim*, but esp. pp. 344–65.

83 TNA: PRO FO371/141825: V1015/2: letter by P. M. Crosthwaite, Beirut, to Sir Roger Stevens of FO, 25 April 1959. Robert McClintock reasoned that Nasser's stand on Communism was of 'priceless advantage' and above all Nasser 'had saved Syria from Communism'.

84 TNA: PRO FO1110/1251: PR146/65: letter by F. J. Leishman, Tehran, to D. C. Hopson of FO, 1 October 1959.

85 TNA: PRO FO371/164061: EB1692/3: draft note, 'UK Delegation Brief for the Twelfth Session of the Counter-Subversion Committee of CENTO', undated, c. 1962.

86 TNA: PRO FO371/164060: EB1691/1: letter by B. A. B. Burrows, Ankara, to G. H. Hiller of FO, 15 February 1962.

87 TNA: PRO FO1110/1236: PR1125/43: letter 'Transmission "X"' by FO to the Regional Information Office, Middle East (attached to the British Embassy in Beirut), 10 September 1959.

88 TNA: PRO FO1110/1236: PR1125/50: letter by press officer in Amman to FO, 25 September 1959; letter by the Regional Information Office in Beirut to FO, 17 October 1959.

89 TNA: PRO FO1110/1236: PR1125/50: letter by the British Embassy in Ankara to FO 30 September 1959.

90 Nuri al-Said, *Arab Independence and Unity* (Baghdad: Government Press, 1943). See also Gallman, *Iraq under General Nurii*, pp. 133–66; Podeh, *Quest for Hegemony*.

91 TNA: PRO FO1110/1041: PR1093/5G: draft note for a talk for the Secretary of State with the Crown Prince of Iraq, 18 January 1957; PRO FO371/121286: V10710/67: BP confidential annex B to BP/CD/D25: report of 'The Counter-Subversion Committee to the Council Regarding Special Proposals Designed to Implement the General Programme of Work' regarding 'Broadcasting', undated, c. 1956.

92 Vaughan, 'Propaganda by Proxy?', pp. 164–5.

93 TNA: PRO FO1110/1353: PR146/95: draft paper, 'Proposals for the Re-orientation of the Functions and Organisation of the Counter-Subversion Office', 12 July 1960. The subjects propagated by Baghdad Radio, fed through the CSO, included the communist attitude to the Palestine question, including Soviet support for Israel; a series of talks on 'the monarchy' and on the 'merits of a religious life containing a few anti-communist angles'; and 'Islam in Soviet Central Asia', the materials of which were supplied by the Iranian counterpart. See TNA: PRO FO371/121288: V10710/105G: letter from Baghdad to L. C. W. Figg, IRD, 1 October 1956.

94 Ibid. The attention to youth and students is noteworthy in that they were often a driver for spreading national revolutionary movements across the region. See also Laqueur, *Communism and Nationalism in the Middle East*, pp. 13–18.

95 TNA: PRO FO371/121284: V10710/33: summary record of the first meeting of the working party on information and counter-subversion held at Baghdad, 21 May 1956.

96 A report of the Central Intelligence Bulletin, 15 April 1958. The document has been declassified under the FOIA at my request (REF: F-2012-00715), 6 June 2012. According to Heikal, Britain and the United States had nine secret radio stations working against Nasser. Heikal, *Nasser*, p. 85.

97 TNA: PRO FO371/121287: V10710/75G: letter by Gordon Waterfield, Ankara, to P. G. D. Adams, Beirut, 28 June 1956.

98 TNA: PRO FO371/121287: V10710/78: letter by R. M. Hadow of FO to G. D. Anderson of Commonwealth Relations Office, 7 August 1956.

99 Ibid. The British adviser on the future planning was noted as a 'high ranking British Broadcasting Corporation expert'.

100 TNA: PRO FO1110/1370: PR10116/4G: memorandum 'Hostile Radio Propaganda from Cairo', 15 February 1961.

101 TNA: PRO FO371/121283: V10710/3G: letter by R. W. J. Hooper, Baghdad, to E. M. Rose of FO, 2 February 1956. Gary Rawnsley notes that the use of medium wave was a 'more reliable' and thus 'more popular' method of transmission for the British. See Rawnsley, 'Overt and Covert', p. 501.

102 Cf. Vaughan, 'Propaganda by Proxy?', pp. 169–70.

103 TNA: PRO FO371/121288: V10710/107G: letter by P. G. D. Adams, Beirut, to J. O. Rennie of IRD, 25 October 1956.

104 Ibid.
105 TNA: PRO FO371/127861: VB1692/3G: jacket 'Committee of Counter-Intelligence Experts', May 1957. The whole jacket of the file has been declassified under the FOIA at my request (REF: 1145-11), 2 December 2011.
106 Eveland, *Ropes of Sand*, pp. 169–70, in which Eveland thought that he had entered 'a madhouse' and that the British plan was 'sheer lunacy'. See also Gallman, *Iraq under General Nuri*, p. 137; Lucas (ed.), *Britain and Suez*, pp. 38–42.
107 *The Iraq Times*, 26 August 1958. Iraqi General Ghazi Daghistani, Deputy Chief of Staff, the chief contact of MI6 in Operation Straggle, confessed at the revolutionary court that the plan had been 'drafted at the British Embassy . . . in agreement with the British Ambassador and at the British Embassy itself'.
108 Ibid.
109 Ibid.
110 John King (ed.), *Inside the Arab Nationalist Struggle: Memoirs of an Iraqi Statesman* (London: I. B. Tauris, 2012), p. 68.
111 Gallman, *Iraq under General Nuri*, pp. 161–2; Eveland, *Ropes of Sand*, pp. 232–3.
112 TNA: PRO FO1110/1251: PR146/65: letter by F. J. Leishman, Tehran, to D. C. Hopson of FO, 1 October 1959.
113 TNA: PRO FO371/121283: V10710/28: letter by P. G. D. Adams, Beirut, to FO, 10 May 1956.
114 OL.101/P.2: draft report, 'The Indigenous Communist Parties and Their Relationship to Subversive Activity in the Baghdad Pact Area', presented by Philip Kirby-Green of MI5, the British representative to the Liaison Committee of the Pact Top Secret, p. 1, 14 July 1958. The document has been released under the FOIA at my request (REF: 1145-11), 31 January 2012.
115 Ibid. pp. 1–2.
116 TNA: PRO FO1110/1251: PR146/65: letter by F. J. Leishman, Tehran, to D. C. Hopson of FO, 1 October 1959. Bakhtiar's view also reflected that of the other members.
117 TNA: PRO FO1110/1353: PR146/41G: minute, 'Future of CSO' by G. F. Hiller, 1 March 1960.
118 Ibid.
119 TNA: PRO FO371/121285: V10710/51: letter by K. S. Bulter, Ankara, to J. O. Rennie of IRD, 20 June 1956.
120 TNA: PRO FO371/121288: V10710/107G: letter by P. G. D. Adams, Beirut, to J. O. Rennie of IRD, 25 October 1956.

121 TNA: PRO FO1110/976: PR146/32 'B': letter by P. G. D. Adams, Beirut, to L. C. W. Figg of IRD, 12 April 1957.

122 TNA: PRO FO371/164061: EB1692/3: draft note, 'UK Delegation Brief for the Twelfth Session of the Counter-Subversion Committee of CENTO', undated, c. 1962.

123 Eveland, *Ropes of Sand*, p. 53.

124 TNA: PRO FO1110/227: PR2707/G: minute, 'Publicity in Kurdistan', 13 September 1949.

125 TNA: PRO FO371/75471: 5381: telegram from FO to Baghdad, 11 June 1949. See also TNA: PRO FO371/75471: 5381: telegram from Sir Henry Mack, Baghdad, to FO, 29 April 1949.

126 TNA: PRO FO195/2650: 1026/33/50: letter by Sir Henry Mack to G. W. Furlonge of FO, 8 November 1950.

127 TNA: PRO FO1110/227: PR2707/38/G: letter by F. R. H. Murray to H. Trevelyan, Baghdad, 18 October 1949.

128 TNA: PRO FO248/1497: E1822/14: report 'The Kurdish Problem', undated, c. 1950.

129 TNA: PRO FO371/132747: E1821/13: report 'The Kurdish Problem', undated, c. August–November 1958.

130 TNA: PRO FO1110/227: PR2707/38/G: letter by F. R. H. Murray to H. Trevelyan, Baghdad, 18 October 1949.

131 The Foreign Office recognised that Turkey was the most adamant; next Iran and then Iraq, which gave some autonomy.

132 TNA: PRO FO371/144805: RK1822/1: letter by L. M. Minford, Ankara, to E. J. W. Barnes of FO, 29 January 1959.

133 TNA: PRO FO371/82318: EP10111/1/G: minute by H. M. Carless, 27 September 1950. The information was passed on to MI6 and MI5.

134 TNA: PRO FO371/121646: VQ1015/84/G: letter by Miss B. Richards of FO to Col. H. G. G. Niven of WO, 8 January 1957; letter by Col. H. G. G. Niven of WO to Miss B. Richards of FO, 14 January 1957.

135 For the earlier period, see TNA: PRO FO248/1523: E1821/8: letter by G. W. Furlonge of FO to B. A. B. Burrows, Washington, 26, February 1951.

136 See Chapter 3.

137 Cf. TNA: PRO KV4/470: the Liddell Diaries, 29 December 1948; Document of 16/9/34 in Asseily and Asfahani, *Face in the Crowd*, pp. 84–5.

138 Asseily and Asfahani, *Face in the Crowd*, pp. 74–6, 78, 80, 89–92, 94–5, 104.

139 TNA: PRO FO371/98532: letter by the British Embassy, Moscow, to the FO, 23 October 1952; PRO FO371/132747: E1821/13: report 'The Kurdish Problem', undated, c. August–November 1958, which also recorded 'the small groups of Kurdish intellectuals active in European capitals such as Paris, which are penetrated by Communists'.

140 This point was raised by Andrew and Mitrokhin in *Mitrokhin Archive II*, p. 9.

141 Vladislav Zubok, 'SPY vs. SPY: The KGB vs. the CIA, 1960–1962', *Cold War International History Project Bulletin*, vol. 4 (1994), p. 29.

142 Vladislav Zubok, *A Failed Empire: The Soviet Union in the Cold War from Stalin to Gorbachev* (Chapel Hill, NC: University of North Carolina Press, 2007), p. 110.

143 Andrew and Mitrokhin, *Mitrokhin Archive II*, p. 175. See also Pavel Sudoplatov, Anatoli Sudoplatov with Jerrold L. Schecter and Leona P. Schecter, *Special Tasks: The Memoirs of an Unwanted Witness* (London: Little, Brown, 1994), pp. 259–64.

144 Zubok, 'SPY vs. SPY', p. 29.

145 TNA: PRO FO371/121646: VQ1015/84G: letter by N. F. B. Shaw, Office of the Military Attaché of the British Embassy, Baghdad, to the Under-Secretary of State, War Office, 4 September 1956.

146 TNA: PRO FO371/149746: draft report by MI5 to FO 'Special Study II: Effects on the Security of the CENTO Area of the Relationship between International Communism and Radical Arab Nationalism', 3 March 1960.

147 Telegram (classified SECRET) by the British Embassy, Istanbul, to FO, 18 July 1958, in Massoud Barzani, *Mustafa Barzani and the Kurdish Liberation Movement, 1931–1961* (Basingstoke: Palgrave Macmillan, 2003), pp. 167–8.

148 TNA: PRO FO371/132747: E1821/1: letter by Chancery in Ankara to FO, 15 August 1958. Although it is beyond the scope of this research, Barzani was indeed at the centre of regional politics from the mid-1960s until his death in 1979. Documentary evidence and oral testimonies indicate that Barzani was considered as an agent by SAVAK and also by MOSSAD against the Ba'ath government of Iraq. See the Harvard Iranian Oral History Project (HIOHP): memoirs of General Hassan Alavi-Kia, interviewed by Habib Lajordee, Paris, France, 1 March 1983, transcript 2, sequence 36; the US Department of State Archive: EO12958: memorandum

by Harold Saunders, US Department of State, for General Haig, 'Supporting the Kurdish Rebellion', 27 March 1972, available at <http://2001-2009.state.gov/documents/organization/70886.pdf> (last accessed 29 August 2016); Black and Morris, *Israel's Secret Wars*, p. 184.

149 TNA: PRO FO1110/1016: PR1034/23G: letter by R. A. Burrows, Tehran, to G. S. Bozman of IRD, 30 August 1957.

150 TNA: PRO FO1110/977: PR146/126G: letter by J. W. Russell, Tehran, to F. R. H. Murray of IRD, 2 November 1957.

151 TNA: PRO FO1110/850: PR10523/4: planning report of the CSO, CENTO, 'Global Publicity for Iran', 22 November 1962

152 In 1958 the Iranian government inaugurated a 'powerful new transmitter for international broadcasts', and 'another high-powered short-wave transmitter and four more medium-wave ones' followed afterwards. See Mohammed Reza Shah Pahlavi, *Mission for My Country* (London: Hutchinson, 1961), p. 152. TNA: PRO FO1110/1185: PR1034/27: letter 'Iran Radio: Anti-Communist Propaganda' by D. J. Makinson, Tehran, to FO, 1 December 1959.

153 TNA: PRO FO1110/1128: PR1034/7G: letter by G. Micklethwait, Tehran, to H. M. Carless of FO, 12 December 1958.

154 Ladjevardi, *Memoirs of Fatemeh Pakravan*, p. 20.

155 TNA: PRO FO371/121288: V10710/105G: letter from Baghdad to L. C. W. Figg, IRD, 1 October 1956.

156 TNA: PRO FO371/121285: V10710/64: BP confidential annex A to BP/SC/3/R2: report, 'Statement by Professor Furazanfar of the Iranian Delegation in the Counter-Subversion Committee Afternoon Session', 26 June 1956.

157 Ibid.

158 TNA: PRO FO1110/1251: PR146/65: letter by D. J. Speares, Tehran, to H. M. Carless of FO, 8 October 1959.

159 TNA: PRO FO371/127861: VB1692/3G: jacket 'Committee of Counter-Intelligence Experts', May 1957. The whole jacket of the file has been declassified under the FOIA at my request (REF: 1145-11), 2 December 2011.

160 TNA: PRO FO371/170252: EB1692/9: document 'CENTO Counter-Subversion Office: Terms of Reference', undated, annex to letter, 16 December 1963.

161 TNA: PRO FO1110/1814:PR10523/35G: letter by G. F. N. Reddaway of IRD, Beirut, to C. F. R. Barclay of FO, 17 March 1964.

162 TNA: PRO FO1110/1251: PR146/48: minute by Peter Joy, 6 August 1959. A classified US document states: 'The primary objective of security in Iran is preservation of the monarchy. Other main objectives are to counter the Soviet threat and to counter the threat from other countries in the area; i.e., Iraq and the UAR. It is from the latter country, as personified by Nasser, that the Shah sees the biggest threat to Iran in this decade. By contrast, the Iranian attitude toward the Soviets is more relaxed than it was in 1960.' The *Asnad-I Laneh-yi Jasusi* (the documents taken from the US embassy in Tehran in 1979) (hereafter *Asnad*), vol. 60, p. 5, report by 'United States Military Information Control Committee: Security in the Government of Iran', by Donald S. Harris, the Secretary, 7 February 1966.

163 HIOHP, Memoirs of General Hassan Alavi-Kia, interviewed by Habib Lajordee, transcript 1, sequence 7.

164 TNA: PRO FO1110/1353: PR146/13: report by Peter Joy, Ankara, to H. M. Carless of FO, 'CENTO Liaison Visit (CSO)', 26 January 1960.

165 HIOHP, Memoirs of General Hassan Alavi-Kia, interviewed by Habib Lajordee, transcript 1, sequence 12; Ladjevardi, *Memoirs of Fatemeh Pakravan*, p. 20. Also cf. TNA: PRO FO1110/1353: PR146/13: report by Peter Joy, Ankara, to H. M. Carless of FO, 'CENTO Liaison Visit (CSO)', 26 January 1960.

166 TNA: PRO FO1110/1353: PR146/7G: letter by D. J. Speares, Tehran, to D. C. Hopson of IRD, 4 January 1960.

167 Ibid.

168 TNA: PRO FO1110/1251: PR146/48: minute by Peter Joy, 6 August 1959.

169 TNA: PRO FO1110/1383: PR10134/41A: letter by D. J. Makinson, Tehran, to C. F. R. Barclay of IRD, 13 January 1962.

170 Ibid.

171 TNA: PRO FO1110/1383: PR1034/41: letter by D. J. Makinson, Tehran, to D. C. Hopson of FO, 6 December 1961. Relationships gradually improved towards the end of 1961, and the BBC also had a role in repairing them by giving the Iranians broadcasting training and constant visits to London.

172 TNA: PRO FO1110/1353: PR146/13: letter by Peter Joy, Ankara, H. M. Carless of FO, 26 January 1960.

173 Cf. TNA: PRO T220/676: file entitled 'Broadcasting Facilities to Countries in Middle East and Propaganda Activities Elsewhere', 1956–7. The file has been released under the FOIA at my request

(REF: 10/915&10/920), 1 February 2011. Cyprus was a prime example of this.

174 TNA: PRO FO1110/1557: PR10523/7: letter by B. L. Strachan of IRD to H. J. Spence, Ankara, 31 August 1962; letter by D. J. Makinson, Tehran to B. L. Strachan of IRD, 17 September 1962.

175 TNA: PRO FO1110/1557: PR10523/7: letter by A. C. Elwell of IRD to D. J. Makinson, Tehran, 17 October 1962.

176 Ibid.

Chapter 6

1 TNA: PRO KV4/472: the Liddell Diaries, 6 November 1950. Guy Liddell was the Deputy Director-General of MI5 (1946–51).

2 Dareini, *Rise and Fall of the Pahlavi Dynasty*, p. 270. General Hussein Fardust was a childhood friend of the Shah, who supervised the development of the Iranian Intelligence Community.

3 Walton, *Empire of Secrets*, pp. 26–9.

4 Ibid. *passim*, but see pp. 146–7, 271.

5 Ibid. p. 146.

6 Thomas Plate and Andrea Darvi, *Secret Police: The Inside Story of a Network of Terror* (London: Robert Hale, 1981), p. 9.

7 TNA: PRO CO885/119: record of the Conference of Colonial Commissioners of Police at the Police College, Ryton-on-Dunsmore, April 1951, p. 15.

8 Cf. Quarrie, *World's Secret Police*, pp. 108–29.

9 'Appendix I: The Maxwell-Fyfe Directive', in Laurence Lustgarten and Ian Leigh, *In from the Cold: National Security and Parliamentary Democracy* (Oxford: Oxford University Press, 1994), p. 517. Emphasis added.

10 Ibid.

11 Eliza Manningham-Buller, *Securing Freedom* (London: Profile, 2012), pp. 44–5.

12 TNA: PRO CAB134/3: AC (O) (50) 16: letter by Sir Frank Newsam to Sir Gladwyn Jebb of FO, 14 April 1950.

13 TNA: PRO KV4/473: the Liddell Diaries, 7 February 1951.

14 TNA: PRO KV4/473: the Liddell Diaries, 7 March 1951.

15 TNA: PRO KV4/473: the Liddell Diaries, 17 May 1951.

16 A case which acted against the British can be seen in Egypt in the early 1950s. See Chapter 3.

17 The organisations were later known as the Supreme Coordination

Council (SCC), the State Security Council (SSC) and the Special Information Bureau (SIB), which was also known as the Special Intelligence Office (SIO). See Dareini, *Rise and Fall of the Pahlavi Dynasty*, p. 200.

18 As there is no backup from archival sources, his memoirs (written in Farsi but later translated into English and published in Delhi) must be treated with caution. However, his memoirs reveal some unusual aspects of the training that he experienced in Britain.

19 Dareini, *Rise and Fall of the Pahlavi Dynasty*, p. 146.

20 Training in summary and report assessment; protective security; classification of sources; report writing; and the overview of the British system, including the JIC. See ibid. pp. 159–61.

21 Ibid. pp. 161–4. In the course of his visits in Britain, he also received '48 hours of special military training' at Plymouth, where he 'underwent gun-shooting special training by a military expert', who explained 'all parts of the pistols and pledged that whoever was trained there would be easily able to carry out accurate assassinations even if strict security measures were imposed'. Ibid. p. 151.

22 Ibid. p. 158.

23 Minute by Patrick Dean to Secretary of State, 16 December 1955. Obtained under the FOIA at my request (REF: 1258-12), 8 March 2013.

24 When an MI5 officer, P. G. B. Giles, was sent to the Canal Zone as the DSO, Guy Liddell noted that Giles's 'aim and object would be to obtain sources of information, the most profitable being bribe-able remnants of the Egyptian Police'. TNA: PRO KV4/474: the Liddell Diaries, 2 January 1952.

25 On the Egyptian coup in 1952, Michael Thornhill suggests that the British government 'may well have been sounded out' about the coup from a *Sunday Times* journalist, who was approached by Egypt's Military Attaché in London. Thornhill, *Road to Suez*, pp. 93–4.

26 Bloch and Fitzgerald, *British Intelligence and Covert Action*, p. 127.

27 Earnest Oney, former CIA officer, noted that 'Five Eyes' 'was based on an agreement between the United States and the Commonwealth countries as to relatively free exchange of information, as well as an agreement not to carry on operational activities in each other's countries. For example, CIA would not carry on any clandestine activities in England or in Australia or New Zealand, and those

countries would not carry on clandestine activities in the United States. It was a gentleman's agreement. Maybe a little more than a gentleman's agreement. I think it was formalized. But that was the basis for the cooperation.' OHOFIS: Earnest Oney, interviewed by Seyyed Vali Reza Nasr, Maryland, 22 and 29 May 1991, script no. 1, p. 26.

28 This can be seen from the agreement reached with General Razmara. See Chapter 2. Some exceptions in Iraq, where espionage in the host country was considered risky but conducted as a necessity, are noted in Chapter 3.

29 Cavendish, *Inside Intelligence*, p. 141.

30 Andrew, *Defence of the Realm*, pp. 478–9.

31 Private information obtained through an interview.

32 Cavendish, *Inside Intelligence*, pp. 140–2.

33 Cf. Dareini, *Rise and Fall of the Pahlavi Dynasty*, pp. 143–63.

34 Deacon, 'C', p. 139.

35 KCLHMA: GB0099 Woodhouse Papers 8/1: draft of his autobiography, *Something Ventured*, 16 August 1976, p. 101. It noted: 'I employed in the humble capacity of translator a young Parsee from Bombay called Shapur Reporter, who also worked for the Times. He had been a school-fellow of the Shah, and later rose to eminence (which included a knighthood) as the Shah's go-between in all sorts of major contracts, principally for arms, between Britain and Iran.' See Dareini, *Rise and Fall of the Pahlavi Dynasty*, pp. 146–7, which notes that Reporter, whose family migrated from India, was born in Tehran in 1921 and later knighted. See also TNA: PRO HO334/391: BNA38416, R.60203: certificate of naturalisation, 'Shapoor Ardeshirji Reporter', 9 August 1955. Some classified records, confiscated by the revolutionary forces in 1979, concerning him as a British agent throughout the period, have been published online, available at <http://www.shahbazi.org/pages/Reporter5.htm> (last accessed 29 August 2016).

36 Dareini, *Rise and Fall of the Pahlavi Dynasty*, pp. 146–7. Richard Deacon claims that Shapoor Reporter had an important role as 'a key man' in the coup of 1953. Deacon, 'C', pp. 113–14.

37 TNA: PRO DEFE23/198: HDS/PO/1077, letter to PUS, signed by HDS, 28 April 1978, which noted that Sir Shapoor Reporter was 'employed by MTS as a representative and consultant in Tehran with the full knowledge of the Iranian Government . . . His very considerable abilities lay in the access he had to the highest levels

of the Iranian Government and the Military and he is an acknowledged expert in the Persian language ... Sir Shapoor's job was therefore to set up appropriate meetings in Tehran with members of the Iranian Government, attend any negotiating meetings and then follow up after the negotiating team had left in order to clear any misunderstandings or complete any work left undone by the negotiating team.' TNA: PRO DEFE23/198, HDS/PO/860, loose minute to PUS, 'Shapoor Reporter' by HDS, 16 March 1978, which notes: 'Sir Shapoor had advised that if closely questioned by taxman on his activities he would plead the Official Secrets Act because of his involvement with MI6.' His role in selling British arms to Iran is quoted in Mark Phythian, *The Politics of British Arms Sales since 1964* (Manchester: Manchester University Press, 2000), p. 89. See also David Leigh and Rob Evans, 'Biography: Shapoor Reporter', *The Guardian*, 8 June 2007; Dorril, *MI6*, p. 654.

38 Cf. TNA: PRO DEFE23/217: the whole file entitled 'Defence Sales to Iran: Lieutenant Colonel D. A. Randel; Sir Shapoor Reporter', 1 January 1974–31 December 1978.

39 Sir Sam Falle notes that 'the unfortunate man genuinely liked England, which he often visited, and, most unwisely, he tried to imitate the British'. Falle, *My Lucky Life*, p. 164.

40 Cf. Rathmell, *Secret War in the Middle East*, p. 119; Patrick Seale, *The Struggle for Syria* (London: I. B. Tauris, 1965); King, *Inside the Arab Nationalist Struggle*, p. 66.

41 TNA: PRO FO371/134202: YQ1015/197: report by J. M. Hunter, Baghdad, to FO, annex D, 'List of 108 Persons to Be Tried by Military Tribunal', 12 August 1958.

42 Cf. Birdwood, *Nuri As-Said*, p. 271n.

43 Waldemar Gallman, US Ambassador in Iraq, recalls: 'Qazzaz was among the first to be arrested by Qasim and among the first of Nuri's associates to be tried publicly by Qasim's military tribunal. I watched his trial on television. He stood erect and strong for hours under a barrage of charges, accusations, and tauntings. He made no apologies. He did not ask for mercy. He maintained throughout the trial what he had done, he had done from conviction, to save his country and his people from communism, and if he had it to do over again he would do the same. As he and everyone who watched the proceedings anticipated, he was sentenced to death and hanged.' Gallman, *Iraq under General Nuri*, p. 96.

44 *The Iraq Times*, 26 August 1958. He was released from prison and moved to Britain. See Eveland, *Ropes of Sand*, p. 291, n.*.

45 Quote from email exchange.

46 Rathmell, *Secret War in the Middle East*, p. 2.

47 Ashton, *King Hussein of Jordan*, p. 38.

48 Ibid. p. 50; Gallman, *Iraq under General Nuri*, p. 139.

49 TNA: PRO KV4/237: SIME/POL.F.1041/B: letter by C. P. C. de Wesselow of SIME to DG, 24 July 1949; PRO FO371/82314: EP1017/4G: minute by Sir William Strang, 9 February 1950.

50 TNA: PRO FO248/1568: minute by Sir Roger Stevens, 19 November 1956.

51 TNA: PRO FO371/134201: VQ1015/152: telegram by Sir Roger Stevens to FO, 26 July 1958.

52 Waldemar Gallman notes that 'the actual figure was generally believed to have been higher'. See Gallman, *Iraq under General Nuri*, p. 78. Duncan McIntosh, Police Adviser in Iraq, put in place the precautionary security measures over the Suez Crisis. See TNA: PRO FO371/121646: VQ1015/80G: telegram by Sir Michael Wright to FO, 6 September 1956.

53 Gallman, *Iraq under General Nuri*, p. 75.

54 King, *Inside the Arab Nationalist Struggle*, pp. 273–4.

55 Dareini, *Rise and Fall of the Pahlavi Dynasty*, p. 150.

56 Ibid. p. 152.

57 It noted that 'the teacher believed that Iran should avoid money-consuming big industrial projects and instead implement small and medium-sized projects in order to save hard currency and create as many jobs as possible to solve one of the country's big problems, unemployment . . .'. Ibid. p. 153.

58 Mohamed Heikal, *The Return of the Ayatollah* (London: Andre Deutsch, 1981), pp. 86–7.

59 In his memoir, Magan states: 'I felt particularly nervous of the Iraqi Army which might try to seize power and which I felt that the Iraqi intelligence authorities had not got sufficiently covered.' Magan, *Middle Eastern Approaches*, pp. 146–7.

60 TNA: PRO CAB158/34: JIC (58) 102: JIC report, 'Reasons for the Failure of the Iraqi Intelligence Services to Give Warning of the Revolution of July 14', 8 October 1958; TNA: PRO CAB159/16: JIC (54) 67th meeting, 'Liaison with Iraq', 29 July 1954.

61 Cf. Falle, *My Lucky Life*, pp. 181–7, 205. This point is also noted in Hashimoto, 'British Security Liaison in the Middle East', pp. 848–74.

62 Falle, *My Lucky Life*, p. 163.

63 Gallman, *Iraq under General Nuri*, pp. 6, 101.

64 TNA: PRO KV4/474: the Liddell Diaries, 9 June 1952.

65 According to Al-Asmari, 'spying on the private lives of individuals is illegal and inadmissible according to Quran'. See Abdulaziz Al-Asmari, 'Origins of an Arab and Islamic Intelligence Culture', in Davies and Gustafson (eds), *Intelligence Elsewhere*, p. 98.

66 TNA: PRO KV4/473: the Liddell Diaries, 8 October 1951.

67 TNA: PRO FO371/136452: RK1015/3: telegram by Sir James Bowker, Ankara, to FO, 20 January 1958.

68 The Shah himself authorised SAVAK to conduct such operations, and SAVAK received a '200 to 300 page report daily' on Princess Ashraf's boyfriend. Dareini, *Rise and Fall of the Pahlavi Dynasty*, p. 119.

69 Ibid. p. 223.

70 TNA: PRO KV4/473: the Liddell Diaries, 8 October 1951, in which Guy Liddell notes: 'one of their main troubles is that the [Jordanian] Police have not got the co-operation of the public, and another thing, of course, is that most of their Ministers are probably corrupt'.

71 O'Connell, *King's Counsel*, p. 4.

72 OHOFIS: Richard Helms, interviewed by William Burr, Washington DC, 10 and 24 July 1985, script no. 1, p. 12.

73 According to a classified CIA report, the Shah himself took a 'deep and personal interest in the day to day operations' of the various intelligence and security organisations and made 'all major, and many minor, decisions in this field'. *Asnad*, vol. 60, p. 5, report by 'United States Military Information Control Committee: Security in the Government of Iran', by Donald S. Harris, the Secretary, 7 February 1966. See also an oral testimony by the CIA station chief in Tehran in the late 1950s and early 1960s, OHOFIS: Colonel Gratian Yatsevitch, interviewed by William Burr, Washington DC, 5 November 1988 and 12 January 1989, script no. 1, p. 33.

74 Bakhtiar was later attacked by a SAVAK officer and killed in his exile in Iraq in August 1970. Cf. Ladjevardi, *Memoirs of Fatemeh Pakravan*, p. 21, n.16; Dareini, *Rise and Fall of the Pahlavi Dynasty*, p. 227; OHOFIS: Oney, interviewed by Seyyed Vali Reza Nasr, Maryland, 22 and 29 May 1991, script no. 2, p. 5.

75 As a result, SIME reported that between about '600 and 800' officers in the Iranian Armed Forces (the total number of officers was

approximately 10,000) were arrested and that 'twenty-one' were executed and 'more are expected'.

76 TNA: PRO FO371/109989: EP1017/4G: report by David Stewart 'Arrests of Officers of the Persian Armed Forces', 9 December 1954. Emphasis added.

77 Author unknown, 'Late News Briefs', *Sunday Independent*, vol. LII, 86, 4 February 1959. See also Falle, *My Lucky Life*, pp. 230–1; Gallman, *Iraq under General Nuri*, p. 96.

78 Falle, *My Lucky Life*, p. 169.

79 Humphrey Trevelyan, *The Middle East in Revolution* (London: Macmillan, 1970), pp. 136–7; Birdwood, *Nuri Al-Said*, pp. 269–70; Gallman, *Iraq under General Nuri*, p. 203.

80 Manningham-Buller, *Securing Freedom*, pp. 48–9.

81 Hoare, *Camp 020*, pp. 1–30. It was Colonel 'Tin Eye' Stephens's subordinate who conducted such ill-treatment and brutality there.

82 Similarly, there was a lack of documentary evidence in the case of the colonies. See Walton, *Empire of Secrets*, pp. 250–8.

83 OHOFIS: Oney, interviewed by Seyyed Vali Reza Nasr, Maryland, 22 and 29 May 1991, script no. 3, p. 3. 'One of the most difficult things to do with police and intelligence officers, interrogators outside of Europe and the Americas, one of the hardest things is to persuade them that you cannot beat useful information out of people . . . Good interrogation, you don't do it by pulling out fingernails. You don't do it by beating people. You know, you beat anybody long enough, he would confess to anything that you're looking for, and in intelligence interrogation you're not looking for confessions that you can try somebody for in court. You're looking for information that will lead you through a network and ultimately to whoever is running the operation. You don't get useful information by torturing people.' Ibid., script no. 3, p. 4.

84 The Digital National Security Archive (DNSA), The George Washington University: report 'KUBARK Counter-Intelligence Interrogation' by US Army, July 1963, pp. 82, 94, available at <http://www.gwu.edu/~nsarchiv/NSAEBB/NSAEBB122/CIA%20 Kubark%2061-112.pdf> (last accessed 29 August 2016).

85 Quoted in Plate and Darvi, *Secret Police*, p. 55.

86 Dareini, *Rise and Fall of the Pahlavi Dynasty*, p. 270.

87 OHOFIS: Oney, interviewed by Seyyed Vali Reza Nasr, Maryland, 22 and 29 May 1991, script no. 2, p. 5.

88 Falle, *My Lucky Life*, p. 126.

89 TNA: PRO KV4/473: the Liddell Diaries, 8 November 1951.

90 Batatu, *Old Social Classes*, p. 568. See also Laqueur, *Communism and Nationalism in the Middle East*, pp. 195–7.

91 Batatu, *Old Social Classes*, p. 568.

92 TNA: PRO FO371/75130: E3419: letter from Sir H. Mack, Baghdad, to Ernest Bevin, 3 March 1949, which notes: 'Yusuf Salman Yusuf is believed to have twice visited the USSR and the efficiency of his organisation makes it probable that he received his revolutionary training there. There is some evidence that Yahuda Siddiq was about to leave for the USSR at the time of his arrest, while both Shabibi and Bassim were reported to have been sent to Kirkuk during 1946 to create trouble among the Iraq Petroleum Company workers.'

93 TNA: PRO FO371/75130: E2117: telegram from FO to Sir Henry Mack, Baghdad, 5 March 1949.

94 TNA: PRO FO371/75130: E5390: telegram by FO to Baghdad, 4 May 1949, which notes: 'the Communists themselves may bring harm upon Iraq's good name'.

95 Quoted in Batatu, *Old Social Classes*, p. 569.

96 Ibid.

97 It was noted that this had been introduced by the British High Commissioner, Sir Henry Dobbs. TNA: PRO FO624/153: minute by Sir Henry Mack, 8 March 1949; PRO FO371/75130: E3202: telegram from Sir H. Mack, Baghdad, to FO, 9 March 1949.

98 TNA: PRO FO371/75130: E6818: telegram from Sir H. Mack, Baghdad, to FO, 2 June 1949.

99 TNA: PRO FO248/1569: minute by J. T. Fearnley, 11 March 1956.

100 Ibid.

101 TNA: PRO FO248/1569: minute by HM Ambassador, 19 March 1956.

102 TNA: PRO FO248/1569: minute by E. P. N. de Haan, 12 March 1956.

103 Although it is beyond the period of this research, Richard Deacon claims in his biography of Sir Maurice Oldfield that Oldfield as 'C' also advised the Shah on 'intelligence matters' and he was content with the activities of 'the much condemned SAVAK'. Deacon, 'C', p. 113.

104 David McDowall, *A Modern History of the Kurds*, 3rd edn (London: I. B. Tauris, 2004), p. 169. Note that amongst the three, the Turks were the most sensitive on this matter. '[T]he Turks are extremely sensitive about the Kurdish minority ... if

he [Mr Baker] wants to obtain cooperation from the Turkish authorities he would, we suggest, be well advised not to show too great a public interest in the Kurdish problem.' TNA: PRO FO371/144805: letter by L. M. Minford, Ankara, to E. J. W. Barnes of FO, London, 29 January 1959.

105 McDowall, *Modern History of the Kurds*, p. 252. One of the KDPI leaders, Azia Yusifi, was detained until 1977, when he was released due to his ill health. See ibid. p. 260n.

106 TNA: PRO FO371/153093: press cutting from the *Daily Telegraph*, 'Turks Release Tribesmen', 23 November 1960, which notes: 'The last rebellion of the Turkish Kurds occurred in 1926 in the time of Kemal Ataturk.' After over five months in custody, 193 Kurds were released, and 55 Kurdish leaders were 'charged with holding their fanatically-religious followers almost in slavery and inciting them to rebellion'. On Turkey's counter-subversive measures against the Kurds, see Chikara Hashimoto and Egemen Bezci, 'Do the Kurds Have "no friends but the mountains"? Turkey's Secret War against Communists, Soviets and the Kurds', *Middle Eastern Studies*, vol. 52, no. 4 (2016), pp. 640–55.

107 *Hansard*, HC Deb, vol. 624, c102W, 30 May 1960, available at <http://hansard.millbanksystems.com/written_answers/1960/may/30/central-treaty-organisation-turkey-and#S5CV06 24P0_19600530_CWA_69> (last accessed 29 August 2016).

108 Ibid. See also TNA: PRO FO371/149686: EB10113/1: note for supplementary, draft reply, 27 May 1960.

Conclusion

1 Trevelyan, *Middle East in Revolution*, p. ix. Lord Trevelyan was the British Ambassador in Cairo (1955–6) and in Baghdad (1958–61).

2 MECA, St Antony's College, Oxford: Geoffrey Wheeler Collection GB165-0298: unpublished memoirs, 'Fifty Years of Asia', p. 283, undated. Original emphasis. Geoffrey Wheeler was the Oriental Counsellor of the British Embassy in Tehran (1946–50).

3 Quoted in Darby, *British Defence Policy*, p. 22.

4 Cf. Wm. Roger Louis and Roger Owen (eds), *A Revolutionary Year: The Middle East in 1958* (New York: I. B. Tauris, 2002); Ferrea and Louis, *The Iraqi Revolution of 1958*.

5 Cf. AP, Beirut, *The Tuscaloosa News*, 21 September 1959, available

at <http://news.google.com/newspapers?nid=1817&dat=195909
21&id=OokfAAAAIBAJ&sjid=85kEAAAAIBAJ&pg=7016,273
8827> (last accessed 29 August 2016).

6 Asseily and Asfahani, *Face in the Crowd*, p. 147. See also Eveland, *Ropes of Sand*, p. 321. After 1958, when General Fouad Chehab, a former Commander of the Army, became the Lebanese president, the Army, instead of the Sûreté Générale, assumed the main responsibility for internal security in Lebanon.

7 IWM: Private Papers of Patrick Coghill, 'Before I Forget . . .', vol. 2.

8 Cf. TNA: PRO FO371/175633: EB1692/1G: report 'UK Submission to CENTO Liaison Committee: Assessment of the Threat of Communist Subversion in the CENTO Area', 1 January 1964; PRO FO371/180719: EB1692/2: report '13th Session of CENTO Liaison Committee', undated.

9 Private information obtained through an interview.

10 Cf. Prados, *Safe for Democracy*.

11 Cf. Andrew and Mitrokhin, *Mitrokhin Archive*; Andrew and Mitrokhin, *Mitrokhin Archive II*.

12 Michael Herman notes: 'Most intelligence agencies now conduct foreign liaison of some kind; indeed access to bigger partners may be the main justification for some agencies in small powers.' Herman, *Intelligence Power*, p. 203. See also Lander, 'International Intelligence Cooperation', p. 481.

13 Cf. Cormac, *Confronting the Colonies*.

14 Walton, *Empire of Secrets*, p. 304.

Appendix

1 TNA: PRO KV4/234: 56b: attachment to note, 'Future Organisation of SIME' by Percy Sillitoe to Secretary of JIC, 17 August 1946; 82A: attachment to note, 'Statement to CIGS' by Douglas Roberts to Percy Sillitoe, 25 November 1946.

Bibliography

Printed Primary Sources

Dwight D. Eisenhower Presidential Library (DDEL), Abilene, Kansas
The Imperial War Museum (IWM), London
The India Office Library Records (IOLR), the British Library, London
The King's College London Liddell Hart Military Archives, London
Magdalene College, Oxford
Middle East Centre Archive (MECA), St Antony's College, Oxford
The National Archives (TNA), London
National Archives & Records Administration (NARA), Washington DC
The Turkish State Archives [Başbakanlık Devlet Arşivleri Genel Müdürlüğü], Ankara

Digital/Online Primary Sources

Asnad-I Laneh-yi Jasusi (the documents taken from the US embassy in Tehran in 1979)
The CIA Freedom of Information Act Electronic Reading Room
Classified records, confiscated by the Iranian revolutionary forces in 1979, available at <http://www.shahbazi.org/pages/Reporter5.htm>
The Digital National Security Archive (DNSA), The George Washington University
The Doolittle Report, *Report on Covert Activities of the Central Intelligence Agency*, available at <http://cryptome.org/cia-doolittle.pdf>
The US Department of State Archive

Oral Testimonies

The Harvard Iranian Oral History Project (HIOHP)
The Oral History Office of Foundation for Iranian Studies (OHOFIS)

Published Sources

Hansard, Parliamentary Debates (HC Deb).
Royal Air Force Historical Society, 'Seminar – Cold War Intelligence Gathering', *RAF Historical Society Journal*, vol. 23 (2010), p. 62.
Royal Air Force Historical Society, 'Seminar – The RAF in the Mediterranean Region', *RAF Historical Society Journal*, vol. 38 (2007), p. 123.
Royal Institute of International Affairs, *The Baghdad Pact: Origins and Political Setting* (London: Information Department of the Royal Institute of International Affairs, 1956).
White Paper, *Defence: Outline of Future Policy*, Cmnd. 124 (London: Her Majesty's Stationery Office, reprinted 1964).

Published Diplomatic and Miscellaneous Documents

Aldrich, Richard J. (ed.), *Espionage, Security and Intelligence in Britain, 1945–1970* (Manchester: Manchester University Press, 1998).
Asseily, Youmna and Ahmad Asfahani (eds), *A Face in the Crowd* (London: Stacey International, 2007).
Goldsworthy, David (ed.), *British Documents on the End of Empire: The Conservative Government and the End of Empire, 1951–1957: Part I: International Relations* (London: HMSO, 1994).
Hyam, Ronald (ed.), *British Documents on the End of Empire: The Labour Government and the End of Empire, 1945–1951: Part III: Strategy, Politics and Constitutional Change* (London: HMSO, 1992).
Hyam, Ronald and Wm. Roger Louis (eds), *British Documents on the End of Empire: The Conservative Government and the End of Empire, 1957–1964* (London: The Stationery Office, 2000).
Leary, William (ed.), *The Central Intelligence Agency: History and Documents* (Tuscaloosa: University of Alabama Press, 1984).
Ovendale, Ritchie (ed.), *British Defence Policy since 1945* (Manchester: Manchester University Press, 1994).

Wilber, Donald, 'Clandestine Service History: Overthrow of Premier Mossadeq of Iran, November 1952–August 1953', *Foreign Policy Bulletin*, vol. 11, no. 3 (2000), pp. 90–104.

Published Memoirs, Autobiographies and Diaries

Attlee, Clement, *As It Happened* (London: William Heinemann, 1954).

Beeston, Richard, *Looking for Trouble: The Life and Times of a Foreign Correspondent* (London: Tauris Parke, 2006).

Blake, George, *No Other Choice* (London: Jonathan Cape, 1990).

Catterall, Peter (ed.), *The Macmillan Diaries: The Cabinet Years 1950–195* (London: Pan Books, 2004).

Cavendish, Anthony, *Inside Intelligence: The Revelations of an MI6 Officer* (London: HarperCollins, 1990).

Copeland, Miles, *The Game of Nations* (New York: Simon & Schuster, 1969).

Copeland, Miles, *The Game Player* (London: Aurum Press, 1989).

Dareini, Ali Akbar (ed.), *The Rise and Fall of the Pahlavi Dynasty: Memoirs of Former General Hussein Fardust* (Delhi: Motilal Banarsidass, 1999).

Dodds-Parker, Douglas, *Political Eunuch* (Ascot: Springwood, 1986).

Dulles, Allen, *The Craft of Intelligence* (New York: Signet, 1965).

Dzhirkvelov, Ilya, *Secret Servant: My Life with the KGB and the Soviet Elite* (London: Simon & Schuster, 1987).

Eden, Anthony, *Full Circle: The Memoirs of Sir Anthony Eden* (London: Cassell, 1960).

Eveland, Wilbur Crane, *Ropes of Sand: America's Failure in the Middle East* (London: W. W. Norton, 1980).

Falle, Sam, *My Lucky Life: In War, Revolution, Peace and Diplomacy* (Oxford: ISIS, 2004).

Fanon, Frantz, *A Dying Colonialism* (Harmondsworth: Penguin, 1965).

Gallman, Waldemar, *Iraq under General Nuri: My Recollections of Nuri al-Said, 1954–58* (Baltimore: Johns Hopkins University Press, 1964).

Gladwyn, Lord, *The Memoirs of Lord Gladwyn* (London: Weidenfeld & Nicolson, 1972).

Horne, Alistair, *But What Do You Actually Do?* (London: Weidenfeld & Nicolson, 2011).

Johnston, Charles, *The Brink of Jordan* (London: Hamish Hamilton, 1972).

King, John (ed.), *Inside the Arab Nationalist Struggle: Memoirs of an Iraqi Statesman* (London: I. B. Tauris, 2012).

Ladjevardi, Habib (ed.), *Memoirs of Fatemeh Pakravan* (Cambridge, MA: Harvard University, Center for Middle Eastern Studies, 1998).

Lees, Roger, *In the Shade of the Peepul Tree* (private publication, 1998).

Lunt, James, *The Arab Legion, 1923–1957* (London: Constable, 1999).

Magan, William, *Middle Eastern Approaches* (Norwich: Michael Russell, 2001).

Manningham-Buller, Eliza, *Securing Freedom* (London: Profile, 2012).

Mayhew, Christopher, *A War of Words: A Cold War Witness* (London: I. B. Tauris, 1998).

Mure, David, *Practise to Deceive* (London: William Kimber, 1977).

Nasser, Gamal Abdel, *The Philosophy of the Revolution* (Buffalo, NY: Economica, 1959).

Nutting, Anthony, *No End of a Lesson: The Story of Suez* (London: Constable, 1967).

O'Connell, Jack, *King's Counsel: A Memoir of War, Espionage, and Diplomacy in the Middle East* (New York: W. W. Norton, 2011).

Pahlavi, Mohammed Reza Shah, *Mission for My Country* (London: Hutchinson, 1961).

Parsons, Anthony, *They Say the Lion: Britain's Legacy to the Arabs: A Personal Memory* (London: Jonathan Cape, 1986).

Philby, Kim, *My Silent War* (St Albans: Panther, 1969).

Rafizadeh, Mansur, *Witness* (New York: William Morrow, 1987).

Roosevelt, Kermit, *Countercoup: The Struggle for the Control of Iran* (New York: McGraw-Hill, 1979).

El Sadat, Anwar, *Revolt on the Nile* (London: Allan Wingate, 1957).

al-Said, Nuri, *Arab Independence and Unity* (Baghdad: Government Press, 1943).

Sansom, A. W., *I Spied Spies* (London: George G. Harrap, 1965).

Shuckburgh, Evelyn, *Descent to Suez: Diaries 1951–56* (London: Weidenfeld & Nicolson, 1986).

Sillitoe, Percy, *Cloak without Dagger* (London: Cassell, 1955).

Smiley, David, *Irregular Regular* (Norwich: Michael Russell, 1994).

Sudoplatov, Pavel, Anatoli Sudoplatov with Jerrold L. Schecter and Leona P. Schecter, *Special Tasks: The Memoirs of an Unwanted Witness* (London: Little, Brown, 1994).

Trevelyan, Humphrey, *The Middle East in Revolution* (London: Macmillan, 1970).

Woodhouse, Christopher, *Something Ventured* (London: Granada, 1982).

Wright, Peter, *Spycatcher* (Richmond, VIC: William Heinemann, 1987).

Young, Peter *Bedouin Command with the Arab Legion 1953–1956* (London: William Kimber, 1956).

Printed Secondary Sources

Monographs, Edited Works and Theses

Aburish, Said, *Beirut Spy* (London: Bloomsbury, 1990).

Aid, Matthew, *The Secret Sentry* (New York: Bloomsbury, 2009).

Aldrich, Richard J., *GCHQ* (London: Harper, 2011).

Aldrich, Richard J., *The Hidden Hand* (Woodstock: Overlook, 2001).

Anderson, David and David Killingray (eds), *Policing and Decolonisation: Politics, Nationalism, and the Police, 1917–65* (Manchester: Manchester University Press, 1992).

Andrew, Christopher, *The Defence of the Realm: The Authorized History of MI5* (London: Allen Lane, 2009).

Andrew, Christopher, *Secret Service: The Making of the British Intelligence Community* (Sevenoaks: Sceptre, 1986).

Andrew, Christopher and Vasili Mitrokhin, *The Mitrokhin Archive* (London: Allen Lane, 1999).

Andrew, Christopher and Vasili Mitrokhin, *The Mitrokhin Archive II* (London: Allen Lane, Penguin, 2005).

Ashton, Nigel J., *Eisenhower, Macmillan and the Problem of Nasser* (London: Macmillan, 1996).

Ashton, Nigel J., *Kennedy, Macmillan and the Cold War: The Irony of Interdependence* (New York: Palgrave Macmillan, 2002).

Ashton, Nigel J., *King Hussein of Jordan: A Political Life* (London: Yale University Press, 2008).

Barzani, Massoud, *Mustafa Barzani and the Kurdish Liberation Movement, 1931–1961* (Basingstoke: Palgrave Macmillan, 2003).

Batatu, Hanna, *The Old Social Classes and the Revolutionary Movements of Iraq* (Princeton: Princeton University Press, 1978).

Beckett, Ian F. W., *Modern Insurgencies and Counter-Insurgencies* (London: Routledge, 2001).

Bennett, Huw, *Fighting the Mau Mau: The British Army and Counter-Insurgency in the Kenya Emergency* (Cambridge: Cambridge University Press, 2013).

Birdwood, Lord, *Nuri As-Said: A Study in Arab Leadership* (London: Cassell, 1959).

Black, Ian and Benny Morris, *Israel's Secret Wars: A History of Israel's Intelligence Services* (New York: Grove Weidenfeld, 1991).

Bloch, Jonathan and Patrick Fitzgerald, *British Intelligence and Covert Action* (London: Junction Books, 1983).

Bower, Tom, *The Perfect English Spy* (London: Heinemann, 1995).

Bullock, Alan, *Ernest Bevin: Foreign Secretary, 1945–1951* (London: W. W. Norton, 1983).

Caroz, Yaacov, *The Arab Secret Services* (London: Corgi, 1978).

Carruthers, Susan L., *Winning Hearts and Minds: British Governments, the Media and Colonial Counter-Insurgency, 1944–60* (Leicester: Leicester University Press, 1995).

Cesarani, David, *Major Farran's Hat: Murder, Scandal, and Britain's Secret War against Jewish Terrorism, 1945–1948* (London: William Heinemann, 2009).

Charters, David, *The British Army and Jewish Insurgency in Palestine, 1945–47* (London: Macmillan, 1989).

Cockerill, A. W., *Sir Percy Sillitoe* (London: W. H. Allen, 1975).

Cohen, Michael J., *Fighting World War Three from the Middle East* (London: Frank Cass, 1997).

Comber, Leon, *Malaya's Secret Police 1945–60: The Role of the Special Branch in the Malayan Emergency* (Clayton, VIC: Monash University Press, 2008).

Cormac, Rory, *Confronting the Colonies: British Intelligence and Counterinsurgency* (London: Hurst, 2013).

Cradock, Percy, *Know Your Enemy* (London: John Murray, 2002).

Curry, John, *The Security Service 1908–1945: The Official History* (Kew: PRO, 1999).

Dann, Uriel, *King Hussein and the Challenge of Arab Radicalism: Jordan, 1955–1967* (Oxford: Oxford University Press, 1989).

Darby, Phillip, *British Defence Policy East of Suez, 1947–1968* (London: Oxford University Press, 1973).

Davies, Philip H. J., *The British Secret Service* (Oxford: ABC-Clio, 1996).

Davies, Philip H. J., *MI6 and the Machinery of Spying* (Frank Cass: London, 2004).

Davies, Philip H. J. and Kristian Gustafson (eds), *Intelligence Elsewhere* (Washington DC: Georgetown University Press, 2013).

Deacon, Richard, *'C': A Biography of Sir Maurice Oldfield* (London: Futura, 1984).

Defty, Andrew, *Britain, America and Anti-Communist Propaganda,*

1945–1958: The Information Research Department (London: Routledge, 2003).

Devereux, David R., *The Formulation of British Defence Policy towards the Middle East, 1948–56* (London: Macmillan, 1990).

Dimitrakis, Panagiotis, *Failed Alliances of the Cold War* (London: I. B. Tauris, 2012).

Dockrill, Saki, *Britain's Retreat from East of Suez* (Basingstoke: Palgrave Macmillan, 2002).

Dorril, Stephen, *MI6: Inside the Covert World of Her Majesty's Secret Intelligence Service* (London: Free Press, 2000).

Dover, Rob, Michael Goodman and Claudia Hillebrand (eds), *Routledge Companion to Intelligence Studies* (London: Routledge, 2014).

Dylan, Huw, *Defence Intelligence and the Cold War* (Oxford: Oxford University Press, 2014).

Ferrea, Robert A. and Wm. Roger Louis (eds), *The Iraqi Revolution of 1958* (London: I. B. Tauris, 1991).

Fieldhouse, D. K., *Western Imperialism in the Middle East, 1914–1958* (Oxford: Oxford University Press, 2006).

Foot, M. R. D., *SOE: An Outline History of the Special Operations Executive 1940–1946* (London: Pimlico, 1999).

French, David, *The British Way in Counter-Insurgency, 1945–1967* (Oxford: Oxford University Press, 2011).

Gasiorowski, Mark J. and Malcolm Byrne (eds), *Mohammad Mosaddeq and the 1953 Coup in Iran* (New York: Syracuse University Press, 2004).

Gaunson, A. B., *The Anglo-French Clash in Lebanon and Syria, 1940–45* (London: Macmillan, 1987).

Goodman, Michael, *The Official History of the Joint Intelligence Committee, vol. 1* (London: Routledge, 2014).

Grob-Fitzgibbon, Benjamin, *Imperial Endgame* (London: Palgrave Macmillan, 2011).

Harris, George, *The Origins of Communism in Turkey* (Stanford: Stanford University Press, 1967).

Haslam, Jonathan, *Russia's Cold War* (London: Yale University Press, 2011).

Haynes, John Earl and Harvey Klehr, *VENONA* (New Haven, CT: Yale University Press, 1999).

Hazan, Baruch, *Soviet Propaganda: A Case Study of the Middle East Conflict* (Jerusalem: Israel University Press, 1976).

Heikal, Mohamed H., *Cutting the Lion's Tail: Suez: Through Egyptian Eyes* (London: Andre Deutsch, 1986).

Heikal, Mohamed, *Nasser: The Cairo Documents: The Private Papers of Nasser* (London: New English Library, 1972).

Heikal, Mohamed, *The Return of the Ayatollah* (London: Andre Deutsch, 1981).

Hennessy, Peter, *Never Again: Britain 1945–1951* (London: Vintage, 1992).

Hennessy, Peter, *The Secret State: Preparing for the Worst, 1945–2010*, 2nd edn (London: Penguin, 2010).

Herman, Michael, *Intelligence Power in Peace and War* (Cambridge: RIIA, 1996).

Herman, Michael, *Intelligence Services in the Information Age* (London: Frank Cass, 2001).

Hinchcliffe, Peter, John T. Ducker and Maria Holt, *Without Glory in Arabia* (London: I. B. Tauris, 2006).

Hinsley, F. H. and C. A. G. Simkins, *British Intelligence in the Second World War, vol. 4: Security and Counter-Intelligence* (London: Her Majesty's Stationery Office, 1990).

Hoare, Oliver (ed.), *Camp 020: MI5 and the Nazi Spies* (Richmond: PRO, 2000).

Howard, Michael, *British Intelligence in the Second World War, vol. 5: Strategic Deception* (London: Her Majesty's Stationery Office, 1990).

Ismael, Tareq, *The Communist Movement in the Arab World* (London: Routledge, 2005).

Jackson, Robert, *High Cold War* (Sparkford: Patrick Stephens, 1998).

Jeffery, Keith, *MI6: The History of the Secret Intelligence Service, 1909–1949* (London: Bloomsbury, 2010).

Jones, Clive, *Britain and the Yemen Civil War 1962–65: Foreign Policy and the Limits of Covert Action* (Brighton: Sussex Academic Press, 2004).

Kahana, Ephraim and Muhammad Suwaed (eds), *The A to Z of Middle Eastern Intelligence* (Lanham, MD: Scarecrow, 2009).

Kedourie, Elie, *The Chatham House Version and other Middle-Eastern Studies* (London: Weidenfeld & Nicolson, 1970).

Kelly, Saul and Anthony Gorst (eds), *Whitehall and the Suez Crisis* (London: Frank Cass, 2000).

Kent, John, *British Imperial Strategy and the Origins of the Cold War 1944–49* (Leicester: Leicester University Press, 1993).

Kitson, Frank, *Low Intensity Operations: Subversion, Insurgency and Peacekeeping* (London: Faber and Faber, 1971).

Kyle, Keith, *Suez: Britain's End of Empire in the Middle East* (London: St Martin's Press, 1991).

Lapping, Brian, *End of Empire* (London: Guild, 1985).

Laqueur, Walter, *Communism and Nationalism in the Middle East* (London: Routledge and Kegan Paul, 1956).

Lashmar, Paul, *Spy Flights of the Cold War* (Annapolis, MD: Naval Institute Press, 1996).

Lashmar, Paul and James Oliver, *Britain's Secret Propaganda War 1948–1977* (London: Sutton, 1999).

Levey, Zach and Elie Podeh (eds), *Britain and the Middle East: From Imperial Power to Junior Partner* (Brighton: Sussex Academic Press, 2008).

Lewis, Julian, *Changing Direction*, 2nd edn (London: Frank Cass, 2002).

Longrigg, Stephen, *Syria and Lebanon under French Mandate* (Oxford: Oxford University Press, 1958).

Louis, Wm. Roger, *The British Empire in the Middle East, 1945–1951* (Oxford: Clarendon Press, 1984).

Louis, Wm. Roger (ed.), *Imperialism: The Robinson and Gallagher Controversy* (London: New Viewpoints, 1976).

Louis, Wm. Roger and Roger Owen (eds), *A Revolutionary Year: The Middle East in 1958* (New York: I. B. Tauris, 2002).

Louis, Wm. Roger and Roger Owen (eds), *Suez 1956: The Crisis and Its Consequences* (Oxford: Oxford University Press, 1989).

Lucas, W. Scott, *Divided We Stand: Britain, the US and the Suez Crisis* (London: Hodder & Stoughton, 1991).

Lustgarten, Laurence and Ian Leigh, *In from the Cold: National Security and Parliamentary Democracy* (Oxford: Oxford University Press, 1994).

McDowall, David, *A Modern History of the Kurds*, 3rd edn (London: I. B. Tauris, 2004).

Macintyre, Ben, *A Spy among Friends* (London: Bloomsbury, 2014).

Mackenzie, William, *The Secret History of SOE: The Special Operations Executive, 1940–1945* (London: St Ermin's Press, 2000).

McNamara, Robert, *Britain, Nasser and the Balance of Power in the Middle East 1952–1967* (London: Frank Cass, 2003).

Maddrell, Paul, *Spying on Science* (Oxford: Oxford University Press, 2006).

Monroe, Elizabeth, *Britain's Moment in the Middle East, 1914–1971* (London: Chatto & Windus, 1981).

Moravej, K., 'The SAVAK and the Cold War: Counter-Intelligence and Foreign Intelligence, 1957–1968' (PhD thesis, University of Manchester, 2011).

Nassif, Nicholas, *Ser Aldawlah: fousol fe tarekh ala'men ala'am 1945–1977* [*State Secret: Chapters in the History of the Sûreté Générale in Lebanon, 1945–1977*] (Lebanon: General Security, 2013).

Ovendale, Ritchie, *Britain, the United States and the Transfer of Power in the Middle East, 1945–1962* (London: Leicester University Press, 1996).

Petersen, Tore T., *The Middle East between the Great Powers* (London: Macmillan, 2000).

Phythian, Mark, *The Politics of British Arms Sales since 1964* (Manchester: Manchester University Press, 2000).

Plate, Thomas and Andrea Darvi, *Secret Police: The Inside Story of a Network of Terror* (London: Robert Hale, 1981).

Podeh, Elie, *The Quest for Hegemony in the Arab World: The Struggle over the Baghdad Pact* (Leiden: E. J. Brill, 1995).

Popplewell, Richard J., *Intelligence and Imperial Defence* (London: Frank Cass, 1995).

Porter, Bernard, *Plots and Paranoia* (London: Unwin Hyman, 1989).

Prados, John, *Safe for Democracy: The Secret War of the CIA* (Chicago: Ivan R. Dee, 2006).

Primakov, Yevgeni, *Russia and the Arabs* (New York: Basic Books, 2009).

Quarrie, Bruce, *The World's Secret Police* (London: Octopus, 1986).

Rathmell, Andrew, *Secret War in the Middle East: The Covert Struggle for Syria, 1949–61* (London: I. B. Tauris, 1995).

Richelson, Jeffrey, *Foreign Intelligence Organizations* (Cambridge, MA: Ballinger, 1988).

Richelson, Jeffrey and Desmond Ball, *The Ties That Bind* (Boston: Allen & Unwin, 1985).

Seale, Patrick, *The Struggle for Syria* (London: I. B. Tauris, 1965).

Shelley, Adam, 'British Intelligence in the Middle East, 1939–46' (PhD thesis, University of Cambridge, 2008).

Sirrs, Owen, *A History of the Egyptian Intelligence Service: A History of the Mukhabarat, 1910–2009* (London: Routledge, 2010).

Smith, Bradley, *The Ultra-Magic Deals: And the Most Secret Special Relationship, 1940–1946* (Novato, CA: Presidio, 1993).

Smith, Simon, *Britain's Revival and Fall in the Gulf* (London: Routledge, 2004).

Souza, Corinne, *Baghdad's Spy: A Personal Memoir of Espionage and Intrigue from Baghdad to London* (London: Mainstream, 2003).

Tarbush, Mohammad A., *The Role of the Military in Politics: A Case Study of Iraq to 1941* (London: KPI, 1985).

Thomas, Martin, *The French Empire at War, 1940–45* (Manchester: Manchester University Press, 1998).

Thomas, Martin, *The French Empire between the Wars: Imperialism, Politics and Society* (Manchester: Manchester University Press, 2005).

Thomas, Martin, *Empires of Intelligence: Security Service and Colonial Disorder after 1914* (London and Los Angeles: University of California Press, 2008).

Thornhill, Michael, *Road to Suez: The Battle of the Canal Zone* (Phoenix Mill: Sutton, 2006).

Vaughan, James, *The Failure of American and British Propaganda in the Arab Middle East, 1945–1957: Unconquerable Minds* (Basingstoke: Palgrave, 2005).

Walton, Calder, *Empire of Secrets* (London: HarperCollins, 2013).

West, Nigel, *The Friends: Britain's Post War Secret Intelligence Operations* (London: Weidenfeld & Nicolson, 1988).

West, Nigel, *Historical Dictionary of British Intelligence* (Lanham, MD: Scarecrow, 2005).

Wheelock, Keith, *Nasser's New Egypt: A Critical Analysis* (London: Atlantic Books, 1960).

Wilford, Hugh, *America's Great Game: The CIA's Secret Arabists and the Shaping of the Modern Middle East* (New York: Basic Books, 2013).

Yaqub, Salim, *Containing Arab Nationalism: The Eisenhower Doctrine and the Middle East* (Chapel Hill, NC: University of North Carolina Press, 2004).

Zabih, Sepehr, *The Communist Movement in Iran* (Los Angeles: University of California Press, 1966).

Zubok, Vladislav, *A Failed Empire: The Soviet Union in the Cold War from Stalin to Gorbachev* (Chapel Hill, NC: University of North Carolina Press, 2007).

Articles and Book Chapters

Al-Asmari, Abdulaziz, 'Origins of an Arab and Islamic Intelligence Culture', in Philip H. J. Davies and Kristian Gustafson (eds), *Intelligence Elsewhere* (Washington DC: Georgetown University Press, 2013), pp. 89–112.

Aldrich, Richard J., 'Intelligence, Anglo-American Relations and the Suez Crisis, 1956', *INS*, vol. 9, no. 3 (1994), pp. 544–54.

Aldrich, Richard J., 'Legacies of Secret Service: Renegade SOE and the Karen Struggle in Burma, 1948–50', *INS*, vol. 14, no. 4 (1999), pp. 130–48.

Aldrich, Richard J., 'Never-Never Land and Wonderland? British and American Policy on Intelligence Archives', *Contemporary Record*, vol. 8, no. 1 (1994), pp. 133–52.

Aldrich, Richard J., 'Secret Intelligence for a Post-War World: Reshaping the British Intelligence Community, 1944–51', in Richard J. Aldrich (ed.), *British Intelligence, Strategy and the Cold War, 1945–51* (London: Routledge, 1992), pp. 15–49.

Aldrich, Richard J., 'Soviet Intelligence, British Security and the End of the Red Orchestra: The Fate of Alexander Rado', *INS*, vol. 6, no. 1 (1991), pp. 196–217.

Aldrich, Richard J., 'Unquiet in Death: The Post-War Survival of the "Special Operations Executive", 1945–51', in Anthony Gorst, Lewis Johnman and Scott Lucas (eds), *Contemporary British History, 1931–1961* (London: Pinter, 1991), pp. 193–217.

Alon, Yoav, 'Historiography of Empire: The Literature on Britain in the Middle East', in Zach Levey and Elie Podeh (eds), *Britain and the Middle East: From Imperial Power to Junior Partner* (Brighton: Sussex Academic Press, 2008), pp. 33–47.

Anderson, David M., 'Mau Mau in the High Court and the "Lost" British Empire Archives: Colonial Conspiracy or Bureaucratic Bungle?', *The Journal of Imperial and Commonwealth History*, vol. 39, no. 5 (2011), pp. 699–716.

Andrew, Christopher, 'Churchill and Intelligence', *INS*, vol. 3, no. 3 (1988), pp. 181–93.

Arditti, Roger, 'Security Intelligence in the Middle East (SIME): Joint Security Intelligence Operations in the Middle East, c. 1939–58', *INS*, vol. 31, no. 3 (2016), pp. 369–96.

Ashton, Nigel J., 'Harold Macmillan and the "Golden Days" of Anglo-American Relations Revisited, 1957–63', *Diplomatic History*, vol. 29, no. 4 (2005), pp. 691–723.

Ashton, Nigel J., 'The Hijacking of a Pact: The Formation of the Baghdad Pact and Anglo-American Tensions in the Middle East, 1955–1958', *Review of International Studies*, vol. 19, no. 2 (1993), pp. 123–37.

Ashton, Nigel J., 'Macmillan and the Middle East', in Richard Aldous and Sabine Lee (eds), *Harold Macmillan and Britain's World Role* (Basingstoke: Macmillan, 1996), pp. 37–65.

Axelgard, Frederick, 'US Support for the British Position in Pre-Revolutionary Iraq', in Robert Fernea and Wm. Roger Louis (eds), *The Iraqi Revolution of 1958* (London: I. B. Tauris, 1991), pp. 77–94.

Balfour-Paul, Glen, 'Britain's Informal Empire in the Middle East', in Judith M. Brown and Wm. Roger Louis (eds), *The Oxford History of the British Empire: vol. IV, The Twentieth Century* (Oxford: Oxford University Press, 1999), pp. 490–514.

Blackwell, Stephen J., 'A Transfer of Power? Britain, the Anglo-American Relationship and the Cold War in the Middle East, 1957–1962', in Michael F. Hopkins, M. Kandiah and G. Staerck (eds), *Cold War Britain, 1945–1964: New Perspectives* (Basingstoke: Palgrave, 2003), pp. 168–79.

Boyd, Douglas, 'Sharq Al-Adna/The Voice of Britain: The UK's "Secret" Arabic Radio Station and Suez War Propaganda Disaster', *Gazette: The International Journal for Communication Studies*, vol. 65, no. 6 (2003), pp. 443–55.

Charters, David, 'British Intelligence in the Palestine Campaign, 1945–47', *INS*, vol. 6, no. 1 (1991), pp. 115–40.

Cohen, Michael J., 'From "Cold" to "Hot" War: Allied Strategic and Military Interests in the Middle East after the Second World War', *Middle Eastern Studies*, vol. 43, no. 5 (2007), pp. 725–48.

Cohen, Michael J., 'The Strategic Role of the Middle East after the War', in Michael J. Cohen and Martin Kolinsky (eds), *Demise of the British Empire in the Middle East* (London: Frank Cass, 1998), pp. 23–37.

Cormac, Rory, 'Organizing Intelligence: An Introduction to the 1955 Report on Colonial Security', *INS*, vol. 25, no. 6 (2010), pp. 800–22.

Cormac, Rory, 'The Pinprick Approach: Whitehall's Top-Secret Anti-Communist Committee and the Evolution of British Covert Action Strategy', *Journal of Cold War Studies*, vol. 16, no, 3 (2014), pp. 5–28.

Cormac, Rory, 'A Whitehall "Showdown"?: Colonial Office–Joint Intelligence Committee Relations in the Mid-1950s', *The Journal of Imperial and Commonwealth History*, vol. 39, no. 2 (2011), pp. 249–67.

Darwin, John, 'An Undeclared Empire: The British in the Middle East, 1918–39', *Journal of Imperial and Commonwealth History*, vol. 27, no. 2 (1999), pp. 159–76.

Davies, Philip H. J., 'Organizational Politics and the Development of Britain's Intelligence Producer/Consumer Interface', *INS*, vol. 10, no. 4 (1995), pp. 113–32.

Davies, Philip H. J., 'The SIS Singapore Station and the Role of the Far East Controller: Secret Intelligence Structure and Process in Post-War Colonial Administration', *INS*, vol. 14, no. 4 (1999), pp. 105–29.

Davies, Philip H. J., 'From Special Operations to Special Political Action: The "Rump SOE" and SIS Post-War Covert Action Capability 1945–1977', *INS*, vol. 15, no. 3 (2000), pp. 55–76.

Deery, Philip, 'Confronting the Cominform: George Orwell and the Cold War Offensive of the Information Research Department, 1948–50', *Labour History*, vol. 73 (1997), pp. 219–25.

Dimitrakis, Panagiotis, 'British Intelligence and the Cyprus Insurgency, 1955–1959', *IJIC*, vol. 21, no. 2 (2008), pp. 375–94.

Dovey, H. O., 'The False Going Map at Alam Haifa', *INS*, vol. 4, no. 1 (1989), pp. 165–8.

Dovey, H. O., 'Maunsell and Mure', *INS*, vol. 8, no. 1 (1993), pp. 60–77.

Dovey, H. O., 'The Middle East Intelligence Centre', *INS*, vol. 4, no. 4 (1989), pp. 800–12.

Dovey, H. O., 'Operation Condor', *INS*, vol. 4, no. 2 (1989), pp. 357–73.

Dovey, H. O., 'Security in Syria, 1941–45', *INS*, vol. 6, no. 2 (1991), pp. 418–46.

Dovey, H. O., 'The Unknown War: Security in Italy, 1943–45', *INS*, vol. 3, no. 2 (1988), pp. 285–311.

Dylan, Huw, 'The Joint Intelligence Bureau: (Not So) Secret Intelligence for the Post-War World', *INS*, vol. 27, no. 1 (2012), pp. 27–45.

Easter, David, 'Spying on Nasser: British Signals Intelligence in Middle East Crises and Conflicts, 1956–67', *INS*, vol. 28, no. 6 (2013), pp. 824–44.

Franzen, Johan, 'Losing Hearts and Minds in Iraq: Britain, Cold War Propaganda and the Challenge of Communism, 1945–58', *Historical Research*, vol. 83, no. 222 (2010), pp. 747–62.

Gallagher, John and Ronald Robinson, 'The Imperialism of Free Trade', *The Economic History Review*, vol. 6, no. 1 (1953), pp. 1–15.

Goodman, Michael, 'The British Way in Intelligence', in Matthew Grant (ed.), *The British Way in Cold Warfare: Intelligence, Diplomacy and the Bomb, 1945–1975* (London: Continuum, 2009), pp. 127–40.

Goodman, Michael, 'Learning to Walk: The Origins of the UK's Joint Intelligence Committee', *IJIC*, vol. 21, no. 1 (2008), pp. 40–58.

Gorst, Anthony, '"We must cut our coat according to our cloth": The Making of British Defence Policy, 1945–8', in Richard J. Aldrich (ed.), *British Intelligence, Strategy and the Cold War, 1945–51* (London: Routledge, 1992), pp. 143–63.

Gorst, Anthony and W. Scott Lucas, 'The Other Collusion: Operation Straggle and Anglo-American Intervention in Syria, 1955–56', *INS*, vol. 4, no. 3 (1989), pp. 576–95.

Hashimoto, Chikara, 'British Security Liaison in the Middle East: The

Introduction of Police/Security Advisers and the Lebanon–Iraq–Jordan "Anti-Communist Triangle" from 1949 to 1958', *INS*, vol. 27, no. 6 (2012), pp. 848–74.

Hashimoto, Chikara, 'Emir Farid Chehab: Chief of Lebanese Secret Police', in Paul Maddrell, Christopher Moran, Ioanna Iordanou and Mark Stout (eds), *Spy Chiefs: Volume II. Intelligence Leaders in Europe, the Middle East, and Asia* (Washington DC: Georgetown University Press, 2018).

Hashimoto, Chikara, 'Fighting the Cold War or Post-Colonialism?: Britain in the Middle East from 1945 to 1958: Looking through the Records of the British Security Service', *The International History Review*, vol. 36, no. 1 (2014), pp. 19–44.

Hashimoto, Chikara and Egemen Bezci, 'Do the Kurds Have "no friends but the mountains"? Turkey's Secret War against Communists, Soviets and the Kurds', *Middle Eastern Studies*, vol. 52, no. 4 (2016), pp. 640–55.

Jalal, Ayesha, 'Towards the Baghdad Pact: South Asia and Middle East Defence in the Cold War, 1947–1955', *The International History Review*, vol. 11, no. 3 (1989), pp. 409–33.

Jasse, Richard, 'The Baghdad Pact: Cold War or Colonialism?', *Middle Eastern Studies*, vol. 27, no. 1 (1991), pp. 140–56.

Jones, Matthew, 'The "Preferred Plan": The Anglo-American Working Group Report on Covert Action in Syria, 1957', *INS*, vol. 19, no. 3 (2004), pp. 401–15.

Kent, John, 'The Egyptian Base and the Defence of the Middle East, 1945–54', *Journal of Imperial and Commonwealth History*, vol. 21, no. 3 (1993), pp. 45–65.

Lander, Stephen, 'International Intelligence Cooperation: An Inside Perspective', *Cambridge Review of International Affairs*, vol. 17, no. 3 (2004), pp. 481–93.

Lockhart, John Bruce, 'The Relationship between Secret Services and Government in a Modern State', *RUSI Journal*, vol. 119, no. 2 (1974), pp. 3–8.

Louis, Wm. Roger, 'Britain and the Overthrow of the Mosaddeq Government', in Mark J. Gasiorowski and Malcolm Byrne (eds), *Mohammad Mosaddeq and the 1953 Coup in Iran* (New York: Syracuse University Press, 2004), pp. 126–77.

Louis, Wm. Roger and Ronald Robinson, 'The Imperialism of Decolonization', *The Journal of Imperial and Commonwealth History*, vol. 22, no. 3 (1994), pp. 462–511.

Lucas, W. Scott, 'The Path to Suez: Britain and the Struggle for the

Middle East, 1953–56', in Ann Deighton (ed.), *Britain and the First Cold War* (London: Macmillan, 1990), pp. 253–72.

Lucas, W. Scott and Ray Kakeyh, 'Alliance and Balance: The Anglo-American Relationship and Egyptian Nationalism, 1950–57', *Diplomacy and Statecraft*, vol. 7, no. 3 (1996), pp. 631–51.

Lucas, W. Scott and Alistair Morey, 'Hidden "Alliance": The CIA and MI6 before and after Suez', *INS*, vol. 15, no. 2 (2000), pp. 95–120.

Lucas, W. Scott and C. J. Morris, 'A Very British Crusade: The Information Research Department and the Beginning of the Cold War', in Richard J. Aldrich (ed.), *British Intelligence, Strategy and the Cold War, 1945–51* (London: Routledge, 1992), pp. 85–110.

McKnight, David, 'Western Intelligence and SEATO's War on Subversion, 1956–63', *INS*, vol. 20, no. 2 (2005), pp. 288–303.

Maddrell, Paul, 'British Intelligence through the Eyes of the Stasi: What the Stasi's Records Show about the Operations of British Intelligence in Cold War Germany', *INS*, vol. 27, no. 1 (2012), pp. 46–74.

Maddrell, Paul, 'What We Have Discovered about the Cold War Is What We Already Knew: Julius Mader and the Western Secret Services during the Cold War', *Cold War History*, vol. 5, no. 2 (2005), pp. 235–58.

Mawby, Spencer, 'The "Big Lie" and the "Great Betrayal": Explaining the British Collapse in Aden', in Nigel J. Ashton (ed.), *The Cold War in the Middle East: Regional Conflict and the Superpowers, 1967–73* (London: Routledge, 2007), pp. 167–87.

Mawby, Spencer, 'The Clandestine Defence of Empire: British Special Operations in Yemen 1951–64', *INS*, vol. 17, no. 3 (2002), pp. 105–30.

Merrick, Ray, 'The Russia Committee of the British Foreign Office and the Cold War, 1946–47', *Journal of Contemporary History*, vol. 20, no. 3 (1985), pp. 453–68.

Murphy, Philip, 'Creating a Commonwealth Intelligence Culture: The View from Central Africa, 1945–1965', *INS*, vol. 17, no. 3 (2002), pp. 131–62.

Murphy, Philip, 'Intelligence and Decolonization: The Life and Death of the Federal Intelligence and Security Bureau, 1954–63', *The Journal of Imperial and Commonwealth History*, vol. 29, no. 2 (2001), pp. 101–30.

Northedge, F. S., 'Britain and the Middle East', in Ritchie Ovendale (ed.), *The Foreign Policy of the British Labour Governments, 1945–1951* (Leicester: Leicester University Press, 1984), pp. 149–80.

Onslow, Sue, 'Unreconstructed Nationalists and a Minor Gunboat Operation: Julian Amery, Neil McLean and the Suez Crisis', *Contemporary British History*, vol. 20, no. 1 (2006), pp. 73–99.

Ovendale, Ritchie, 'Egypt and the Suez Base Agreement', in John W. Young (ed.), *The Foreign Policy of Churchill's Peacetime Administration 1951–1955* (Leicester: Leicester University Press, 1988), pp. 135–58.

Ovendale, Ritchie, 'William Strang and the Permanent Under-Secretary's Committee', in John Zametica (ed.), *British Officials and British Foreign Policy, 1945–50* (Leicester: Leicester University Press, 1990), pp. 212–27.

Pipes, Daniel, 'Dealing with Middle Eastern Conspiracy Theories', *Orbis*, vol. 36, no. 1 (1992), pp. 41–56.

Podeh, Elie, 'The Perils of Ambiguity: The United States and the Baghdad Pact', in David W. Lesch (ed.), *The Middle East and the United States* (Boulder, CO: Westview Press, 2003), pp. 100–19.

Popplewell, Richard, '"Lacking Intelligence": Some Reflections on Recent Approaches to British Counter-Insurgency, 1900–1960', *INS*, vol. 10, no. 2 (1995), pp. 336–52.

Rawnsley, Gary, 'Overt and Covert: The Voice of Britain and Black Radio Broadcasting in the Suez Crisis, 1956', *INS*, vol. 11, no. 3 (1996), pp. 497–522.

Reid, Brian Holden, 'The "Northern Tier" and the Baghdad Pact', in John W. Young (ed.), *The Foreign Policy of Churchill's Peacetime Administration 1951–1955* (Leicester: Leicester University Press, 1988), pp. 159–79.

Sanjian, Ara, 'The Formulation of the Baghdad Pact', *Middle Eastern Studies*, vol. 33, no. 2 (1997), pp. 226–66.

Scott, Len and Peter Jackson, 'Journeys in Shadows', in Len Scott and Peter Jackson (eds), *Understanding Intelligence in the Twenty-First Century* (London: Routledge, 2004), pp. 1–28.

Sluglett, Peter, 'Formal and Informal Empire in the Middle East', in Robin W. Winks (ed.), *The Oxford History of the British Empire: vol. V, Historiography* (Oxford: Oxford University Press, 1999), pp. 416–36.

Smith, Lyn, 'Covert British Propaganda: The Information Research Department: 1947–77', *Millennium: Journal of International Studies*, vol. 9, no. 1 (1980), pp. 67–83.

Smith, Raymond and John Zametica, 'The Cold Warrior: Clement Attlee Reconsidered, 1945–7', *International Affairs*, vol. 61, no. 2 (1985), pp. 237–52.

Stack, Neville, 'CENTO – The Unknown Alliance', *RUSI Journal*, vol. 117, no. 3 (1972), pp. 51–3.

Thatcher, Nicholas, 'Reflections on US Foreign Policy towards Iraq in the 1950s', in Robert Fernea and Wm. Roger Louis (eds), *The Iraqi Revolution of 1958* (London: I. B. Tauris, 1991), pp. 62–76.

Van Puyvelde, Damien and Sean Curtis, '"Standing on the Shoulders of Giants": Diversity and Scholarship in Intelligence Studies', *INS*, vol. 31, no. 7 (2016), pp. 1040–54.

Vaughan, James, '"A Certain Idea of Britain": British Cultural Diplomacy in the Middle East, 1945–57', *Contemporary British History*, vol. 19, no. 2 (2005), pp. 151–68.

Vaughan, James, '"Cloak without Dagger": How the Information Research Department Fought Britain's Cold War in the Middle East, 1948–56', *Cold War History*, vol. 4, no. 3 (2004), pp. 56–84.

Vaughan, James, 'Propaganda by Proxy?: Britain, America, and Arab Radio Broadcasting, 1953–1957', *Historical Journal of Film, Radio, and Television*, vol. 22, no. 2 (2002), pp. 157–72.

Wagner, Steven, 'British Intelligence and the "Fifth" Occupying Power: The Secret Struggle to Prevent Jewish Illegal Immigration to Palestine', *INS*, vol. 29, no. 5 (2014), pp. 698–726.

Wagner, Steven, 'British Intelligence and the Jewish Resistance Movement in the Palestine Mandate, 1945–46', *INS*, vol. 23, no. 5 (2008), pp. 629–57.

Walton, Calder, 'British Intelligence and the Mandate of Palestine: Threats to British National Security Immediately after the Second World War', *INS*, vol. 23, no. 4 (2008), pp. 435–62.

Wark, Wesley, 'Coming in from the Cold: British Propaganda and Red Army Defectors, 1945–1952', *The International History Review*, vol. 9, no. 1 (1987), pp. 48–72.

West, Nigel, '"Venona": The British Dimension', *INS*, vol. 17, no. 1 (2002), pp. 117–34.

Wilford, Hugh, 'The Information Research Department: Britain's Secret Cold War Weapon Revealed', *Review of International Studies*, vol. 24, no. 3 (1998), pp. 353–69.

Yitzhak, Ronen, 'The Beginnings of Transjordanian Military Intelligence: A Neglected Aspect of the 1948 War', *Middle East Journal*, vol. 57, no. 3 (2003), pp. 449–68.

Zamir, Meir, 'The "Missing Dimension": Britain's Secret War against France in Syria and Lebanon, 1942–45 – Part II', *Middle Eastern Studies*, vol. 46, no. 6 (2010), pp. 791–899.

Zubok, Vladislav, 'SPY vs. SPY: The KGB vs. the CIA, 1960–1962', *Cold War International History Project Bulletin*, vol. 4 (1994), pp. 22–33.

Newspapers
The Guardian
The Iraq Times
The Observer
The Telegraph
The Tuscaloosa News

Appendix: Security Intelligence Middle East Charter[1]

1. Security Intelligence Middle East (SIME) is an inter-service organisation and a part of the Security Service (MI5).
2. Head/SIME is responsible to the Director-General of the Security Service, and for local policy and executive action to the Middle East Defence Committee jointly and individually.
3. SIME is responsible for the collection, collation and dissemination to the interested and appropriate Service and Civil Authorities of Security Intelligence affecting British interests in the Middle East. It is also responsible for such executive action as may be approved by the Service and/or Civil Authority concerned.
4. SIME will, with the approval of the relevant authorities, maintain representatives under appropriate Service or other suitable cover wherever they are considered to be necessary throughout the Middle East area. Such representatives are responsible to Head/SIME from whom they receive directions and funds, and locally to their respective Service Commanders and/or Civil Authorities.
5. SIME will maintain close relations with MI6 in the Middle East to ensure thorough integration of all security information affecting the area. It will also maintain liaison as required with the Police and/or Security Authorities of the countries within the area, and with all representatives and links of the Security Service.
6. SIME cannot be called upon to reveal its sources of information to any other organisation or outside authority. It is, however, within the discretion of Head/SIME to do so in a case where he considers it desirable or expedient and subject

to obtaining the consent of any other organisation which may control or have an interest in the source. In important cases the matter should be referred to the Director-General of the Security Service.

7. Head/SIME will be a member of the Joint Intelligence Committee, Middle East.

8. SIME has an establishment sponsored by the Army which allows for any appointment to be held by a member of any of the three Services or of the Security Service.

9. The Army will continue to furnish Field Intelligence funds upon estimates submitted by Head/SIME. It will also provide accommodation and other services.

Index

EU representative:
Easy Access System Europe
Mustamäe tee 50, 10621 Tallinn, Estonia
Gpsr.requests@easproject.com

www.ingramcontent.com/pod-product-compliance
Lightning Source LLC
Chambersburg PA
CBHW060150280326
41932CB00012B/1706